MAKE EVERY DAY
A CELEBRATION!

It's another year, and that means there are 365 reasons to celebrate. From the family traditions and seasonal holidays you look forward to all year long, to the everyday moments in between, **TASTE OF HOME HOLIDAY & CELEBRATIONS** gives you timeless recipes, invaluable menu-planning guidance and fun, no-fuss decoration and party-favor ideas to make any occasion simply spectacular!

'TIS THE SEASON. Easy-to-follow menus and can-do recipes take the stress out of the busiest time of year. Let this comprehensive section of festive dishes make the season merry. Greet St. Nicholas' arrival with a fun and family-friendly brunch...mingle and nosh with friends at a holiday book swap...feast on a timeless Christmas dinner featuring Roast Goose with Sweet Glaze...and ring in the Chinese New Year with an authentic Asian buffet.

GIVING THANKS. Add a few more recipes to your list of Thanksgiving dinner staples with our showstopping menu featuring an impressive Turducken with all the trimmings. Round out the meal with any of the freshly baked loaves, rolls and savory quick breads showcased in A Cornucopia of Breads and make your finale particularly grand with the rich, decadent treats on display in Autumn Cheesecakes.

EASTER GATHERINGS. Usher in spring with a feast of fun festivities and mouthwatering menus. A vintage Easter dinner, complete with succulent Pineapple-Glazed Ham, will bring back fond memories. For dessert, delight guests with playful mini pies and tarts. Indulge in all your favorites—Banana Cream Pies, Pecan French Silk Pies and Strawberry-Rhubarb Cream Cheese Tarts to name just a few—pared down for single-serving enjoyment.

SPECIAL CELEBRATIONS. From Valentine's Day to Halloween, the year is filled with reasons to gather your family and friends. Let the celebrations continue with this jam-packed chapter featuring a Haunted Fairy Tale Forest Halloween, family-friendly ideas for Spring Break Fun, a Farmers Market Feast and many more colorful, memory-making inspirations.

DECORATING IDEAS. Find inspiration for simple but simply stunning table toppers, party favors and decor. From easy-to-make gourd and apple candleholders to a whimsical fabric banner, it couldn't be easier to add the perfect finishing touches to your event.

With gotta-try eats, mood-setting decorations and perfect party themes, **TASTE OF HOME HOLIDAY & CELEBRATIONS** will help you make magical memories throughout the whole year.

Would you like to see one of your family-favorite recipes featured in a future edition of this timeless treasury of holiday and special occasion recipes? Turn to page 256 for all the details.

taste of home
HOLIDAY & CELEBRATIONS
2012

Taste of Home Books
© 2012 Reiman Media Group, LLC
5400 S. 60th St., Greendale WI 53129

International Standard Book Number (13):
978-0-89821-944-9
International Standard Serial Number:
1535-2781

For other Taste of Home
books and products, visit
ShopTasteofHome.com

■ **EDITORIAL**
Editor-in-Chief **Catherine Cassidy**

Executive Editor/Print & Digital Books **Stephen C. George**
Creative Director **Howard Greenberg**
Editorial Services Director **Kerri Balliet**

Senior Editor/Print & Digital Books **Mark Hagen**
Editor **Sara Rae Lancaster**
Associate Creative Director **Edwin Robles Jr.**
Art Director **Gretchen Trautman**
Craft Editor **Shalana Frisby**
Content Production Manager **Julie Wagner**
Copy Chief **Deb Warlaumont Mulvey**
Copy Editors **Mary C. Hanson, Alysse Gear, Joanne Weintraub**
Contributing Copy Editor **Valerie Berg Phillips**
Food Editor **Mary King**
Associate Food Editor **Jenni Sharp**
Recipe Content Manager **Colleen King**
Assistant Photo Coordinator **Mary Ann Koebernik**
Recipe Testing **Taste of Home Test Kitchen**
Food Photography **Taste of Home Photo Studio**
Editorial Assistant **Marilyn Iczkowski**

■ **BUSINESS**
Vice President, Publisher **Jan Studin, jan_studin@rd.com**
Regional Account Director **Donna Lindskog, donna_lindskog@rd.com**
Eastern Account Director **Joanne Carrara**
Eastern Account Manager **Kari Nestor**
Account Manager **Gina Minerbi**
Midwest & Western Account Director **Jackie Fallon**
Midwest Account Manager **Lorna Phillips**
Michigan Sales Representative **Linda C. Donaldson**
Southwestern Account Representtive **Summer Nilsson**

Corporate Digital and Integrated Sales Director, N.A. **Steve Sottile**
Associate Marketing Director, Integrated Solutions **Katie Gaon Wilson**
Digital Sales Planner **Tim Baarda**

General Manager, Taste of Home Cooking Schools **Erin Puariea**

Direct Response Advertising **Katherine Zito, David Geller Associates**

Vice President, Creative Director **Paul Livornese**
Executive Director, Brand Marketing **Leah West**
Senior Marketing Manager **Vanessa Bailey**
Associate Marketing Manager **Betsy Connors**

Vice President, Magazine Marketing **Dave Fiegel**

■ **READER'S DIGEST NORTH AMERICA**
Vice President, Business Development **Jonathan Bigham**
President, Books and Home Entertaining **Harold Clarke**
Chief Financial Officer **Howard Halligan**
Vice President, General Manager, Reader's Digest Media **Marilynn Jacobs**
Chief Content Officer, Milwaukee **Mark Jannot**
Chief Marketing Officer **Renee Jordan**
Vice President, Chief Sales Officer **Mark Josephson**
Vice President, Chief Strategy Officer **Jacqueline Majers Lachman**
General Manager, Milwaukee **Frank Quigley**
Vice President, Marketing and Creative Services **Elizabeth Tighe**
Vice President, Chief Content Officer **Liz Vaccariello**

■ **THE READER'S DIGEST ASSOCIATION, INC.**
President and Chief Executive Officer **Robert E. Guth**

■ **COVER PHOTOGRAPHY**
Photographer **Dan Roberts**
Food Styling Manager **Sarah Thompson**
Set Styling Manager **Stephanie Marchese**

ON THE FRONT COVER Vanilla Bean Cake with White Chocolate Ganache (p. 188).

ON THE BACK COVER Kale & Bacon Salad with Honey-Horseradish Vinaigrette (p. 11), Clove-Studded Oranges (p. 15), Rustic Tomato Cheese Tart (p. 9).

TABLE OF CONTENTS

tis*the*season

The holidays are steeped in tradition, from the exchange of Christmas greetings and carefully wrapped presents to time-honored dishes made but once a year. Whether you're looking to add to your special memories or start a new tradition, you'll find plenty of festive inspiration, including tasty recipes and heartwarming party ideas, right here.

If you have ever dreamed of treating your family to a sumptuous and traditional Christmas dinner with all the festive trimmings—including the Christmas goose—this meal is made for you!

Your table will look as pretty as a Norman Rockwell painting when it is dressed with a classically elegant meal that features succulent Roast Goose with Sweet Glaze. Best of all, sharing the table with the impressive bird are a host of savory side dishes that include Fig & Nut Harvest Stuffing, Great Grain Salad, Rotkohl, and Broccoli with Garlic, Bacon & Parmesan.

YULETIDE FEAST

CHRISTMAS TRADITIONS

A FEW WEEKS BEFORE

- Prepare two grocery lists: one for nonperishable items to purchase now and one for perishable items to purchase a few days before Christmas Day.
- Order a 10- to 12-pound domestic goose from your butcher.

TWO DAYS BEFORE

- Buy remaining grocery items.
- Make citrus slices for Grapefruit Layer Cake.

CHRISTMAS EVE

- Set the table.
- Prepare the vinaigrette for the Great Grain Salad; cover and chill.
- Prepare glaze for Roast Goose with Sweet Glaze; cover and chill.
- Bake cakes for Grapefruit Layer Cake. Wrap each cake tightly in plastic wrap; store in a large resealable plastic bag.
- Assemble Fruit & Nut Harvest Stuffing; cover and chill.
- For Rotkohl (Red Cabbage), clean and shred cabbage; refrigerate in a resealable plastic bag.
- Prepare vinaigrette for Kale & Bacon Salad with Honey-Horseradish Vinaigrette. Place in a covered container; chill.
- Remove broccoli florets from the head for Broccoli with Garlic, Bacon & Parmesan; wash and dry. Place in a resealable plastic bag; chill.

CHRISTMAS DAY

- In the morning, prepare Great Grain Salad; cover and chill.
- Prepare frosting for Grapefruit Layer Cake. Assemble cake; refrigerate until serving.
- Bake the Roast Goose with Sweet Glaze. Reheat glaze; baste and continue baking as directed.
- As guests arrive, bake Honeyed Fig & Ricotta Appetizers alongside goose.
- Bake Fruit & Nut Harvest Stuffing alongside goose.
- Remove the goose and stuffing from the oven. Increase the temperature to 375º. Bake Rustic Tomato Cheese Tart.
- Prepare Rotkohl (Red Cabbage).
- Prepare Broccoli with Garlic, Bacon & Parmesan.
- Assemble Kale & Bacon Salad with Honey-Horseradish Vinaigrette.
- For dessert, serve Grapefruit Layer Cake.

rustic tomato cheese tart

My fresh tomato tart is perfect when you want garden-fresh flavor—even in the winter! The crust stays nice and crisp and the toppings are bursting with fresh spices and Christmas colors.

MOJI DABNEY
EGG HARBOR TOWNSHIP, NEW JERSEY

7   sheets phyllo dough (14 inches x 9 inches)
⅓   cup olive oil
7   tablespoons crumbled goat cheese
1   cup thinly sliced sweet onion
1   cup (4 ounces) shredded fontina cheese
4   plum tomatoes, thinly sliced
2   tablespoons minced chives
1   tablespoon minced fresh basil or 1 teaspoon dried basil
¼   teaspoon salt
¼   teaspoon pepper

1. Place one sheet of phyllo dough on a parchment-lined baking sheet. Brush phyllo with oil and sprinkle with 1 tablespoon crumbled goat cheese. (Keep the remaining phyllo covered with plastic wrap and a damp towel to prevent it from drying out.) Repeat layers, brushing oil all the way to edges.

2. Sprinkle onion over top to within 1 in. of edges; sprinkle with fontina cheese. Arrange tomato slices in a slightly overlapping pattern over fontina cheese. Sprinkle with chives, basil, salt and pepper. Bring up edges of tart over filling.

3. Bake at 375° for 30-35 minutes or until the crust is golden brown.

YIELD: 12 SERVINGS.

roast goose with sweet glaze

(PICTURED ON PAGE 7)

While goose is thought of as a traditional Christmas entree, some people do not care for its dark meat. My recipe will change their mind in one bite. The sweet citrus glaze complements the rich poultry perfectly.

COLLEEN STURMA | MILWAUKEE, WISCONSIN

1 domestic goose (10 to 12 pounds)

1 teaspoon salt

2 small navel oranges, quartered

1 small onion, quartered

2 garlic cloves

¾ cup orange marmalade

3 tablespoons Dijon mustard

2 tablespoons reduced-sodium soy sauce

1 tablespoon brown sugar

½ teaspoon pepper

1. Sprinkle goose and inside cavity with salt. Prick skin well with a fork. Place the oranges, onion and garlic in cavity. Tuck wings under goose; tie drumsticks together. Place breast side up on a rack in a roasting pan.

2. Bake, uncovered, at 350° for 2¾ to 3¼ hours or until a thermometer reads 180°. Cover loosely with foil if goose browns too quickly. If necessary, drain fat from pan as it accumulates.

3. In a small saucepan, combine the marmalade, mustard, soy sauce, brown sugar and pepper. Cook and stir over medium heat until heated through. During the last 15 minutes of cooking, baste some of the glaze over goose.

4. Place goose on a serving platter; cover and let stand for 15 minutes before carving. Just before serving, brush with remaining glaze.

YIELD: 10 SERVINGS.

rotkohl (red cabbage)

(PICTURED ON PAGE 6)

Red cabbage is one of my family's favorite German dishes! It goes well with many meats, especially those served for special occasions. The longer it cooks, the better!

CATHY LEMMON | QUINLAN, TEXAS

½ teaspoon whole peppercorns

2 bay leaves

2 whole cloves

2 medium onions, chopped

¼ cup butter, cubed

1 garlic clove, minced

1 cup dry red wine or grape juice

1 medium head red cabbage, shredded

3 medium apples, chopped

1½ teaspoons salt

¼ teaspoon pepper

2 tablespoons red wine vinegar

1. Place the peppercorns, bay leaves and cloves on a double thickness of cheesecloth; bring up corners of cloth and tie with string to form a bag.

2. In a Dutch oven, saute onions in butter until tender. Add garlic; cook 1 minute longer. Add wine, stirring to loosen browned bits from pan. Add the cabbage, apples, salt, pepper and spice bag.

3. Bring to a boil. Reduce heat; cover and simmer, for 30-35 minutes or until cabbage is tender, stirring occasionally. Stir in vinegar. Discard spice bag. Serve with a slotted spoon.

YIELD: 7 SERVINGS.

kale & bacon salad
with honey-horseradish vinaigrette

Totally scrumptious and packed with nutrition, this salad was my response to friends who asked how they could incorporate kale into their diets without sacrificing taste. It is also wonderful with collard or mustard greens, prepared in the same fashion, or with a mix of spinach and arugula or watercress.

ELIZABETH WARREN | OKLAHOMA CITY, OKLAHOMA

10 kale leaves, stems removed and thinly sliced

¼ cup loosely packed basil leaves, thinly sliced

½ cup alfalfa sprouts

4 bacon strips, cooked and crumbled

½ cup crumbled feta cheese

½ medium ripe avocado, peeled and thinly sliced

1 hard-cooked egg, chopped

1 cup grape tomatoes, chopped

VINAIGRETTE

⅓ cup olive oil

3 tablespoons lemon juice

2 tablespoons prepared horseradish

2 tablespoons honey

1½ teaspoons garlic powder

1½ teaspoons spicy brown mustard

¼ teaspoon crushed red pepper flakes

⅛ teaspoon pepper

Dash salt

1. Divide kale and basil among eight salad plates. Top with sprouts, bacon, cheese, avocado, egg and tomatoes.

2. In a small bowl, whisk the vinaigrette ingredients. Drizzle over the salads; serve immediately.

YIELD: 8 SERVINGS.

broccoli with garlic, bacon & parmesan

(PICTURED ON PAGE 7)

This simple yet sophisticated side dish uses just a few basic ingredients.
The way the bold garlic flavor blends with the smoky bacon makes ordinary broccoli irresistible.

ERIN CHILCOAT | SMITHTOWN, NEW YORK

8   thick-sliced bacon strips, chopped

2   bunches broccoli, cut into florets

6   tablespoons olive oil

10   garlic cloves, minced

½   teaspoon crushed red pepper flakes

2   cups reduced-sodium chicken broth

¼   cup grated Parmesan cheese

1. In a large skillet, cook bacon over medium heat until crisp. Remove to paper towels with a slotted spoon; drain, reserving the drippings.

2. In the same skillet, saute broccoli in drippings and oil just until lightly browned. Add garlic and pepper flakes; cook 2 minutes longer. Stir in broth; cook and stir over medium-low heat for 30-35 minutes or until broccoli is tender and broth is absorbed. Stir in bacon; sprinkle with cheese.

YIELD: 8 SERVINGS.

great grain salad

(PICTURED ON PAGE 6)

I can't think of a better dish to round out a meal. My grain salad features all my favorite nuts, seeds and fruits. Try adding grilled chicken to make it a meal on its own.

RACHEL DUEKER | GERVAIS, OREGON

3   cups water

½   cup medium pearl barley

½   cup uncooked wild rice

⅔   cup uncooked basmati rice

½   cup slivered almonds

½   cup sunflower kernels

½   cup salted pumpkin seeds or pepitas

½   cup each golden raisins, chopped dried apricots and dried cranberries

⅓   cup minced fresh parsley

4   teaspoons grated orange peel

VINAIGRETTE

⅔   cup walnut oil

⅔   cup raspberry vinegar

2   teaspoons orange juice

2   teaspoons pepper

1   teaspoon salt

1. In a large saucepan, bring water to a boil. Add barley and wild rice. Reduce heat; cover and simmer for 55-65 minutes or until tender. Meanwhile, cook basmati rice according to package directions. Cool barley and rices to room temperature.

2. In a large bowl, combine the almonds, sunflower kernels, pumpkin seeds, dried fruit, parsley and orange peel; add barley and rices.

3. In a small bowl, whisk the vinaigrette ingredients. Pour over the salad and toss to coat. Cover and refrigerate for at least 2 hours.

YIELD: 12 SERVINGS (¾ CUP EACH).

grapefruit layer cake

I grew up in Florida where we had 10 grapefruit trees and were constantly trying to use the fruit in different ways. This luscious cake was one of my "grapefruit experiments." A nice, bright citrus taste shines through in every moist bite.

SARA PLESO
SPARTA, TENNESSEE

OVEN-DRIED CITRUS SLICES

- 2 grapefruit slices
- 2 orange slices
- 1 teaspoon sugar

CAKE

- ¾ cup butter, softened
- 1½ cups sugar
- 2 eggs
- 1 teaspoon vanilla extract
- ½ teaspoon grated lemon peel
- 3 cups cake flour
- 3 teaspoons baking powder
- ¾ teaspoon salt
- ¼ teaspoon baking soda
- ¾ cup 2% milk
- ½ cup white grapefruit juice

FROSTING

- 3 packages (two 8 ounces, one 3 ounces) cream cheese, softened
- 2 tablespoons butter, softened
- 8 cups confectioners' sugar
- 2 tablespoons plus 2 teaspoons grated grapefruit peel
- 2 teaspoons grated lemon peel
- 2 teaspoons grated orange peel
- ½ teaspoon vanilla extract

1. Place grapefruit and orange slices on a greased and foil-lined baking sheet. Sprinkle with sugar. Bake at 170° for about 2 hours or until dried (fruit will be slightly tacky). Remove to wire racks. Let stand for 2-3 days or until completely dried.

2. In a large bowl, cream butter and sugar until light and fluffy, about 5 minutes. Add eggs, one at a time, beating well after each addition. Stir in vanilla and lemon peel; mix well. Combine the flour, baking powder, salt and baking soda; add to creamed mixture alternately with milk and grapefruit juice. Beat just until combined.

3. Transfer to two greased and floured 9-in. round baking pans. Bake at 350° for 21-24 minutes or until a toothpick inserted near the center comes out clean. Cool for 10 minutes before removing to wire racks to cool completely.

4. In a large bowl, beat cream cheese and butter until fluffy. Add the confectioners' sugar, citrus peels and vanilla; beat until smooth.

5. Cut each cake horizontally into two layers. Spread frosting between layers and over top and sides of cake. Garnish with citrus slices.

YIELD: 16 SERVINGS.

honeyed fig & ricotta appetizers

Stave off hungry guests' growling stomachs with these tasty bites. Don't let their upscale appearance fool you—the warm appetizers are really quite simple to make.

TASTE OF HOME TEST KITCHEN

½ cup ricotta cheese

1 teaspoon sugar

¼ teaspoon ground cinnamon

¼ teaspoon ground nutmeg

24 gingersnap cookies

8 dried figs

¼ cup honey

1. In a small bowl, combine the ricotta cheese, sugar, cinnamon and nutmeg. Spread 1 teaspoon over each cookie. Arrange on a foil-lined baking sheet.

2. Cut each fig into three slices; place on cheese mixture. Drizzle fig slices with honey. Bake at 350° for 4-6 minutes or until heated through. Serve immediately.

YIELD: 2 DOZEN.

fruit & nut harvest stuffing

If you're looking for a dish to win over family and friends, you can't go wrong with my fruit and nut stuffing. I made it for the first Thanksgiving I celebrated with my fiance's extended family. It was a hit!

AMY BURTON | CARY, NORTH CAROLINA

1 pound bulk pork sausage

1 large onion, chopped

2 celery ribs, chopped

1 medium tart apple, peeled and chopped

3 garlic cloves, minced

3 tablespoons minced fresh sage

2 tablespoons minced fresh rosemary

2 tablespoons minced fresh thyme

2 teaspoons each poultry seasoning, ground ginger and allspice

⅛ teaspoon crushed red pepper flakes

1 package (12 ounces) unseasoned stuffing cubes

3½ cups chicken broth

½ cup butter, melted

½ cup finely chopped dried apricots

½ cup chopped hazelnuts

½ cup chopped almonds

½ cup raisins

1. In a large skillet, cook the sausage, onion and celery over medium heat until sausage is no longer pink; drain. Add the apple, garlic and seasonings; cook 1 minute longer.

2. Place stuffing cubes in a large bowl. Stir in the broth, butter, apricots, nuts, raisins and sausage mixture. Transfer to a greased 13-in. x 9-in. baking dish.

3. Cover and bake at 350° for 30 minutes. Uncover; bake 10-15 minutes longer or until lightly browned.

YIELD: 13 SERVINGS.

HOMEMADE POULTRY SEASONING

Out of poultry seasoning? Don't worry. When a recipe calls for it, you can make your own at home with this simple recipe that yields 1 teaspoon of poultry seasoning. In a small container, simply combine 3/4 teaspoon rubbed sage and 1/4 teaspoon dried thyme or marjoram.

clove-studded oranges

It turns out DIY Christmas decorations aren't a new craze after all. Just check out these clove-studded oranges, a popular holiday decoration during the 15th century. Simple yet elegant, they lend no-fuss color and interest to tabletops, mantles and bowls.

☐ a selection of oranges, grapefruits, clementines and other citrus fruits

☐ toothpicks

☐ whole cloves

1. Gently poke holes in the fruit with a toothpick in the pattern or design you want.

2. Fill each toothpick hole with a single clove.

3. Arrange the fruits in a bowl or vase, on a platter, or as desired.

TIME-HONORED TRADITIONS

Pomanders, a clove-studded fruit, were traditionally made at Christmas and New Year's and given as gifts. They represented a wish of prosperity for the receiver. The word pomander comes from the French pomme (which means apple, also the root of Pomona, the Roman goddess of fruits, and pommel, the decorative hilt of a word or dagger,) and ambre, which means golden in color.

It's the most wonderful time of the year, but it's also one of the busiest. Why spend more time than necessary working in the kitchen when you can let your slow cooker do the work?

Feast on an array of home-style favorites all prepared with a set-it-and-forget-it attitude. With your slow cooker at your side and a tiny bit of preparation, you will not only free up space in the oven, but you'll find that it's a snap to set a memorable meal in the table with less effort than imagined.

After all, dishes like moist and tender Glazed Rosemary Pork Roast and Applesauce Sweet Potatoes serve up all the comforting flavors of a traditional Christmas dinner, but without all the fuss. Simply turn the pages for even more scrumptious ideas that make the most of your time, your holiday and your all-time favorite kitchen appliance!

NO-FUSS HOLIDAY DINNER

Glazed Rosemary Pork Roast (p. 18)
Applesauce Sweet Potatoes (p. 18)

SLOW COOKER
SEASONAL FARE

applesauce sweet potatoes

(PICTURED ON PAGE 17)

During the holidays, using my slow cooker not only frees up oven space, but time, too! Sweet potatoes are a must on our family menu, and this no-fuss version has everyone thinking I spent hours in the kitchen.

PAMELA ALLEN | MARYSVILLE, OHIO

2 pounds sweet potatoes, peeled and sliced

1½ cups unsweetened applesauce

⅔ cup packed brown sugar

3 tablespoons butter, melted

1 teaspoon ground cinnamon

½ cup chopped glazed pecans, optional

Place sweet potatoes in a 4-qt. slow cooker. Combine the applesauce, brown sugar, butter and cinnamon; pour over sweet potatoes. Cover and cook on low for 4-5 hours or until potatoes are tender. Sprinkle with pecans if desired. Serve with a slotted spoon.

YIELD: 8 SERVINGS.

glazed rosemary pork roast

(PICTURED ON PAGE 17)

For a change of pace, I'll serve this special pork roast at holiday gatherings. It's a welcome break from traditional turkey or ham, and when dressed with an herb-infused glaze featuring rosemary, thyme and sage, its flavor is unbeatable.

JOYCE MANIER | BEECH GROVE, INDIANA

1 boneless whole pork loin roast (3 pounds)

1 tablespoon butter

1 teaspoon olive oil

1 large onion, sliced

1 tablespoon brown sugar

1 tablespoon minced fresh rosemary

1 teaspoon dried thyme

1 teaspoon rubbed sage

1 teaspoon grated orange peel

½ teaspoon pepper

¼ teaspoon salt

⅔ cup apricot jam

½ cup orange juice

1 bay leaf

1. Cut roast in half. In a large skillet, brown roast in butter and oil on all sides. Transfer to a 4- or 5-qt. slow cooker.

2. Add onion to the same skillet; cook and stir until tender. Stir in the brown sugar, herbs, orange peel, pepper and salt. Spread over pork. Combine jam and orange juice; pour over top. Add bay leaf.

3. Cover and cook on low for 4 hours or until a meat thermometer reads 160°. Discard bay leaf.

YIELD: 8 SERVINGS.

make-ahead eggnog

Homemade eggnog is a tradition in many families during the holiday season. Our slow cooker version shaves off calories and time spent preparing it.

TASTE OF HOME
TEST KITCHEN

6 cups whole milk

1 cup egg substitute

⅔ cup sugar

2 teaspoons rum extract

1½ teaspoons pumpkin pie spice

French vanilla whipped topping, optional

Additional pumpkin pie spice

In a 3-qt. slow cooker, combine first five ingredients. Cover and cook on low for 2-3 hours or until heated through. Serve eggnog in mugs; dollop with whipped topping and sprinkle with additional pumpkin pie spice if desired.

YIELD: 9 SERVINGS (¾ CUP)

USE YOUR NOGGIN: NEW USES FOR EGGNOG

If you think eggnog is just for sipping, think again! While many prefer their eggnog "straight up," some aficionados take a more inventive approach to enjoying the rich and creamy beverage.

- Use eggnog in place of milk when making French toast.

- Replace your usual coffee creamer with a few tablespoons of eggnog or make an eggnog latte.

- Use it to make thick and frosty homemade ice cream.

- Replace the milk in your breakfast smoothie with eggnog for added flavor and extra creaminess.

old-fashioned tapioca

My family loves old-fashioned tapioca, but I don't always have the time to make it.
That's why I developed this simple recipe that allows us to enjoy the comforting dessert more often.

RUTH PETERS | BEL AIR, MARYLAND

8 cups 2% milk

1 cup pearl tapioca

1 cup plus 2 tablespoons sugar

⅛ teaspoon salt

4 eggs

1½ teaspoons vanilla extract

Sliced fresh strawberries and whipped cream, optional

1. In a 4- to 5-qt. slow cooker, combine the milk, tapioca, sugar and salt. Cover and cook on low for 4-5 hours.

2. In a large bowl, beat the eggs; stir in a small amount of hot tapioca mixture. Return all to the slow cooker, stirring to combine. Cover and cook 30 minutes longer or until a thermometer reads 160°. Stir in vanilla.

3. Serve with strawberries and whipped cream if desired.

YIELD: 18 SERVINGS.

slow-cooker lasagna

My friend first made this recipe using a store-bought marinara sauce.
I created a homemade sauce, and it has been a big hit whenever I serve it.

SHERI OGANOWSKI | DAYTON, OHIO

1 pound ground turkey

1 pound bulk Italian sausage

¾ cup chopped sweet onion

3 garlic cloves, minced

3 cans (15 ounces each) tomato sauce

1 can (28 ounces) crushed tomatoes, undrained

⅓ cup sugar

3 tablespoons dried parsley flakes, divided

2 teaspoons dried basil

3 teaspoons dried oregano, divided

½ teaspoon salt, divided

¼ cup dry red wine or beef broth

3 cups (12 ounces) shredded part-skim mozzarella cheese

2½ cups ricotta cheese

1 cup grated Parmesan cheese

1 package (9 ounces) no-cook lasagna noodles

1. In a Dutch oven, cook the turkey, sausage, onion and garlic over medium heat until meat is no longer pink; drain. Stir in the tomato sauce, crushed tomatoes, sugar, 2 tablespoons parsley, basil, 2 teaspoons oregano and ¼ teaspoon salt. Bring to a boil. Reduce heat; simmer, uncovered, for 45 minutes. Add wine; cook 15 minutes longer.

2. Meanwhile, in a large bowl, combine the cheeses and the remaining parsley, oregano and salt.

3. Spread 2¼ cups meat mixture into a 6-qt. slow cooker. Arrange five noodles over sauce, breaking to fit if necessary. Spread 1⅓ cups of cheese mixture over noodles. Repeat layers twice. Top with remaining meat mixture.

4. Cover and cook on low for 4-5 hours or until noodles are tender.

YIELD: 10 SERVINGS.

SLOW COOKER SECRETS

Unless the recipe instructs you to stir in or add ingredients, refrain from lifting the lid while the slow cooker is cooking. Every time you lift the lid, steam is lost and you add 15 to 30 minutes of cooking time.

spiced split pea soup

A hint of curry adds the perfect amount of kick to this family-pleasing soup.
Just assemble the ingredients in the slow cooker, then go about your day while it simmers.

SUE MOHRE | MT. GILEAD, OHIO

4 cups reduced-sodium chicken broth

1 cup dried green split peas

2 medium potatoes, chopped

2 medium carrots, halved and thinly sliced

1 medium onion, chopped

1 celery rib, thinly sliced

3 garlic cloves, minced

3 bay leaves

4 teaspoons curry powder

1 teaspoon ground cumin

½ teaspoon coarsely ground pepper

½ teaspoon ground coriander

1 can (28 ounces) diced tomatoes, undrained

1. In a 4-qt. slow cooker combine the first 12 items.

2. Cover and cook on low for 7-9 hours or until peas are tender. Add tomatoes; heat through. Discard bay leaves.

YIELD: 10 SERVINGS (2½ QUARTS).

sweet & sour turkey meatballs

Pomegranates are my favorite winter fruit, so I try to enjoy them in many different ways. Here is one of my favorite recipes that uses the juice to flavor tender meatballs.

CHRISTINE WENDLAND | BROWNS MILLS, NEW JERSEY

4 thick-sliced peppered bacon strips

1 egg, beaten

½ cup seasoned bread crumbs

3 tablespoons minced fresh cilantro

1 teaspoon salt

1 teaspoon white pepper

2 pounds ground turkey

1 jar (18 ounces) apricot preserves

1 can (14½ ounces) diced tomatoes, undrained

1 bottle (8 ounces) taco sauce

½ cup pomegranate juice

1. Place bacon in a food processor; cover and process until finely chopped. In a large bowl, combine the egg, bread crumbs, cilantro, salt and pepper. Crumble turkey and bacon over mixture and mix well. Shape into 1-in. balls.

2. Place in two ungreased 15-in. x 10-in. x 1-in. baking pans. Bake at 400° for 8-10 minutes or until a thermometer reads 165° and juices run clear.

3. In a 4-qt. slow cooker, combine the preserves, tomatoes, taco sauce and juice. Stir in meatballs. Cover and cook on high for 2-3 hours or until heated through.

YIELD: ABOUT 5½ DOZEN.

butternut squash with whole grain pilaf

Fresh thyme really shines in this hearty slow-cooked side dish featuring tender butternut squash, nutritious whole grain pilaf and vitamin-packed baby spinach.

TASTE OF HOME TEST KITCHEN

1 cup Kashi whole grain pilaf

1 medium butternut squash (about 3 pounds), cut into ½-inch cubes

1 can (14½ ounces) vegetable broth

1 medium onion, chopped

½ cup water

3 garlic cloves, minced

2 teaspoons minced fresh thyme or ½ teaspoon dried thyme

½ teaspoon salt

¼ teaspoon pepper

1 package (6 ounces) fresh baby spinach

Place pilaf in a 4-qt. slow cooker. In a large bowl, combine the squash, broth, onion, water, garlic, thyme, salt and pepper. Cover and cook on low for 4-5 hours or until pilaf is tender, adding spinach during the last 30 minutes of cooking.

YIELD: 12 SERVINGS (¾ CUP EACH).

SQAUSH STORAGE TIPS

The most common varieties of winter squash are butternut, acorn, hubbard, spaghetti and turban. Look for squash that feel heavy for their size and have hard, deep-colored rinds free of blemishes. Unwashed winter squash can be stored in a dry, cool, well-ventilated place for up to 1 month.

moist corn spoon bread

One bite and you'll want to pair this comforting side dish with all your holiday meals!
It's more moist than traditional corn pudding made in the oven, plus the cream cheese is a nice addition.

TASTE OF HOME TEST KITCHEN

1 package (8 ounces) cream cheese, softened

2 tablespoons sugar

1 cup 2% milk

½ cup egg substitute

2 tablespoons butter, melted

½ teaspoon salt

¼ teaspoon cayenne pepper

⅛ teaspoon pepper

2 cups frozen corn

1 can (14¾ ounces) cream-style corn

1 cup yellow cornmeal

1 cup (4 ounces) shredded Monterey Jack cheese

3 green onions, thinly sliced

1. In a bowl, beat the cream cheese and the sugar until smooth. Gradually beat in the milk. Gently beat in the egg substitute, butter, salt, cayenne and pepper until blended. Stir in the remaining ingredients.

2. Pour into a greased 3-qt. slow cooker. Cover and cook on low for 4-5 hours or until a toothpick inserted near the center comes out clean.

YIELD: 8 SERVINGS.

crab & artichoke dip

Whenever my girlfriends and I got together, this rich and creamy dip always accompanied our favorite bottle of wine. Because the recipe relies on the convenience of a slow cooker, it's a great addition to holiday gatherings, too!

CONNIE MCKINNEY | MARSHALL, MISSOURI

3 cups fresh baby spinach

1 can (14 ounces) water-packed artichoke hearts, rinsed, drained and chopped

1 package (8 ounces) cream cheese, softened

2 cups (8 ounces) shredded Havarti cheese

1 can (6 ounces) lump crabmeat, drained

½ cup sour cream

⅛ teaspoon salt

⅛ teaspoon pepper

Assorted crackers

1. In a large saucepan, bring ½ in. of water to a boil. Add spinach; cover and boil for 3-5 minutes or until wilted. Drain.

2. In a 1½-qt. slow cooker, combine the artichokes, cheeses, crabmeat, sour cream, salt, pepper and spinach. Cover and cook on low for 2-3 hours or until cheese is melted. Serve with crackers.

YIELD: 3½ CUPS.

garlic & herb mashed potatoes

Can you keep a secret? Cream cheese is the "secret ingredient" in these comforting spuds. Simply mix, mash and let them simmer in the slow cooker.

FRIEDA BLIESNER | MCALLEN, TEXAS

4 pounds Yukon Gold potatoes (about 12 medium), peeled and cubed

1 package (8 ounces) cream cheese, softened and cubed

1 cup (8 ounces) sour cream

½ cup butter, cubed

⅓ cup heavy whipping cream

3 tablespoons minced chives

3 garlic cloves, minced

1 tablespoon minced fresh parsley

1 teaspoon minced fresh thyme

½ teaspoon salt

¼ teaspoon pepper

1. Place potatoes in a Dutch oven and cover with water. Bring to a boil. Reduce heat; cover and cook for 10-15 minutes or until tender. Drain. Mash potatoes with cream cheese, sour cream, butter and cream. Stir in the remaining ingredients.

2. Transfer to a greased 3- or 4-qt. slow cooker. Cover and cook on low for 2-3 hours or until heated through.

YIELD: 10 SERVINGS.

LEFTOVER MAKEOVER

It's hard to imagine there would be any Garlic & Herb Mashed Potatoes left over, but if there are, freeze the excess in muffin cups. Once they're frozen, remove the single servings and store in resealable plastic freezer bags. During the week, pull out as many servings as you need and reheat them in the microwave.

beef osso bucco

Treat holiday guests to elegant comfort food at its best. Our hearty beef entree boasts a thick, savory sauce complemented by the addition of gremolata, a chopped herb condiment made of lemon zest, garlic and parsley.

TASTE OF HOME
TEST KITCHEN

½ cup all-purpose flour

½ teaspoon pepper

¾ teaspoon salt, divided

6 beef shanks (14 ounces each)

2 tablespoons butter

1 tablespoon olive oil

½ cup white wine or beef broth

1 can (14½ ounces) diced tomatoes, undrained

1½ cups beef broth

2 medium carrots, chopped

1 medium onion, chopped

1 celery rib, sliced

1 tablespoon dried thyme

1 tablespoon dried oregano

2 bay leaves

3 tablespoons cornstarch

¼ cup cold water

GREMOLATA

⅓ cup minced fresh parsley

1 tablespoon grated lemon peel

1 tablespoon grated orange peel

2 garlic cloves, minced

1. In a large resealable plastic bag, combine the flour, pepper and ½ teaspoon salt. Add beef, a few pieces at a time, and shake to coat.

2. In a large skillet, brown beef in butter and oil. Transfer meat and drippings to a 6-qt. slow cooker. Add wine to skillet, stirring to loosen browned bits from pan; pour over meat. Add the tomatoes, broth, carrots, onion, celery, thyme, oregano, bay leaves and remaining salt.

3. Cover and cook on low for 7-9 hours or until meat is tender. Discard bay leaves.

4. Skim fat from cooking juices; transfer juices to a large saucepan. Bring to a boil. Combine cornstarch and water until smooth; gradually stir into the pan. Bring to a boil; cook and stir for 2 minutes or until thickened.

5. In a small bowl, combine the gremolata ingredients. Serve beef with gremolata and sauce.

YIELD: 6 SERVINGS.

Rise and shine! St. Nick made a visit last night, so it's time to celebrate this morning with a family breakfast your gang will remember for years to come. Better yet..turn this tasty brunch into an annual tradition with friends and neighbors and kick off the holiday season in a delicious way!

As the kids race to the mantle to empty their stockings, you'll have no trouble serving up decadent French toast or a hearty breakfast casserole. If your guests have to eat and run that morning, you can also consider no-fuss Blueberry Pancake Snack Mix, Sweet Potato Cranberry Doughnuts or frosty Cherry Cobbler Smoothies. You'll find all of these change-of-pace brunch ideas and more in this colorful section!

EASY EYE-OPENERS

A JOLLY ST. NICK'S BRUNCH

toffee apple french toast with caramel syrup

(PICTURED ON PAGE 27)

I adapted Mom's recipe to include one of my all-time much-loved flavor treats: caramel apples!

SUZANNE FORSBERG | MANTECA, CALIFORNIA

8 cups cubed French bread

3 medium tart apples, peeled and chopped

1 envelope (.74 ounce) instant spiced cider mix

1 package (8 ounces) cream cheese, softened

¾ cup packed brown sugar

¼ cup sugar

1¾ cups 2% milk, divided

2 teaspoons vanilla extract, divided

½ cup milk chocolate English toffee bits

5 eggs

1½ cups sugar

¾ cup buttermilk

½ cup butter, cubed

2 tablespoons corn syrup

1 teaspoon baking soda

2 teaspoons vanilla extract

1. Place half of the bread cubes in a greased 13-in. x 9-in. baking dish. Top with apples and sprinkle with cider drink mix. In a small bowl, beat the cream cheese, sugars, ¼ cup milk and 1 teaspoon vanilla until smooth. Stir in toffee. Spread over apples. Top with remaining bread cubes.

2. In another bowl, whisk the eggs and remaining milk and vanilla. Pour over top. Cover and refrigerate overnight.

3. Remove from the refrigerator 30 minutes before baking. Bake, uncovered, at 350° for 40-45 minutes or until a knife inserted near the center comes out clean. Let stand for 10 minutes before serving.

4. Meanwhile, in a Dutch oven, combine the sugar, buttermilk, butter, corn syrup and baking soda. Bring to a boil over medium heat, stirring constantly. Cook, stirring occasionally, until mixture turns a golden amber color, about 7 minutes. Remove from the heat; stir in vanilla. Serve with French toast.

YIELD: 12 SERVINGS (1½ CUPS SYRUP).

blueberry pancake snack mix

My no-fuss, kid-friendly recipe is easy to mix and perfect for busy families who are on the go.

AYSHA SCHURMAN | AMMON, IDAHO

3 cups Corn Chex

2 cups Wheat Chex

1 cup Rice Chex

2 cups dried blueberries

1 cup chopped walnuts

⅓ cup maple syrup

¼ cup butter, melted

1. In a microwave-safe bowl, combine the first five ingredients. In another bowl, combine syrup and butter. Pour over cereal mixture; toss to coat.

2. Microwave on high for 5 minutes, stirring after each minute. Spread onto waxed paper to cool. Store in an airtight container.

YIELD: 2 QUARTS.

EDITOR'S NOTE: *This recipe was tested in a 1,100-watt microwave.*

sweet potato-cranberry doughnuts

I grew up near Idaho, where "spudnuts" are made from mashed potatoes. I reworked a recipe to feature sweet potatoes and cranberries.

JONI HILTON
ROCKLIN, CALIFORNIA

¼ cup sugar

1½ teaspoons active dry yeast

1 teaspoon ground cinnamon

½ teaspoon salt

4 to 4½ cups all-purpose flour

1 cup 2% milk

¼ cup shortening

2 tablespoons water

2 eggs

½ cup mashed sweet potatoes

½ cup finely chopped dried cranberries

Oil for deep-fat frying

1 cup confectioners' sugar

2 to 3 tablespoons apple cider or juice

1. In a large bowl, combine the sugar, yeast, cinnamon, salt and 1½ cups flour. In a small saucepan, heat the milk, shortening and water to 120°-130°; add to dry ingredients. Beat on medium speed for 2 minutes. Add the eggs, mashed potatoes and cranberries; beat 2 minutes longer. Stir in enough remaining flour to form a firm dough.

2. Do not knead. Place in a greased bowl, turning once to grease the top. Cover and let rise in a warm place until doubled, about 1 hour.

3. Punch dough down. Turn onto a lightly floured surface; roll out to ½-in. thickness. Cut with a floured 2½-in. doughnut cutter; reroll scraps. Place 1-in. apart on greased baking sheets. Cover and let rise until doubled, about 30 minutes.

4. In an electric skillet or deep fryer, heat oil to 375°. Fry doughnuts, a few at a time, until golden brown on both sides. Drain on paper towels. Combine confectioners' sugar and apple cider; dip warm doughnuts in glaze.

YIELD: 2 DOZEN.

cherry cobbler smoothies

(PICTURED ON PAGE 26)

*It's been said that breakfast is the most important meal of the day. I want to make it count,
so I created this fruity and refreshing smoothie packed with good-for-you cherries and vanilla yogurt.*

SHERRY MOTE | MARIETTA, GEORGIA

2 cups vanilla yogurt

½ cup orange juice

¼ cup honey

1 teaspoon vanilla extract

1 teaspoon almond extract

2 cups ice cubes

2 cups frozen pitted dark sweet cherries

2 teaspoons ground cinnamon

1. In a blender, combine all ingredients; cover and process for 30 seconds or until smooth. Pour into chilled glasses; serve immediately.

YIELD: 5 SERVINGS.

apple salad with peanut butter dressing

*Kids of all ages will beg for second helpings of this fun and festive salad.
It's great for bringing little ones into the kitchen because the ingredient list is simple,
no baking is involved and the entire dish comes together oh-so easily!*

TERRI MERRITTS | NASHVILLE, TENNESSEE

4 medium apples, chopped

½ teaspoon lemon juice

1 medium banana, peeled and sliced

1 small carrot, shredded

¼ cup dried mango, chopped

2 tablespoons flaked coconut

½ cup chopped walnuts, optional

DRESSING

¼ cup brown sugar

¼ cup sour cream

¼ cup heavy whipping cream

2 tablespoons creamy peanut butter

1. In a large bowl, toss apples with lemon juice. Add the banana, carrot, mango, coconut and walnuts if desired. Combine dressing ingredients; pour over apple mixture and toss to coat. Chill until serving.

YIELD: 8 CUPS.

BROWN-SUGAR BASICS

Always store brown sugar in an airtight container. If you find you need to soften the sugar, simply place a slice of bread or an apple wedge with the sugar in a covered container. It may take a day or two until the sugar returns to a useable consistancy. If you're in a hurry, however, you can microwave the sugar on high for 20-30 seconds. Repeat if necessary, but watch carefully! The sugar can begin to melt if it's in the microwave too long.

cheese grits & sausage breakfast casserole

I can't resist this breakfast casserole. It combines all my favorites into one dish: creamy grits, tangy cheese, rich eggs and flavorful sausage! It's a perfect alternative to more traditional breakfast bakes.

MANDY RIVERS | LEXINGTON, SOUTH CAROLINA

2 pounds bulk Italian sausage

2 cups water

2 cups chicken broth

½ teaspoon salt

1¼ cups quick-cooking grits

1 pound sharp cheddar cheese, shredded

1 cup 2% milk

1½ teaspoons garlic powder

1 teaspoon rubbed sage

6 eggs, beaten

Paprika, optional

1. In a large skillet, cook sausage over medium heat until no longer pink; drain.

2. In a large saucepan, bring the water, broth and salt to a boil. Slowly stir in grits. Reduce heat; cook and stir for 5-7 minutes or until thickened. Remove from the heat. Add cheese, milk, garlic powder and sage, stirring until cheese is melted. Stir in sausage and eggs. Transfer to a greased 13-in. x 9-in. baking dish; sprinkle with paprika if desired.

3. Bake, uncovered, at 350° for 40-45 minutes or until a knife inserted near the center comes out clean. Let stand for 10 minutes before serving.

YIELD: 12 SERVINGS.

orange-glazed bacon

(PICTURED ON PAGE 27 & AT RIGHT)

Just when you thought bacon couldn't get any tastier, our Test Kitchen staff whipped up this easy recipe starring your favorite breakfast meat drizzled with a sweet orange glaze.

TASTE OF HOME TEST KITCHEN

¾ cup orange juice

¼ cup honey

1 tablespoon Dijon mustard

¼ teaspoon ground ginger

⅛ teaspoon pepper

1 pound bacon strips

1. In a small saucepan, combine the first five ingredients. Bring to a boil; cook until liquid is reduced to ⅓ cup.

2. Place bacon on a rack in an ungreased 15-in. x 10-in. x 1-in. baking pan. Bake at 350° for 10 minutes; drain.

3. Drizzle half of glaze over bacon. Bake for 10 minutes. Turn bacon and drizzle with remaining glaze. Bake 5-10 minutes longer or until golden brown. Place bacon on waxed paper until set. Serve warm.

YIELD: 8 SERVINGS.

christmas morning oatmeal

I found this recipe on line and was convinced I was eating yummy apple crisp for breakfast! Even when I cut down on the butter, this hearty oatmeal remained moist, scrumptious and worked great when cooked overnight.

MONICA LORD | COLLEGEVILLE, PENNSYLVANIA

⅓ cup packed brown sugar

1 teaspoon ground cinnamon

½ teaspoon ground nutmeg

2 medium apples, peeled and sliced

¾ cup dried cranberries

2 tablespoons butter, cubed

2 cups old-fashioned oats

2 cups water

2 cups cranberry-apple juice

½ teaspoon salt

1. In a small bowl, combine the brown sugar, cinnamon and nutmeg. Add apples and cranberries; toss to coat. Transfer to a 3-qt. slow cooker. Dot with butter.

2. In a large bowl, combine the oats, water, juice and salt; pour over apple mixture. Cover and cook on low for 7-8 hours or until liquid is absorbed.

YIELD: 6 SERVINGS.

COOKING WITH OATS

Before either old-fashioned or quick-cooking oats are processed, the hull is removed and they are cleaned, toasted and cleaned again. At this point, they are referred to as groats. Old-fashioned oats are groats that are steamed and flattened with huge rollers. They take about 15 minutes to cook. Quick-cooking oats are groats that have been cut into two or three pieces before being steamed and rolled. They take about 5 minutes to prepare. Both can be used interchangeably, although old-fashioned oats often give recipes a more satisfying texture.

new year's kick-off omelet

*For over 30 years, we've hosted a New Year's breakfast for family and friends.
The main attraction used to be Belgian waffles...until I came up with this omelet
that is baked in the oven and then rolled up, sliced and served.*

SHARON BALLOU | RANDALL, MINNESOTA

18   eggs

½   teaspoon salt

¼   teaspoon pepper

1   cup 2% milk

½   cup cream cheese, softened

1   cup (4 ounces) shredded
    Colby cheese

¾   cup cubed fully cooked ham

¾   cup chopped tomatoes

½   cup chopped fresh
    mushrooms

3   green onions, thinly sliced

1. Line a greased 15-in. x 10-in. x 1-in. baking pan with parchment paper; grease the paper and set aside.

2. In a large bowl, whisk the eggs, salt and pepper. In a small bowl, beat milk and cream cheese until smooth; add to egg mixture. Pour into prepared pan.

3. Bake at 350° for 15-20 minutes or until set. Turn omelet onto a work surface; peel off parchment paper. Sprinkle omelet with cheese, ham, tomatoes, mushrooms and green onions; roll up jelly-roll style, starting with a long side. Place on a serving platter. Let stand for 5 minutes before serving.

YIELD: 10 SERVINGS.

W ho doesn't like to curl up by the fireplace with a good book? Add a few new titles to your shelf this holiday season by inviting your friends over for a holiday book swap.

As you trade gently read books, nibble and nosh on a savory buffet of elegant appetizers.

Marinated Antipasto Medley serves a rainbow of colors and flavors, while being light enough to leave room for heartier bites, such as Seafood Cakes with Herb Sauce, Moroccan Stuffed Mushrooms and Spicy Beef Satay.

BITES 'N' BOOKS

A HOLIDAY BOOK SWAP

moroccan stuffed mushrooms

(PICTURED ON PAGE 34)

*Coriander and cumin update familiar stuffed mushrooms, while the addition
of fluffy couscous gives these bite-size snacks a little more heft.*

RAYMONDE BOURGEOIS | SWASTIKA, ONTARIO

24 medium fresh mushrooms

½ cup chopped onion

⅓ cup finely shredded carrot

1 teaspoon canola oil

1 garlic clove, minced

½ teaspoon salt

½ teaspoon ground cumin

¼ teaspoon ground coriander

¾ cup vegetable broth

2 tablespoons dried currants

½ cup uncooked couscous

2 tablespoons minced fresh parsley

2 tablespoons minced fresh mint

1. Remove stems from mushrooms and finely chop stems; set caps aside. In a large nonstick skillet, saute the onion, carrot and chopped stems in oil until crisp-tender.

2. Add the garlic, salt, cumin and coriander. Cook and stir for 1 minute. Add broth and currants; bring to a boil. Stir in couscous. Remove from the heat; cover and let stand for 5-10 minutes or until broth is absorbed. Fluff with a fork. Stir in parsley and mint. Stuff into mushroom caps.

3. Place on a foil-lined baking sheet. Bake at 400° for 10-15 minutes or until mushrooms are tender.

YIELD: 2 DOZEN.

spicy beef satay

(PICTURED ON PAGE 34)

The fragrant spices and full flavors of North African cuisine make these appetizers a tasty party food.

ROXANNE CHAN | ALBANY, CALIFORNIA

1 cup white wine vinegar

¾ cup sugar

½ cup water

1 tablespoon orange marmalade

¼ teaspoon grated orange peel

¼ teaspoon crushed red pepper flakes

½ cup finely chopped salted roasted almonds

2 tablespoons minced fresh mint

1 green onion, finely chopped

1 tablespoon lemon juice

1 garlic clove, minced

¼ teaspoon each ground cinnamon, cumin and coriander

1 pound lean ground beef (90% lean)

Minced fresh parsley

1. In a small saucepan, combine the first six ingredients. Bring to a boil. Reduce heat; simmer, uncovered, for about 25 minutes or until reduced to ½ cup.

2. Meanwhile, in a large bowl, combine the almonds, mint, onion, lemon juice, garlic and spices. Crumble beef over mixture and mix well. Divide into 24 pieces. Shape each piece into a 3-in. x 1-in. rectangle; insert onto soaked wooden appetizer skewers.

3. Broil 6 in. from the heat for 2-4 minutes on each side or until a meat thermometer reads 160°. Arrange on a serving platter. Drizzle with sauce mixture and sprinkle with parsley.

YIELD: 2 DOZEN (½ CUP SAUCE).

black forest icebox cookies

You'll want to keep these festive cookies on hand for when holiday company arrives. The rich chocolate wafers are the perfect complement to the creamy filling's sweet-tart tones.

TASTE OF HOME
TEST KITCHEN

- 3 tablespoons sugar
- 4 teaspoons cornstarch
-    Pinch salt
- ¾ cup fresh or frozen pitted tart cherries, thawed and coarsely chopped
- ¾ cup cherry juice blend
- 1½ teaspoons lemon juice
- 1 to 2 drops red food coloring, optional
- ½ cup Mascarpone cheese
- 1 tablespoon confectioners' sugar
- 1 teaspoon cherry brandy
- 1 package (9 ounces) chocolate wafers
- ½ cup semisweet chocolate chips
- ¼ cup heavy whipping cream

1. In a small saucepan, combine sugar, cornstarch and salt. Add the cherries, juice blend and lemon juice. Bring to a boil; cook and stir for 2 minutes or until thickened. Remove from the heat and stir in food coloring if desired. Cool to room temperature.

2. In a small bowl, combine the Mascarpone cheese, confectioners' sugar and brandy. Spread about 1 teaspoon cheese mixture onto 20 wafers; top with 2 teaspoons cherry mixture and remaining wafers. Place on a waxed paper-lined baking pan. Place chocolate chips in a small bowl. In a small saucepan, bring cream just to a boil. Pour over chips; whisk until smooth. Drizzle over cookies. Cover and refrigerate cookies for up to 4 hours before serving.

YIELD: 20 COOKIES.

seafood cakes with herb sauce

(PICTURED ON PAGE 34)

My tasty starter showcases salmon and scallops, but shrimp, lobster or any firm white fish work well, too.

ELIZABETH TRUESDELL | PETALUMA, CALIFORNIA

¾ cup mayonnaise

4½ teaspoons dill pickle relish

1 tablespoon minced chives

1 tablespoon minced fresh parsley

2 teaspoons tomato paste

1 teaspoon grated lemon peel

⅛ teaspoon salt

⅛ teaspoon pepper

SEAFOOD CAKES

1¼ cups panko (Japanese) bread crumbs

1 medium sweet red pepper, finely chopped

1 medium sweet yellow pepper, finely chopped

⅓ cup finely chopped onion

1 egg, lightly beaten

2 tablespoons minced fresh parsley

2 teaspoons minced chives

1 pound bay scallops, coarsely chopped

½ pound salmon fillet, skin removed and coarsely chopped

⅔ cup butter, cubed

Additional finely chopped sweet red and yellow peppers and minced chives

1. Combine the first eight ingredients; set aside ¼ cup. Chill remaining sauce until serving.

2. In a large bowl, combine the bread crumbs, peppers, onion, egg, parsley, chives and reserved sauce. Gently fold in scallops and salmon.

3. With floured hands, shape mixture by 2 tablespoonfuls into ½-in.-thick patties. In a large skillet over medium heat, cook seafood cakes in butter in batches for 2-3 minutes on each side or until golden brown. Transfer to ungreased baking sheets.

4. Bake at 400° for 5-6 minutes or until golden brown. Serve with sauce. Garnish with additional peppers and chives.

YIELD: 40 APPETIZERS (½ CUP SAUCE).

marinated antipasto medley

(PICTURED ON PAGE 34)

People can't stop nibbling on these marinated bites. The recipe's make-ahead convenience is very handy.

LAURIE HUDSON | WESTVILLE, FLORIDA

8 ounces Colby-Monterey Jack cheese, cut into ½-inch cubes

1 jar (10 ounces) pimiento-stuffed olives, drained

1 jar (16 ounces) cocktail onions, drained

1 cup grape tomatoes

6 ounces pepperoni, cut into ½-inch cubes

DRESSING

¼ cup olive oil

2 tablespoons cider vinegar

½ teaspoon sugar

¼ teaspoon salt

¼ teaspoon dried basil

¼ teaspoon dried oregano

⅛ teaspoon garlic powder

⅛ teaspoon pepper

⅛ teaspoon Louisiana-style hot sauce

In a large bowl, combine the first five ingredients. In a small bowl, whisk the dressing ingredients; pour over vegetable mixture and toss to coat. Cover and refrigerate for at least 3 hours. Stir before serving. Serve with a slotted spoon.

YIELD: 9 SERVINGS.

vodka-infused cherry tomatoes

Even those who claim they don't like tomatoes can't resist eating these unique nibbles. They're festive, fancy and so easy.

PATRICIA NIEH
PORTOLA VALLEY, CALIFORNIA

2 pints cherry tomatoes

2 cups vodka

½ cup coarse sea salt, optional

¼ cup coarsely ground pepper, optional

1. Using a skewer, poke a few holes in each tomato. In a container, combine the tomatoes and the vodka. Cover and refrigerate for 2 days.

2. Pour tomatoes and vodka into a shallow serving dish. In a small bowl, combine salt and pepper if desired. Serve tomatoes with toothpicks and if desired, seasoned salt for dipping.

YIELD: 5 DOZEN.

artichoke hummus

I'm never invited to a party without being asked to bring this artichoke hummus dip. I like to serve it with vegetable crudettes, but you can also serve it with toasted pita bread or your favorite crackers.

HOLLY COLE | PARRISH, FLORIDA

1 can (15 ounces) garbanzo beans or chickpeas, rinsed and drained

1 jar (7½ ounces) marinated quartered artichoke hearts, drained

¼ cup tahini

1 tablespoon capers, drained

2 tablespoons lemon juice

4 garlic cloves, minced

2 teaspoons grated lemon peel

1 teaspoon ground cumin

½ teaspoon garlic powder

⅛ teaspoon salt

Dash crushed red pepper flakes, optional

Dash pepper

2 fresh rosemary sprigs, chopped

Place the first 12 ingredients in a food processor; cover and process until smooth. Transfer to a small bowl; stir in rosemary. Serve with vegetables.

YIELD: 2 CUPS.

yogurt cheese dip

It's rare to come across recipes that are perfect for holiday noshing and are good for you. That's why I adore this versatile dip. I served it at a party, and the two gals sitting near it couldn't stop eating it.

CORALEE HUMPHREYS | NEW HARTFORD, NEW YORK

3 cups plain Greek yogurt

1 teaspoon sesame seeds, toasted

½ teaspoon salt

⅛ teaspoon cayenne pepper

⅛ teaspoon ground cumin

1 tablespoon olive oil

1 teaspoon grated lemon peel

Baked pita chips

1. Line a strainer with four layers of cheesecloth or one coffee filter and place over a bowl. Place yogurt in prepared strainer; cover yogurt with edges of cheesecloth. Refrigerate for 8 hours or overnight.

2. Remove yogurt from cheesecloth and discard liquid from bowl. Combine sesame seeds, salt, cayenne and cumin. Spread yogurt on a serving plate. Drizzle with oil. Sprinkle with sesame seed mixture and lemon peel. Serve with pita chips.

YIELD: 2 CUPS.

chocolate-caramel rum coffee

This decadent coffee drink can stand alone as a dessert or a delightful complement to any chocolate or caramel treat! Our family enjoys sipping it after a special dinner or while sitting in front of the fireplace.

JOYCE CONWAY | WESTERVILLE, OHIO

2 cans (12 ounces each) evaporated milk

¾ cup rum

½ cup chocolate syrup

½ cup caramel sundae syrup

¼ cup packed brown sugar

4 cups hot brewed coffee

2 tablespoons coffee liqueur

COFFEE WHIPPED CREAM

1 cup heavy whipping cream

6 tablespoons confectioners' sugar

2 tablespoons coffee liqueur

Coffee beans, optional

1. In a large saucepan, combine the milk, rum, syrups and brown sugar. Cook over medium heat until hot (do not boil). Stir in coffee and liqueur.

2. Meanwhile, in a small bowl, beat cream until it begins to thicken. Add confectioners' sugar; beat until stiff peaks form. Fold in liqueur until combined.

3. Pour coffee mixture into mugs. Garnish with a dollop of coffee whipped cream and coffee beans if desired.

YIELD: 8 SERVINGS.

COFFEE SHOP GARNISH

It's easy to give coffee drinks you make at home that eye-catching coffee shop appearance. Just add a few sprinkles of baking cocoa or instant chocolate drink mix or some decadent chocolate curls for a pretty and elegant finishing touch.

Store baking cocoa or instant chocolate drink mix in a small shaker—like the ones that hold powdered sugar—for speedy sifting. For chocolate curls, use a vegetable peeler to peel off curls from a solid block of chocolate.

cranberry-jalapeno martini

Slightly tart, a little sassy and completely delicious. That's how I describe this creative adult beverage that is ideal for holiday gatherings. Garnish with fresh mint and cranberries for an extra special touch.

KELLI HAETINGER | VIRGINIA BEACH, VIRGINIA

1 cup turbinado (washed raw) sugar

1½ cups cranberry juice, divided

½ cup fresh or frozen cranberries

½ teaspoon chopped seeded jalapeno pepper

Ice cubes

6 cups vodka

Fresh mint leaves and additional cranberries

1. In a large saucepan, combine the sugar, ½ cup cranberry juice, cranberries and jalapeno. Bring to a boil. Reduce the heat; simmer, uncovered, for 3 minutes or until sugar is dissolved. Remove from the heat. Cover and let stand for 20 minutes.

2. Strain liquid; discard the cranberries and jalapeno. Cover and refrigerate syrup for at least 2 hours or until chilled.

3. For each serving, fill a mixing glass or tumbler three-fourths full with ice. Add 3 ounces vodka, 1 tablespoon cranberry juice and 1 tablespoon cranberry syrup; stir until condensation forms on outside of glass. Strain into a chilled cocktail glass. Repeat. Garnish glasses with mint and cranberries if desired.

YIELD: 16 SERVINGS.

goat cheese egg rolls

I love cooking with goat cheese. There is something about its tart flavor and smoothness that make recipes that use it feel extra special. My egg rolls are no exception.

SUSAN NILSSON | STERLING, VIRGINIA

½ cup finely chopped walnuts, toasted

½ cup pitted dates, finely chopped

1 teaspoon ground cardamom

1 teaspoon ground cinnamon

1 log (8 ounces) fresh goat cheese

8 egg roll wrappers

Oil for deep-fat frying

¼ cup raspberry vinaigrette

1 teaspoon reduced-sodium soy sauce

1. In a small shallow bowl, combine the walnuts, dates, cardamom and cinnamon. Cut cheese into eight pieces; shape each piece into a 3-in. log. Roll in walnut mixture.

2. Place one cheese log in the center of one egg roll wrapper. (Keep remaining wrappers covered with a damp paper towel until ready to use.) Fold bottom corner over filling. Fold sides toward center over filling. Moisten remaining corner with water; roll up tightly to seal. Repeat.

3. In an electric skillet or deep-fat fryer, heat oil to 375°. Fry egg rolls, a few at a time, for 3-4 minutes or until golden brown, turning often. Drain on paper towels.

4. Combine vinaigrette and soy sauce; serve with egg rolls.

YIELD: 8 EGG ROLLS (¼ CUP SAUCE).

cranberry hot wings

Cranberry lends seasonal flair as well as a touch of sweetness to these spicy wings. Their popularity with guests makes them my standby recipe for any gathering.

ROBIN HAAS | CRANSTON, RHODE ISLAND

1 can (14 ounces) jellied cranberry sauce, cubed

2 tablespoons ground mustard

2 tablespoons hot pepper sauce

2 tablespoons reduced-sodium soy sauce

2 tablespoons honey

1 tablespoon cider vinegar

2 teaspoons garlic powder

1 teaspoon grated orange peel

3 pounds chicken wings

Blue cheese salad dressing and celery ribs

1. In a 5-qt. slow cooker, combine the first eight ingredients. Cover and cook on low for 45 minutes or until cranberry sauce is melted.

2. Meanwhile, cut wings into three sections; discard wing tip sections. Place wings on a greased broiler pan. Broil 4-6 in. from the heat for 15-20 minutes or until lightly browned, turning occasionally.

3. Transfer wings to slow cooker; toss to coat. Cover and cook on high for 2-3 hours or until tender. Serve wings with salad dressing and celery ribs.

YIELD: ABOUT 1 DOZEN.

EDITOR'S NOTE: *Uncooked chicken wing sections (wingettes) may be substituted for whole chicken wings.*

ham and cheese cream puffs

For a savory spin on a dessert favorite, try my ham and cheese cream puffs. With their luscious cream cheese filling and tender pastry, the bites lend an elegant touch to any appetizer tray.

SONYA GOERGEN | MOORHEAD, MINNESOTA

- 1 carton (8 ounces) spreadable chive and onion cream cheese
- ½ cup mayonnaise
- 3 tablespoons 2% milk
- 1 cup cubed fully cooked ham
- 1 cup (4 ounces) shredded cheddar cheese
- 3 tablespoons chopped sweet red pepper
- 1 tablespoon minced chives
- 1 tablespoon minced fresh parsley
- 1 garlic clove, minced

CREAM PUFFS

- 1 cup water
- ½ cup butter, cubed
- ¼ teaspoon seasoned salt
- ⅛ teaspoon garlic powder
- ⅛ teaspoon onion powder
- 1 cup all-purpose flour
- 4 eggs
- 1 cup (4 ounces) shredded cheddar cheese
- 1 tablespoon minced fresh parsley
- 1 tablespoon minced chives
  Additional minced fresh parsley and chives

1. In a small bowl, beat the cream cheese, mayonnaise and milk until blended. Stir in the ham, cheese, pepper, chives, parsley and garlic. Cover and refrigerate until ready to use.

2. In a large saucepan, bring the water, butter, seasoned salt, garlic powder and onion powder to a boil. Add flour all at once and stir until a smooth ball forms.

3. Remove from the heat; let stand for 5 minutes. Add eggs, one at a time, beating well after each addition. Continue beating until mixture is smooth and shiny. Stir in the cheese, parsley and chives.

4. Drop by teaspoonfuls 2 in. apart onto greased baking sheets. Bake at 400° for 20-25 minutes or until golden brown. Remove to wire racks. Immediately split puffs open; remove tops and set aside. Discard soft dough from inside. Cool puffs.

5. Just before serving, fill cream puffs with ham mixture. Sprinkle with additional parsley and chives.

YIELD: 3 DOZEN.

lemon risotto fritters
with lemon-cilantro dipping sauce

Lemon adds a splash of flavor to these fried Southern favorites. Fresh cilantro really perks up the creamy dipping sauce, making it impossible to eat just one fritter.

DONNA THOMAS | DALLAS, TEXAS

4½ to 5 cups chicken broth

1 small onion, finely chopped

4 tablespoons butter, divided

1 tablespoon olive oil

1½ cups uncooked arborio rice

½ cup white wine or additional chicken broth

1 tablespoon lemon juice

2 teaspoons grated lemon peel

½ teaspoon sea salt

¼ teaspoon pepper

1 cup all-purpose flour

2 eggs

1 cup dry bread crumbs

Oil for deep-fat frying

DIPPING SAUCE

½ cup mayonnaise

1 tablespoon minced fresh cilantro

1 garlic clove, minced

1 teaspoon grated lemon peel

1 teaspoon lemon juice

1. In a large saucepan, heat broth and keep warm. In a large skillet, saute onion in 2 tablespoons butter and oil for 2-3 minutes or until tender. Add rice; cook and stir for 2-3 minutes. Reduce heat; stir in wine and lemon juice. Cook and stir until all of the liquid is absorbed.

2. Add heated broth, ½ cup at a time, stirring constantly. Allow the liquid to absorb between additions. Cook just until risotto is creamy and rice is almost tender. (Cooking time is about 20 minutes.) Add the lemon peel, salt, pepper and remaining butter; cook and stir until heated through. Transfer to a 15-in. x 10-in. x 1-in. baking pan. Cool to room temperature. Cover and refrigerate for 1 hour.

3. Place flour and eggs in separate shallow bowls. Place bread crumbs in another shallow bowl. Shape risotto mixture into 1½ in. balls. Dip fritters in the flour, eggs, then bread crumbs.

4. In an electric skillet or deep fryer, heat oil to 375°. Fry fritters, a few at a time, until golden brown on both sides.

5. In a small bowl, combine sauce ingredients; serve with fritters.

YIELD: 1½ DOZEN (½ CUP SAUCE).

A LESSON IN LEMON JUICE

When a recipe calls for juice from a fresh lemon, you can use either fresh, frozen or bottled lemon juice in equal amounts.

When lemons are in season or you have excess lemons on hand, juice them and freeze the juice in ice cube trays. Measure 1 or 2 tablespoons of juice into each compartment. When frozen, remove the cubes and place them in resealable freezer bags. It's great to have the juice already measured when you're in a hurry!

an inviting idea

Gather your friends for an afternoon of good food and good reads with a holiday book swap. Our "bookish" invitation sets the theme while providing all the necessary details.

- ☐ library cards
- ☐ assorted cardstock and/or pages from a discarded book
- ☐ glue stick
- ☐ ink jet printer (if using a digital collage sheet)

1. Purchase library cards at your local paper store or buy a digital library card collage sheet. If using a digital collage sheet, print the library card images on card stock with an inkjet printer.

2. Hand write your invitation on the cards or, before printing, use a photo editing program to type your invitation on the digital collage sheet.

3. Use a glue stick to mat each library card on your choice of colored card stock. Leave a half inch border around the edges.

4. For the vintage book page backing, either use pages from an old book or use a digital collage sheet of vintage book pages.

5. Use a glue stick to mount the regular book pages on card stock for stability or print the digital book pages on card stock with an inkjet printer.

6. Cut vintage book pages to desired rectangular size for fitting mailing envelopes.

7. Adhere a mounted library card centered on each book page.

CRAFTER'S NOTE: *We found our digital library card collage sheet online at Etsy.com.*

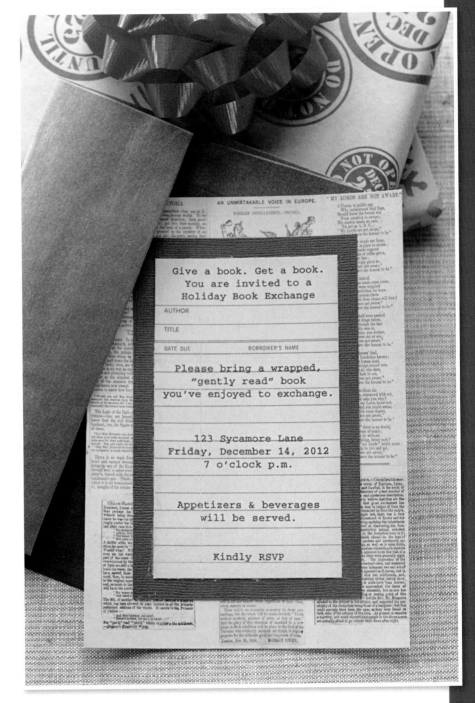

Give a book. Get a book.
You are invited to a
Holiday Book Exchange

AUTHOR

TITLE

DATE DUE   BORROWER'S NAME

Please bring a wrapped,
"gently read" book
you've enjoyed to exchange.

123 Sycamore Lane
Friday, December 14, 2012
7 o'clock p.m.

Appetizers & beverages
will be served.

Kindly RSVP

Nothing rounds out a festive menu quite like a selection of colorful salads and savory side dishes. And when those simple dinner accompaniments feature the freshest and finest produce of the season, your holiday meals are sure to shine! Whether you're planning a yuletide feast or a simple family dinner on a chilly winter night, consider a dish featuring hearty root vegetables, leafy fennel or juicy pomegranate. You will find recipes for sides and salads spotlighting these ingredients and more in this handy chapter.

You might want to consider items such as Artichoke & Green Bean Penne, Fennel-Stuffed Twice Baked Potatoes, Winter Country Soup or even Minted Parsnip Souffles. They make great side dishes as well as light change-of-pace main courses. Regardless of which item you try first, you'll satisfy everyone at your table during this cozy season.

EASY DINNER ADDITIONS
Artichoke & Green Bean Penne (p. 48)

IN-SEASON SIDE DISHES

artichoke & green bean penne

(PICTURED ON PAGE 47)

This pretty side dish goes well with just about any main course...and it even makes a fantastic meatless entree! Featuring colorful produce, toasted almonds and a creamy sauce, it's sure to satisfy.

SARAH PIERCE | SANTA MONICA, CALIFORNIA

3 cups uncooked penne pasta

¾ pound fresh green beans, trimmed and cut into 1-inch pieces

1 cup sliced fresh mushrooms

1 medium sweet red pepper, chopped

3 tablespoons butter, cubed

1 package (8 ounces) frozen artichoke hearts, thawed and quartered

1 carton (8 ounces) Mascarpone cheese

¼ cup heavy whipping cream

¾ teaspoon salt

½ teaspoon pepper

¼ cup slivered almonds, toasted

¼ cup grated Parmesan cheese

1. In a saucepan, cook pasta according to package directions, adding green beans during the last 5 minutes of cooking.

2. Meanwhile, in a Dutch oven, saute mushrooms and red pepper in butter until tender. Reduce heat; stir in the artichokes, Mascarpone cheese, cream, salt and pepper. Heat through (do not boil).

3. Drain beans and pasta; stir into artichoke mixture. Add almonds and toss to coat. Sprinkle with Parmesan cheese.

YIELD: 9 SERVINGS.

holiday sweet potato skins

While we usually enjoy these as snacks, the change-of-pace appetizers make an excellent side dish, too.

DEBORAH PUETTE | LILBURN, GEORGIA

3 large sweet potatoes

2 tablespoons butter, melted

1¼ teaspoons salt

3 tablespoons honey

2 green onions, thinly sliced

5 bacon strips, cooked and crumbled

½ cup dried cranberries

1 cup (4 ounces) shredded Gouda cheese

Sour cream

1. Scrub and pierce sweet potatoes. Microwave on high for 4-6 minutes or until almost tender. When cool enough to handle, cut each potato lengthwise into 4 wedges.

2. Place a 28-in. x 18-in. piece of heavy-duty foil on a large baking sheet. Arrange potatoes in a single layer on foil. Brush with butter; sprinkle with salt and drizzle with honey. Top with a second large piece of foil. Bring edges of foil together; crimp to seal, forming a large domed packet.

3. Bake at 400° for 15-20 minutes or just until fork tender. Carefully uncover; sprinkle with green onions. Broil 4-6 in. from the heat for 4 minutes. Sprinkle with bacon, cranberries and cheese. Broil 1-2 minutes longer or until cheese is melted. Serve with sour cream.

YIELD: 1 DOZEN.

minted parsnip souffles

Parsnip souffles make wonderful use of a root vegetable that is often overlooked. The subtle mint flavor pairs well with a variety of meats.

CATHERINE WILKINSON
DEWEY, ARIZONA

3 eggs

3 tablespoons butter, divided

3 tablespoons all-purpose flour, divided

1½ pounds medium parsnips, peeled and sliced

2 tablespoons finely chopped onion

½ cup water

2 teaspoons lemon juice

3 tablespoons sugar

1 teaspoon salt

1 cup half-and-half cream

2 tablespoons minced fresh mint

1. Separate eggs; let stand at room temperature for 30 minutes. Grease six 8-oz. ramekins with 1 tablespoon butter and dust with 1 tablespoon flour.

2. Place parsnips, onion and water in a microwave-safe bowl. Cover and microwave on high for 5-7 minutes or until parsnips are tender. Let stand for 5 minutes; drain. Place parsnip mixture and lemon juice in a food processor; cover and process until blended. Set mixture aside.

3. In a small saucepan over medium heat, melt remaining butter. Stir in the sugar, remaining flour and salt until blended. Gradually whisk in cream. Bring to a boil, stirring constantly. Cook and stir 1-2 minutes longer or until thickened. Transfer to a large bowl; stir in mint.

4. Stir a small amount of hot mixture into egg yolks; return all to the bowl, stirring constantly. Allow to cool slightly. Stir in parsnip mixture.

5. In another bowl with clean beaters, beat egg whites until stiff peaks form. Stir a fourth of the egg whites into egg yolk mixture until no white streaks remain. Fold in remaining egg whites until combined. Transfer to prepared dishes.

6. Bake at 350° for 20-25 minutes or until the tops are puffed and center appears set. Serve immediately.

YIELD: 6 SERVINGS.

fennel-stuffed twice-baked potatoes

*In my opinion, nothing is as versatile as the potato. I recently decided
to try cooking with fennel and wanted to add the flavor to a baked potato.
The cheese, fennel, garlic and pine nuts lend this appealing side dish delicious Italian flair.*

PAM IVBULS | OMAHA, NEBRASKA

6 large baking potatoes

2 large fennel bulbs, cored and coarsely chopped

¼ cup olive oil

2 teaspoons sugar

1½ teaspoons salt

2 garlic cloves, minced

¼ cup butter, softened

½ cup 1% milk

6 ounces farmer or fontina cheese, shredded

⅓ cup sour cream

Paprika

1. Scrub and pierce the potatoes. Bake at 375° for 1 hour or until tender.

2. Meanwhile, saute fennel in oil until crisp-tender. Add sugar and salt. Cook and stir for 15 minutes. Reduce heat to low; cook 10 minutes longer, stirring frequently. Add garlic; cook and stir for 5 minutes or until fennel is golden brown. Remove from the heat; set aside.

3. Cool potatoes for 5 minutes. When cool enough to handle, cut a thin slice off the top of each potato and discard. Scoop out the pulp, leaving thin shells.

4. In a large bowl, mash pulp with butter. Stir in the milk, cheese, sour cream and fennel mixture. Spoon into potato shells. Place on a baking sheet. Bake, uncovered, at 375° for 20-35 minutes or until heated through. Sprinkle with paprika.

YIELD: 6 SERVINGS.

pomegranate splash salad

*The sparkling pomegranate gems make this salad irresistibly beautiful. My family loves it at
holiday gatherings when pomegranates are in season. Even the kids can't get enough of this delight.*

EMILY JAMISON | CHAMPAIGN, ILLINOIS

4 cups fresh baby spinach

4 cups spring mix salad greens

¾ cup crumbled feta cheese

¾ cup pomegranate seeds

¾ cup fresh or frozen raspberries

⅓ cup pine nuts, toasted

CRANBERRY VINAIGRETTE

½ cup thawed cranberry juice concentrate

3 tablespoons olive oil

2 tablespoons rice vinegar

Dash salt

In a large bowl, combine the first six ingredients. In a small bowl, whisk the vinaigrette ingredients. Serve with salad.

YIELD: 8 SERVINGS.

POMEGRANATE POINTERS

Cut off the crown of the pomegranate and score fruit in quarters, taking care not to cut the juicy red seeds. Place the sections in a bowl of water and soak for 5 minutes. Break the sections open and gently push out the seed clusters. Discard skin and white membrane. Drain water, reserving seeds. Dry on paper towels.

winter country soup

My soup will warm your family up on the chilliest of winter nights. Featuring smoked sausage, beans and other vegetables, it's a hearty way to start a meal or a satisfying lunch all by itself.

JEANNETTE SABO | LEXINGTON PARK, MARYLAND

1 package (14 ounces) smoked sausage, cut into ¼-inch slices

1 large sweet red pepper, cut into ½-inch pieces

8 shallots, chopped

1 tablespoon butter

8 cups chopped fresh kale

8 cups vegetable broth

3 cups frozen corn

1 can (15½ ounces) great northern beans, rinsed and drained

½ teaspoon cayenne pepper

¼ teaspoon pepper

¾ cup uncooked orzo pasta

1. In a Dutch oven, saute the sausage, red pepper and shallots in the butter until vegetables are tender.

2. Add kale; cover and cook for 2-3 minutes or until kale is wilted. Stir in the broth, corn, beans, cayenne and pepper. Bring to a boil. Reduce the heat; simmer, uncovered, for 20 minutes. Return to a boil. Stir in orzo. Cook 8-10 minutes longer or until pasta is tender.

YIELD: 12 SERVINGS (3 QUARTS).

kale quinoa salad

Here's a holiday side dish you can feel good about serving. Kale packs a mighty punch of vitamins, while quinoa delivers a hearty serving of protein. Best of all, the flavor can't be beat!

LISA WARREN | WASHINGTON, WASHINGTON DC

1½ cups water

½ cup tomato juice

1 cup quinoa, rinsed

1 small onion, chopped

1 tablespoon olive oil

1 garlic clove, minced

½ teaspoon crushed red pepper flakes

6 cups coarsely chopped fresh kale

¼ cup pine nuts

¼ cup dried currants

1 tablespoon balsamic vinegar

1 teaspoon lemon juice

1 teaspoon grated lemon peel

¼ teaspoon salt

⅛ teaspoon pepper

1. In a large saucepan, bring water and tomato juice to a boil. Add quinoa. Reduce heat; cover and simmer for 18-22 minutes or until the liquid is absorbed. Remove from the heat; fluff with a fork.

2. In a large skillet, saute onion in oil until tender. Add garlic and pepper flakes; cook 1 minute longer. Stir in kale and cook for 3-4 minutes or until wilted.

3. Stir in pine nuts and currants; cook 2 minutes longer or until kale is tender. Stir in the vinegar, lemon juice, peel, salt and pepper; cook 1-2 minutes longer. Remove from the heat and stir in quinoa. Serve at room temperature.

YIELD: 6 SERVINGS.

EDITOR'S NOTE: *Look for quinoa in the cereal, rice or organic food aisle of your grocery store.*

caramelized pearl onions

I came up with this savory dish on a whim one Christmas when my mother and I craved a vegetable side a little different than our usual Brussels sprouts. We all liked it so much that it now makes a regular appearance on the holiday table.

ERIKA SZYMANSKI | PULLMAN, WASHINGTON

1 pound pearl onions, peeled

2 teaspoons olive oil

½ cup dry red wine or beef broth

¼ cup balsamic vinegar

1 tablespoon cider vinegar

½ teaspoon pepper

¼ teaspoon salt

¼ teaspoon dried thyme

½ cup pomegranate seeds

1 teaspoon snipped fresh dill

In a large skillet, cook onions in oil over medium heat for 8-10 minutes or until browned. Stir in the wine, vinegars, pepper, salt and thyme. Bring to a boil. Reduce heat; simmer, uncovered, for 12-15 minutes or until onions are tender and liquid is evaporated. Stir in pomegranate seeds and dill; heat mixture through.

YIELD: 2½ CUPS.

lemon-macadamia brussels sprouts

*Even kids enjoy Brussels sprouts when they're prepared like this!
The subtle lemon flavor and crunchy macadamia nuts give the side dish plenty of appeal.*

MARCIA DOYLE | POMPANO, FLORIDA

1   pound fresh Brussels sprouts, halved

6   garlic cloves, minced

¼   cup butter, cubed

2   tablespoons olive oil

2   tablespoons red wine vinegar

2   to 3 teaspoons minced fresh tarragon

1   teaspoon minced fresh basil

¼   teaspoon salt

¼   teaspoon pepper

¼   cup chopped macadamia nuts

2   tablespoons lemon juice

1. Place Brussels sprouts in a steamer basket; place in a large saucepan over 1 in. of water. Bring to a boil; cover and steam for 7 minutes or until crisp-tender.

2. Meanwhile, in large skillet, heat butter and oil over medium heat until butter is melted. Add garlic; cook for 1 minute. Stir in the vinegar, tarragon, basil, salt and pepper. Add Brussels sprouts; stir to coat. Transfer to a serving plate. Sprinkle with nuts and drizzle with lemon juice.

YIELD: 4 SERVINGS.

fig-carrot stuffed kabocha squash

*While searching for a new winter squash variety, I stumbled upon kabocha squash—
it really wowed me. The flavor and texture are both rich and beautiful. I improvised
in creating this recipe, and I think the dish really suits the squash quite well.*

CAITLIN STEPHENS-NORTH | MALDEN, MASSACHUSETTS

1   medium kabocha squash (about 3 pounds)

½   teaspoon fennel seed

¼   teaspoon ground fenugreek

¼   teaspoon pepper

    Dash ground nutmeg

    Dash ground cloves

1   tablespoon olive oil

½   teaspoon salt

STUFFING

3   medium carrots, finely chopped

2   shallots, chopped

1   tablespoon olive oil

5   fresh or dried figs, cut into eighths

½   cup water

¼   teaspoon salt

¼   teaspoon ground cinnamon

¼   teaspoon pepper

    Dash ground nutmeg

    Dash ground cloves

3   tablespoons chopped pecans

1. Wash squash; cut into four wedges. Remove loose fibers and seeds from the inside and discard.

2. In a spice grinder or with a mortar and pestle, combine the fennel seed, fenugreek, pepper, nutmeg and cloves; grind until seeds are crushed.

3. Brush squash with oil. Sprinkle with salt and ¾ teaspoon spice mixture. Place in an ungreased 15-in. x 10-in. x 1-in. baking sheet. Bake, uncovered, at 400° for 35-40 minutes or until tender.

4. Meanwhile, in a large skillet, saute carrots and shallots in oil until tender. Stir in the figs, water, salt, cinnamon, pepper, nutmeg, cloves and remaining spice mixture. Bring to a boil. Reduce heat; simmer, uncovered, for 8-10 minutes or until liquid is evaporated and figs are tender. Stir in pecans.

5. Fill squash with stuffing. Bake 10-15 minutes longer or until heated through.

YIELD: 4 SERVINGS.

EDITOR'S NOTE: *Fenugreek is available from Penzeys Spices. Call 800-741-7787 or visit penzeys.com.*

KNOW KABOCHA

Kabocha squash (pronounced kah-bow-cha) is a sweet, pumpkin-shaped winter squash with a wonderfully strong earthy flavor that reminds some of chestnuts and others of pumpkin. It's sweeter than butternut squash and offers a delightfully moist texture. Its thick green skin makes it a great option for braising, steaming and traditional oven-baked cooking methods.

Due to the squash's ability to hold its shape, kabocha is ideal to stuff and bake in the oven. Its soft, fleshy meat however, also makes the squash a great addition to quick breads and even cakes and pies.

beet and sweet potato fries

Oven-baked root vegetables put a colorful and flavorful twist on traditional french fries—and add interest to any meal as a fun side dish.

MARIE RIZZIO
INTERLOCHEN, MICHIGAN

- ½ cup reduced-fat mayonnaise
- 1 teaspoon pink peppercorns, crushed
- ½ teaspoon green peppercorns, crushed
- ½ teaspoon coarsely ground pepper, divided
- 1 large sweet potato (about 1 pound)
- 2 tablespoons olive oil, divided
- ½ teaspoon sea salt, divided
- 2 large fresh beets (about 1 pound)

1. In a small bowl, combine the mayonnaise, peppercorns and ¼ teaspoon ground pepper. Cover and refrigerate until serving.

2. Peel and cut sweet potato in half widthwise; cut each half into ½-in. strips. Place in a small bowl. Add 1 tablespoon oil, ¼ teaspoon salt and ⅛ teaspoon pepper; toss to coat. Spread onto a baking sheet lined with parchment paper.

3. Peel and cut beets in half; cut into ½-in. strips. Transfer to the same bowl; add the remaining oil, salt and pepper. Toss to coat. Spread onto another parchment paper-lined baking sheet.

4. Bake vegetables, uncovered, at 425° for 20-30 minutes or until tender, turning once. Serve with peppercorn mayonnaise.

YIELD: 5 SERVINGS (½ CUP SAUCE).

Do you want to know the secret to a happy holiday? Simple! It's chocolate! Chocolate-covered cherries, chocolate mousse, chocolate tarts, chocolate sauce, chocolate cake...a never-ending list of chocolate goodies makes it easy to spread the joy of the season.

This Christmas, impress your holiday guests with an awe-inspiring Decadent Chocolate Crepe Cake.

The showstopping dessert features layer upon layer of tender chocolate crepes sandwiched between a white chocolate buttercream filling, and is drenched in a semisweet chocolate ganache icing. A towering slice of this treat is enough to make even old Ebenezer Scrooge smile.

HOORAY FOR CHOCOLATE
Decadent Chocolate Crepe Cake (p. 58)

CHOCOLATE CHEER

decadent chocolate crepe cake

(PICTURED ON PAGE 57)

No other dessert has wowed family and friends the way this stunning crepe cake did the first time I made it. A "showstopper" in every sense of the word, it features layers of tender chocolate crepes and rich white chocolate buttercream frosting draped in a semisweet chocolate ganache.

TINA SAWCHUK | ARDMORE, ALBERTA

¾ cup unsalted butter, cubed

8 ounces bittersweet chocolate, coarsely chopped

6 eggs

2½ cups whole milk

3 teaspoons vanilla extract

1½ cups all-purpose flour

⅓ cup sugar

⅛ teaspoon salt

WHITE CHOCOLATE BUTTERCREAM

8 ounces white baking chocolate, chopped

½ cup heavy whipping cream

2¼ cups sugar

1 teaspoon cream of tartar

8 egg whites

2 cups unsalted butter, softened

2 teaspoons vanilla extract

SEMISWEET CHOCOLATE GANACHE

6 ounces semisweet chocolate, chopped

¾ cup heavy whipping cream

2½ teaspoons corn syrup

⅛ teaspoon salt

1. In a microwave, melt butter and chocolate; stir until smooth. Set aside to cool. In a large bowl, whisk the eggs, milk, vanilla and cooled chocolate mixture. Combine the flour, sugar and salt; add to egg mixture and mix well. Cover and refrigerate for 2 hours or overnight. (Batter will appear curdled.)

2. For buttercream, in a microwave, melt white chocolate with cream; stir until smooth. Set aside to cool. In a small bowl, combine sugar and cream of tartar.

3. Place egg whites in a double boiler or metal bowl over simmering water; stir in the sugar mixture. Constantly whisk until mixture reaches 120-130° (do not overheat). Stirring gently, keep at 120-130° for 2 minutes. Immediately transfer to a mixing bowl.

4. With a whisk attachment, beat on high speed for 5 minutes. Reduce speed and beat for 5 additional minutes or until cool and stiff. Transfer to a large bowl.

5. In the same mixing bowl with the whisk attachment, beat butter and vanilla until light and fluffy. Beat in cooled white chocolate mixture. With a spatula, stir a fourth of the meringue into butter mixture until no white streaks remain. Fold in remaining meringue. Cover and refrigerate.

6. Heat a lightly greased 8-in. nonstick skillet over medium heat; pour 2 tablespoons crepe batter into center of skillet. Lift and tilt pan to coat bottom evenly. Cook until top appears dry, about 2 minutes; turn and cook 15-20 seconds longer. Remove to a wire rack. Repeat with remaining batter, greasing skillet as needed.

7. When cool, stack crepes with waxed paper or paper towels in between.

8. To assemble, place one crepe on a cake plate. Spread with 3 tablespoons buttercream. Repeat layers until 10 crepes are used. Refrigerate for 15 minutes. Repeat layering and chilling until 30 crepes are used, ending layers with a crepe. (Save remaining crepes for another use.) Refrigerate.

9. For ganache, place chocolate in a small bowl. In a small saucepan, bring cream, corn syrup and salt just to a boil. Pour over chocolate; whisk until smooth. Cool, stirring occasionally, until ganache reaches a spreading consistency. Spread over top and sides of cake. Refrigerate for 1 hour before serving.

YIELD: 8 SERVINGS.

chocolate cherry truffles

My blue ribbon cherry truffles were the delicious result of a kitchen experiment involving a bottle of kirsch I had received as a gift and some dried cherries I had on hand. Now, it is an annual favorite.

GERRY COFTA
MILWAUKEE, WISCONSIN

1 cup finely chopped dried cherries

¼ cup cherry brandy

11 ounces 53% cacao dark baking chocolate, chopped

½ cup heavy whipping cream

1 teaspoon cherry extract

COATING

4 ounces milk chocolate, chopped

4 ounces dark chocolate, chopped

Melted dark, milk and white chocolate and pearl dust

1. In a small bowl, combine cherries and brandy; cover and let soak for 1 hour or until cherries are softened.

2. Place dark chocolate in a small bowl. In a small saucepan, bring cream just to a boil. Pour over chocolate; whisk until smooth. Stir in extract and soaked cherries with liquid.

3. Let the chocolate cool to room temperature, stirring occasionally. Refrigerate for 1 hour or until firm.

4. Shape into 1-in. balls. Place on baking sheets; cover and refrigerate for at least 1 hour.

5. In a microwave, melt milk chocolate; stir until smooth. Dip half of the balls into milk chocolate, allowing excess to drip off. Place on waxed paper; let stand until set.

6. Melt dark chocolate; stir until smooth. Dip remaining balls into dark chocolate, allowing excess to drip off. Place on waxed paper; let stand until set. Drizzle with melted chocolate and decorate with pearl dust as desired. Store in an airtight container in the refrigerator.

YIELD: 4 DOZEN.

EDITOR'S NOTE: *Pearl dust is available from Wilton Industries. Call 800-794-5866 or visit wilton.com.*

elegant chocolate mousse

(PICTURED AT RIGHT IN PARFAITS)

There is something delightfully simple, yet so satisfying about homemade chocolate mousse. Garnish individual servings with fresh berries or chocolate shavings.

TASTE OF HOME TEST KITCHEN

2½ cups heavy whipping cream, divided

½ cup sugar

4 egg yolks

10 ounces German sweet chocolate, chopped

1 teaspoon vanilla extract

1. In a large saucepan, heat 1½ cups cream and sugar over medium heat until bubbles form around sides of pan. Whisk a small amount of the hot mixture into the egg yolks.

2. Return all to the pan, whisking constantly. Cook and stir over low heat until mixture reaches at least 160° and coats the back of a metal spoon. Remove from the heat. Stir in chocolate and vanilla. Transfer to a large bowl; refrigerate until chilled.

3. In a small bowl, beat remaining cream until stiff peaks form; fold into chocolate mixture. Cover and refrigerate until serving.

YIELD: 6 SERVINGS.

chocolate-raspberry creme brulee

Just when I thought nothing could beat the specialness of creme brulee, I created this decadent version that stars rich chocolate and sweet raspberries. Cracking through the top reveals a smooth and rich custard everyone enjoys.

JAN VALDEZ | CHICAGO, ILLINOIS

8 ounces semisweet chocolate, chopped

4 cups heavy whipping cream

½ cup plus 2 tablespoons sugar, divided

8 egg yolks, beaten

1 tablespoon vanilla extract

30 fresh raspberries

2 tablespoons brown sugar

1. Place chocolate in a small bowl. In a small saucepan, bring cream and ½ cup sugar just to a boil. Pour over chocolate; whisk until smooth. Stir a small amount of hot cream mixture into egg yolks. Return all to the pan, stirring constantly. Remove from the heat; stir in vanilla.

2. Place 3 raspberries in each of ten ungreased 6-oz. ramekins or custard cups. Place in a baking pan; add 1 in. of boiling water to pan. Bake, uncovered, at 325° for 40-50 minutes or until centers are just set (mixture will jiggle). Remove ramekins from water bath; cool 10 minutes. Cover and refrigerate for at least 4 hours.

3. Combine brown sugar and remaining sugar. If using a creme brulee torch, sprinkle custards with sugar mixture. Heat sugar with the torch until caramelized. Serve immediately.

4. If broiling the custards, place ramekins on a baking sheet; let stand at room temperature for 15 minutes. Sprinkle with sugar mixture. Broil 8 in. from the heat for 4-7 minutes or until sugar is caramelized. Refrigerate for 1-2 hours or until firm.

YIELD: 10 SERVINGS.

chocolate-covered cherry parfaits

If you're a fan of the sweet-tart combination of chocolate-covered cherries, you'll be first in line to indulge in this parfait version of the classic candy.

TASTE OF HOME TEST KITCHEN

1 package (12 ounces) frozen pitted dark sweet cherries, thawed

3 tablespoons sugar

4 teaspoons cornstarch

2 tablespoons cherry brandy

1 cup heavy whipping cream

1 package (8 ounces) cream cheese, softened

¼ cup confectioners' sugar

1⅓ cups Elegant Chocolate Mousse (see p. 60)

Chocolate syrup, optional

1. Drain cherries, reserving ⅓ cup liquid; set aside.

2. In a small saucepan, combine the sugar and cornstarch; stir in reserved cherry juice until smooth. Bring to a boil; cook and stir for 1 minute or until thickened. Remove from the heat; stir in cherries and brandy. Cover and refrigerate until chilled.

3. In a small bowl, beat cream until stiff peaks form. In another bowl, beat cream cheese and confectioners' sugar until smooth. Fold in whipped cream.

4. Spoon half of the mousse, cream mixture and cherries into four parfait glasses. Layer with remaining cream mixture, the mousse and cherries. Drizzle with the chocolate syrup if desired.

YIELD: 4 SERVINGS.

two layer baked alaska

The very first dessert I made for company was a baked Alaska.
It was a complete disaster. When I finally got it right, I branched out and
made this two-layered treat, which was a total success and continues to be a favorite.

LORRAINE CALAND | SHUNIAH, ONTARIO

3 ounces semisweet chocolate

⅓ cup shortening

1 cup graham cracker crumbs

¾ cup finely chopped pecans

¼ cup packed dark brown sugar

FILLING

2 cups chocolate ice cream, softened

2 cups strawberry ice cream, softened

CHOCOLATE SAUCE

¼ cup sugar

¼ cup water

2 tablespoons butter

4 ounces semisweet chocolate

MERINGUE

4 egg whites

½ cup sugar

½ teaspoon cream of tartar

1. In a microwave, melt chocolate and shortening; stir until smooth. Stir in the cracker crumbs, pecans and brown sugar. Press onto the bottom and up the sides of a greased 9-in. pie plate. Refrigerate for 30 minutes.

2. Spread chocolate ice cream into crust. Layer with strawberry ice cream. Cover and freeze 1-2 hours or until firm.

3. In a small saucepan, bring the sugar, water and butter to a boil; stirring constantly. Remove from the heat. Add the chocolate; stir until smooth. Cool to room temperature. Drizzle ½ cup over ice cream. Freeze until firm.

4. In a small heavy saucepan, combine the egg whites, sugar and cream of tartar. With a hand mixer, beat on low speed for 1 minute. Continue beating over low heat until egg mixture reaches 160°, about 4 minutes.

5. Transfer to a bowl; beat 5-7 minutes or until stiff glossy peaks form and sugar is dissolved. Immediately spread over frozen pie.   Heat with a creme brulee torch for 3-4 minutes or until meringue is lightly browned. Serve immediately with remaining chocolate sauce.

YIELD: 8 SERVINGS.

sacher torte parfaits

We think you'll agree, these pretty parfaits look and taste like a fancy restaurant dessert, but require
very little fuss—especially if you've already made Elegant Chocolate Mousse for the Chocolate-Covered
Cherry Parfaits on page 61. A tray of these individual desserts will make faces light up with delight.

TASTE OF HOME TEST KITCHEN

1 cup chopped dried apricots

¼ cup Amaretto

3 tablespoons apricot preserves

5 double chocolate cookies, coarsely chopped

1⅓ cups Elegant Chocolate Mousse (see p. 60)

1. Place apricots in a small bowl. Cover with Amaretto; let stand for 15 minutes. Drain; stir in preserves.

2. Divide ½ cup of cookies among four parfait glasses. Top with half of the mousse and apricot mixture. Repeat layers. Top with remaining cookies.

YIELD: 4 SERVINGS.

petit pain au chocolat

I've had this recipe for over 20 years and it's still one of my most treasured. The presentation is just fancy enough for special occasions, yet the recipe is very achievable.

DENISE WHEELER | NEWAYGO, MICHIGAN

1 sheet frozen puff pastry, thawed

½ cup milk chocolate chips

1 egg, beaten

DRIZZLE

¼ cup milk chocolate chips

2 tablespoons butter

1 cup confectioners' sugar

4 teaspoons hot water

1. Unfold puff pastry onto a lightly floured surface. Roll out into a 10-in. square. Cut into four squares.

2. Place 2 tablespoons chocolate chips in the center of each square. Brush edges with egg. Fold one corner over filling to the opposite corner, forming a triangle; press edges to seal. Brush tops with remaining egg. Transfer to a greased baking sheet.

3. Bake at 350° for 18-20 minutes or until golden brown. Remove to a wire rack to cool.

4. In a microwave, melt chocolate chips and butter; stir until smooth. Whisk in confectioners' sugar and enough water to achieve a drizzling consistency. Drizzle over pastries.

YIELD: 4 SERVINGS.

salted dark chocolate tart

When I was little, my grandpa always had a bag of caramels in his truck and a few in his pocket. Whether we were camping or going to a movie, I always enjoyed sharing caramels with him. Now I try to put caramel in as many of my desserts as possible, including this one.

LEAH TACKITT | AUSTIN, TEXAS

1½ cups Oreo cookie crumbs

⅓ cup butter, melted

CARAMEL

¾ cup sugar

3 tablespoons water

⅓ cup heavy whipping cream

2 tablespoons butter, cubed

Dash salt

FILLING

4 cups dark chocolate chips

1¼ cups heavy whipping cream

1 teaspoon vanilla extract

½ teaspoon large-crystal sea salt

1. In a small bowl, combine cookie crumbs and butter; press onto the bottom and up the sides of a greased 9-in. fluted tart pan with removable bottom. Cover and refrigerate for 30 minutes.

2. For caramel, in a small saucepan over medium heat, combine sugar and water. Cook, shaking pan occasionally, until sugar is melted and mixture is almost clear (do not boil).

3. Increase heat to medium high; bring to a boil, without stirring. Cover and boil for 2 minutes, tightly holding lid of pan down. Uncover; shake pan. Cook 1-2 minutes longer or until mixture is amber, shaking pan several times.

4. Remove from the heat; stir in cream (mixture will bubble) until smooth. Stir in butter (mixture will bubble) and salt until blended. Pour into crust; refrigerate for 15 minutes.

5. Place chocolate in a large bowl. In a small saucepan, bring cream just to a boil. Pour over chocolate; whisk until smooth. Stir in vanilla. Let stand for 20 minutes.

6. Pour over caramel. Sprinkle with sea salt. Refrigerate for at least 3 hours. Remove from the refrigerator about 45 minutes before serving.

YIELD: 16 SERVINGS.

kickin' chocolate sauce

Drizzled on ice cream or fresh fruit, here's a chocolate sauce that delivers a subtle kick. Deliciously different and always in demand, it's a recipe you'll prepare often.

RICHARD MASKIELL | ATHENS, OHIO

1 package (11½ ounces) milk chocolate chips

½ cup coconut rum

¼ cup heavy whipping cream

1 teaspoon ground cinnamon

1 teaspoon ground ancho chili pepper

Ice cream or assorted fruit

1. In a microwave, melt chocolate; stir until smooth. Stir in the rum, cream, cinnamon and chili powder.

2. Serve with ice cream or fruit. Refrigerate leftovers.

YIELD: 1½ CUPS.

famous chocolate cupcakes

We could tell you this is the best chocolate cake you will ever try, or you could serve it at your next holiday event and see for yourself. With its tender texture and perfect chocolate flavor, the cake makes an equally perfect cupcake, too.

TASTE OF HOME TEST KITCHEN

4   ounces milk chocolate, chopped
¼   cup hot water
½   cup butter, softened
1   cup sugar
2   eggs
1½ teaspoons vanilla extract
1¼ cups all-purpose flour
¼   cup baking cocoa
¾   teaspoon baking soda
½   teaspoon salt
½   cup buttermilk

PEANUT BUTTER FROSTING

1½ cups creamy peanut butter
½   cup butter, softened
2¼ cups confectioners' sugar
24 miniature peanut butter cups

1. In a small bowl, combine chocolate and hot water. Whisk until smooth. Cool slightly.

2. In a large bowl, cream butter and sugar until light and fluffy. Add eggs, one at a time, beating well after each addition. Beat in vanilla.

3. Combine the flour, cocoa, baking soda and salt. Whisk buttermilk into chocolate mixture. Add dry ingredients to creamed mixture alternately with chocolate mixture, beating well after each addition. Fill paper-lined muffin cups half full.

4. Bake at 350° for 20-22 minutes or until a toothpick inserted near the center comes out clean. Cool for 10 minutes before removing from pans to wire racks to cool completely.

5. For frosting, combine the peanut butter, butter and confectioners' sugar; beat until smooth. Frost cupcakes. Garnish with peanut butter cups.

YIELD: 2 DOZEN.

EDITOR'S NOTE: *Find decorative cupcake liners at fancyflours.com.*

double shot espresso ganache cake

*After trying a similar dessert at a restaurant in Venice, Italy, I knew I had to try and re-create
this rich espresso cake draped in an espresso ganache. My version is close to perfect. Serve generous
slices with a bowl of whipped cream and fresh raspberries, dusted with cocoa, on the side.*

WOLFGANG HANAU | WEST PALM BEACH, FLORIDA

15 ounces bittersweet
chocolate, coarsely chopped

1 cup unsalted butter, cubed

4½ teaspoons brewed espresso

½ teaspoon sugar

6 eggs

ESPRESSO GANACHE

2½ ounces semisweet chocolate,
coarsely chopped

¼ cup heavy whipping cream

1 tablespoon brewed espresso

Optional garnishes: whipped
cream, espresso beans, fresh
raspberries and baking cocoa

1. Place a greased 9-in. springform pan on a double thickness of heavy-duty foil (about 18 in. square). Securely wrap foil around pan.

2. In a heavy saucepan over low heat, melt chocolate and butter. Combine espresso and sugar until sugar is dissolved; stir into chocolate mixture. Cool to lukewarm.

3. In a large bowl, beat eggs on medium speed for 1 minute. Beat on high speed for 4 minutes longer or until thick and lemon-colored. Gradually beat in cooled chocolate mixture until no streaks remain. Pour into prepared pan.

4. Place springform pan in a large baking pan; add 1½ in. of hot water to larger pan. Bake at 400° for 19-22 minutes or until temperature reaches 160° and top appears set. Cool on a wire rack for 10 minutes. Carefully run a knife around edge of pan to loosen; cool 1 hour longer. Refrigerate overnight. Remove sides of pan.

5. For ganache, place chocolate in a small bowl. In a small saucepan, bring cream just to a boil. Pour over chocolate; whisk until smooth. Stir in espresso. Spread over cake. Garnish as desired. Refrigerate leftovers.

YIELD: 16 SERVINGS.

EDITOR'S NOTE: *This recipe does not use flour.*

chocolate tiramisu parfaits

*Chocolate, cake and coffee...what isn't there to love about tiramisu? Our pretty parfaits
take the work out of preparing the tempting dessert, but leave behind all the luscious flavor.*

TASTE OF HOME TEST KITCHEN

⅔ cup heavy whipping cream

1 tablespoon instant espresso
powder

2 tablespoons strong brewed
coffee

8 crisp ladyfinger cookies

1⅓ cups Elegant Chocolate
Mousse (see p.60)

Baking cocoa and chocolate
curls

1. In a small bowl, beat cream and espresso powder until stiff peaks form. Brush coffee over cookies and coarsely chop.

2. Spoon half of the mousse into four parfait glasses. Top with half the cookies and half the whipped cream. Repeat layers. Dust tops with cocoa and garnish with chocolate curls.

YIELD: 4 SERVINGS.

EDITOR'S NOTE: *This recipe was prepared with Alessi brand ladyfinger cookies.*

warm mexican chocolate cakettes

Maybe it's the cute, single serving presentation...or maybe the moist and tender cake...whatever makes this darling dessert so alluring, it's sure to be a winner at your next celebration.

MATT WARREN
MEQUON, WISCONSIN

1   cup all-purpose flour

1   teaspoon baking soda

⅛   teaspoon salt

6   ounces Mexican chocolate, chopped

1   package (1 ounce) instant hot cocoa mix

3   tablespoons boiling water

¼   cup unsalted butter, softened

⅔   cup packed brown sugar

2   eggs

½   cup sour cream

2   tablespoons brewed coffee

½   teaspoon vanilla extract

WHIPPED MARSHMALLOW TOPPING

⅓   cup marshmallow creme

½   cup heavy whipping cream

     Chocolate curls

1. Butter six 8-ounce ovenproof coffee mugs or ramekins.

2. In a small bowl, combine the flour, baking soda and salt; set aside. In a small saucepan, combine the chocolate, cocoa mix and water. Cook and stir over medium heat until smooth; cool.

3. In small bowl, beat butter and brown sugar until well blended. Beat in eggs, one at time, beating well after each addition. Add chocolate mixture; mix well. Add sour cream alternately with dry ingredients, beating well after each addition. Add coffee and vanilla. Divide among prepared cups.

4. Bake at 350° for 25-30 minutes or until set and a knife inserted near the center comes out clean.

5. Meanwhile, in small bowl, stir marshmallow creme until smooth. Add cream; beat until soft peaks form. Refrigerate until serving.

6. Dollop each dessert with marshmallow topping and garnish with chocolate curls. Serve warm.

YIELD: 6 SERVINGS.

molten chocolate cakes with mint fudge sauce

The perfect accompaniment to a generous scoop of vanilla ice cream, my Molten Chocolate Cakes feature my signature mint sauce. Ice cream, chocolate cake and mint fudge sauce—it's the triple threat of desserts!

DIANE HALFERTY | CORPUS CHRISTI, TEXAS

1¼ cups unsalted butter, cubed

10 ounces bittersweet chocolate, chopped

4 eggs

8 egg yolks

3 cups confectioners' sugar

1 cup all-purpose flour

CHOCOLATE MINT SAUCE

5 ounces bittersweet chocolate, chopped

2 ounces unsweetened chocolate, chopped

½ cup hot water

¼ cup corn syrup

1 teaspoon peppermint extract

Vanilla ice cream, optional

1. In a double boiler or metal bowl over hot water, melt butter and chocolate; stir until smooth. In a large bowl, beat the eggs, egg yolks and confectioners' sugar until thick and lemon-colored. Beat in flour until well blended. Gradually beat in butter mixture.

2. Transfer to eight greased 6-oz. ramekins or custard cups. Place ramekins on a baking sheet. Bake at 450° for 15-17 minutes or until a thermometer inserted near the center reads 160° and sides of cakes are set.

3. Meanwhile, in a double boiler or metal bowl over hot water, melt chocolates; stir until smooth. Whisk in the hot water, corn syrup and extract; remove and keep warm.

4. Remove cakes from the oven and let stand for 1 minute. Run a knife around edges of ramekins; invert onto dessert plates. Serve with warm chocolate sauce and vanilla ice cream if desired.

YIELD: 8 SERVINGS.

creamy chocolate rice pudding

While feeling bored one summer afternoon, I decided to create this scrumptious spin on traditional rice pudding. Now, my creative summer treat is a frequent request year-round.

GREGORY ROYSTER | NORTH LAUDERDALE, FLORIDA

4 cups 2% milk

½ cup uncooked long grain rice

½ cup sugar

⅛ teaspoon salt

1 teaspoon vanilla extract

1¾ cups miniature semisweet chocolate chips, divided

⅓ cup heavy whipping cream

Whipped cream, optional

1. In a large saucepan, combine the milk, rice, sugar and salt. Bring to a boil over medium heat. Reduce heat; simmer, uncovered, for 40-45 minutes or until thick and creamy, stirring often. Remove from the heat; stir in vanilla.

2. Place 1 cup chips in a small bowl. In a small saucepan, bring cream just to a boil. Pour over chocolate; whisk until smooth. Slowly stir into rice mixture. Cover and refrigerate for 1 hour.

3. Stir in remaining chips. Spoon into dessert dishes. Cover and refrigerate for at least 4 hours. Serve with whipped cream if desired.

YIELD: 8 SERVINGS.

dark chocolate panna cotta

Everything about this dessert, from the pretty presentation to its silky smooth texture, says "special." Rich chocolate is accented perfectly by the flavor of sweet, ripe berries.

SUSAN ASANOVIC | WILTON, CONNECTICUT

1 can (14 ounces) whole-berry cranberry sauce

5 tablespoons raspberry liqueur, divided

1 envelope unflavored gelatin

1 cup cold 2% milk

4 ounces 53% cacao dark baking chocolate, chopped

1½ cups heavy whipping cream

½ cup sugar

⅛ teaspoon salt

2 teaspoons vanilla extract

Fresh raspberries and mint leaves, optional

1. Place cranberry sauce in a food processor; cover and process until pureed. Strain and discard pulp. Stir in 3 tablespoons of the liqueur; set aside.

2. In a small bowl, sprinkle gelatin over milk; let stand for 1 minute. Meanwhile, place chocolate in another small bowl. In a small saucepan, bring cream, sugar and salt just to a boil. Pour over chocolate; whisk until smooth.

3. Stir a small amount of the chocolate mixture into gelatin mixture until gelatin is completely dissolved. Stir in 1 cup cranberry puree and vanilla. Pour into eight 6-oz. custard cups. Cover and refrigerate for 8 hours or overnight.

4. In a small bowl, combine the remaining cranberry puree and liqueur; cover and refrigerate until serving.

5. Unmold onto serving plates. Serve with sauce and garnish with raspberries and mint if desired.

YIELD: 8 SERVINGS.

'Tis the season for Christmas cookies... and more Christmas cookies! Maybe it's the memory of Grandma's famous sugar cookies, the opportunity to try out a new recipe or the homey aroma of a freshly baked batch of sweets just out of the oven, but something about the Christmas season seems to bring out the baker in each of us.

Double the delight of biting into a warm and gooey cookie such as Cranberry Orange Rugalach, by inviting your friends over for a cookie exchange.

Here, we've gathered a selection of can't-miss, high-yield cookie recipes perfect for sharing the Christmas spirit. You'll even find fun and easy ideas for making your get-together one that your friends will remember throughout the New Year.

COOKIE SWAP CHEER
Cranberry Orange Rugalach (p. 72)

AN OLD-FASHIONED
COOKIE EXCHANGE

cranberry orange rugalach

(PICTURED ON PAGE 70)

A hint of cranberry and splash of orange are wrapped in a buttery cookie, then drizzled with chocolate. Can you say, "heaven?" A platter of the showstopping treats makes any event a celebration.

GINGER SULLIVAN | CUTLER BAY, FLORIDA

1   cup butter, softened

1   package (8 ounces) cream cheese, softened

½   cup sugar

2   egg yolks

½   teaspoon orange extract

½   teaspoon vanilla extract

2½   cups all-purpose flour

¼   teaspoon salt

2   packages (5 ounces each) dried cranberries

1½   cups golden raisins

½   cup orange juice

1   egg, beaten

Melted chocolate, optional

1. In a large bowl, cream the butter, cream cheese and sugar until light and fluffy. Beat in egg yolks and extracts. Combine flour and salt; gradually add to creamed mixture and mix well.

2. Divide dough into four portions. Shape each into a ball, then flatten into a disk. Wrap each in plastic wrap; refrigerate for 2 hours or until firm.

3. Place the cranberries, raisins and juice in a food processor; cover and process until finely chopped. On a lightly floured surface, roll each portion into a 12-in. circle; spread each with ½ cup cranberry mixture. Cut each circle into 12 wedges.

4. Roll up wedges from the wide end and place point side down 1 in. apart on greased baking sheets; brush with egg. Bake at 350° for 10-12 minutes or until lightly browned. Remove to wire racks to cool. Drizzle with melted chocolate if desired. Store in an airtight container.

YIELD: 4 DOZEN.

For Hazelnut Rugalach: *Omit filling ingredients. Spread ¼ cup Nutella over each circle. Proceed as directed.*

For Chocolate-Coconut Rugalach: *Omit filling ingredients. Place 1 cup miniature chocolate chips and 1 cup flaked coconut in a food processor. Cover and pulse until finely chopped. Sprinkle ½ cup mixture over each circle. Proceed as directed.*

For Walnut Rugalach: *Omit filling ingredients. Place 1½ cups chopped walnuts, ⅔ cup packed brown sugar and 1 teaspoon ground cinnamon in a food processor. Cover and pulse until finely chopped. Sprinkle ½ cup mixture over each circle. Proceed as directed.*

MAKING RUGALACH

Rugalach is a traditional Jewish cookie prepared for Hanukkah. The dough for these crescent-shaped cookies is prepared with cream cheese and can contain fruit, raisins, nuts, jam and poppy seeds. By following the recipe above and photos here, your rugalach cookies will turn out with bakery-style perfection.

heavenly chocolate-fudge cake balls

My special treats are similar to the popular cake pops—but without the stick! They're guaranteed to calm any chocolate craving and jazz up holiday goodie trays all at the same time. Best of all, no one will guess how easy they are to make!

LYNN DAVIS | MORENO VALLEY, CALIFORNIA

1 package (18¼ ounces) devil's food cake mix

2 tablespoons hot water

1 teaspoon instant coffee granules

1 cup chocolate fudge frosting

⅓ cup baking cocoa

¼ cup chocolate syrup

1⅓ cups miniature semisweet chocolate chips

2 pounds white candy coating, chopped

Optional toppings: milk chocolate English toffee bits, toasted flaked coconut and crushed candy canes

1. Prepare and bake the cake according to package directions. Cool completely. Crumble cake into a large bowl.

2. In a small bowl, combine hot water and coffee granules; stir until dissolved. Add the frosting, cocoa and chocolate syrup; stir until combined. Add to cake; beat on low speed until blended. Stir in chocolate chips. Shape into 1-in. balls. Arrange on waxed paper-lined baking sheets.

3. In a microwave, melt candy coating; stir until smooth. Dip balls in coating mixture; allow excess to drip off. Place on waxed paper. Sprinkle with toppings of your choice. Let stand until set. Store in airtight containers.

YIELD: 95 CAKE BALLS.

chocolate-covered apricot-pecan pretzels

Salty pretzel rods dipped in a caramel, apricot and pecan mixture, then covered with dark chocolate, make a deliciously different treat during the holidays.

AYSHA SCHURMAN | AMMON, IDAHO

1 package (6 ounces) dried apricots, finely chopped

1⅓ cups chopped pecans, divided

2 packages (11 ounces each) Kraft caramel bits

¼ cup water

42 pretzel rods

3 cups dark chocolate chips

1 tablespoon shortening

1. In a small bowl, combine apricots and ⅔ cup pecans: set aside.

2. In a large heavy saucepan over medium-low heat, melt caramel bits with water, stirring constantly. Spoon caramel over two-thirds of each pretzel, rotating rods to coat all sides; allow excess caramel to drip off.

3. Sprinkle caramel with apricot mixture. Place on a waxed paper-lined baking sheet and refrigerate for 30 minutes or until set.

4. In another heavy saucepan over low heat, melt chips with shortening, stirring constantly. Spoon chocolate over coated ends of pretzels; allow excess to drip off. Return to baking sheet and sprinkle with remaining pecans. Store in airtight containers.

YIELD: 3½ DOZEN.

cranberry caramels

When I make holiday goodies, my sister always asks when I'm sending these cranberry caramels.

JAN RINKER | CRAIG, COLORADO

1 teaspoon plus ¼ cup butter, divided

1 cup sugar

1 cup chopped fresh cranberries

1 cup light corn syrup

½ cup heavy whipping cream

⅛ teaspoon salt

1. Line an 8-in. square dish with foil; grease the foil with 1 teaspoon butter and set aside.

2. In a large heavy saucepan, combine sugar, cranberries, corn syrup, cream, salt and remaining butter. Cook and stir over medium heat until mixture comes to a boil, washing down the sides of the pan using a pastry brush dipped in cold water to eliminate sugar crystals. Once mixture reaches a boil, cook without stirring until a candy thermometer reads 248° (firm-ball stage).

3. Remove from the heat. Pour into prepared pan (do not scrape saucepan). Let stand until firm, about 5 hours or overnight.

4. Using foil, lift candy out of pan. Discard foil; cut candy into 1-in. squares using a buttered knife. Wrap individually in waxed paper; twist ends.

YIELD: 1¼ POUNDS.

EDITOR'S NOTE: *We recommend that you test your candy thermometer before each use by bringing water to a boil; the thermometer should read 212°. Adjust your recipe temperature up or down based on your test.*

neapolitan fudge

If you like Neapolitan ice cream, you'll devour my fudge version of that vanilla, strawberry and chocolate favorite! It makes a great addition to any Christmas candy platter but is well-received any time of year.

FAITH LEONARD | DELBARTON, WEST VIRGINIA

1½ teaspoons butter

1 package (8 ounces) cream cheese, softened

3 cups confectioners' sugar

16 ounces milk chocolate, melted and cooled

VANILLA LAYER

1 package (8 ounces) cream cheese, softened

3 cups confectioners' sugar

16 ounces white baking chocolate, melted and cooled

1 tablespoon vanilla extract

RASPBERRY LAYER

1 package (8 ounces) cream cheese, softened

3 cups confectioners' sugar

16 ounces white baking chocolate, melted and cooled

1 tablespoon raspberry extract

8 to 10 drops food coloring, optional

1. Line a 13-in. x 9-in. baking pan with foil and grease the foil with butter; set aside. In a large bowl, beat cream cheese until fluffy. Gradually beat in confectioners' sugar. Beat in the melted milk chocolate. Spread into a prepared pan. Refrigerate for 10 minutes.

2. For vanilla layer, in a large bowl beat cream cheese until fluffy. Gradually beat in confectioners' sugar. Beat in melted white chocolate and vanilla. Spread over the chocolate layer. Refrigerate for 10 minutes.

3. For raspberry layer, in a large bowl beat cream cheese until fluffy. Gradually beat in the confectioners' sugar. Beat in melted white chocolate and raspberry extract. Tint with food coloring if desired. Spread over top. Cover and refrigerate for at least 8 hours or overnight.

4. Using foil, lift fudge out of pan. Gently peel off foil; cut the fudge into 1-in. squares. Store in an airtight container in the refrigerator.

YIELD: ABOUT 6½ POUNDS.

chai snickerdoodles

*When I think of winter, I think of two things: warm cookies and a chai.
My recipe combines both in a comforting favorite—snickerdoodles!*

EVANGELINE BRADFORD | ERLANGER, KENTUCKY

2 cups sugar

2 teaspoons ground cinnamon

1 teaspoon ground ginger

1 teaspoon ground cardamom

½ teaspoon ground allspice

1 cup butter, softened

2 eggs

1½ teaspoons vanilla extract

2¾ cups all-purpose flour

2 teaspoons cream of tartar

1 teaspoon baking soda

⅛ teaspoon salt

1. In a small bowl, combine the sugar, cinnamon, ginger, cardamom and allspice. Remove ½ cup of sugar mixture to a shallow bowl; set aside.

2. In a large bowl, cream butter and remaining sugar mixture until light and fluffy. Beat in eggs and vanilla. Combine the flour, cream of tartar, baking soda and salt; gradually add to creamed mixture and mix well.

3. Shape into 1½-in. balls; roll in reserved sugar mixture. Place 2 in. apart on parchment paper-lined baking sheets. Bake at 350° for 10-13 minutes or until edges begin to brown. Cool for 2 minutes before removing from pans to wire racks.

YIELD: 6½ DOZEN.

cocoa butter sticks

*Mom has been making these delectable, melt-in-your-mouth cookies
at Christmas time for as long as I can remember. Their wonderful cocoa flavor
and crisp chewy texture make them a standout on any cookie tray.*

REBECCA WILSON | LONGMONT, COLORADO

¾ cup butter, softened

¾ cup sugar

1 egg

1½ cups all-purpose flour

2 tablespoons baking cocoa

1 teaspoon baking powder

¼ teaspoon salt

TOPPING

1 egg

1 tablespoon cold water

3 tablespoons finely chopped almonds

2 tablespoons coarse sugar

1. In a large bowl, cream butter and sugar until light and fluffy. Beat in egg. Combine the flour, cocoa, baking powder and salt; gradually add to creamed mixture and mix well. Cover and refrigerate for at least 2 hours.

2. Divide dough into four portions. On ungreased baking sheets, roll each portion into an 8-in. x 1-in. log. Flatten with a fork dipped in flour to ¼-in. thickness. Whisk egg and water; brush over dough. Combine almonds and sugar; sprinkle over tops. Bake at 350° for 10-14 minutes or until set.

3. Place pans on wire racks. When cool enough to handle, transfer to a cutting board; cut diagonally with a serrated knife into ¾-in. slices. Turn cookies over and place back onto baking sheets. Bake 5 minutes longer to crisp bottoms. Cool on wire racks. Store in an airtight container.

YIELD: ABOUT 3¼ DOZEN.

peppermint meringue cookies

*Green and red swirls set these whimsical delights apart from any other meringue recipe.
They look like they came straight from Candy Land! Each pretty bite packs just the right amount
of refreshing peppermint flavor perfectly complemented by a bottom layer of chocolate.*

TASTE OF HOME TEST KITCHEN

4 egg whites

½ teaspoon cream of tartar

½ teaspoon peppermint extract

¼ teaspoon salt

1 cup sugar

Red and green paste food
coloring, optional

6 ounces dark chocolate candy
coating, chopped

1. Place egg whites in a large bowl; let stand at room temperature for 30 minutes. Add the cream of tartar, peppermint extract and salt; beat on medium speed until soft peaks form. Gradually add sugar, 1 tablespoon at a time, beating on high until stiff glossy peaks form and sugar is dissolved.

2. If desired, using a new small paintbrush, paint four alternating red and green stripes inside a pastry bag fitted with a #2D star tip. Fill bag with meringue. Pipe 1½-in.-diameter cookies onto parchment paper-lined baking sheets, repainting stripes if necessary.

3. Bake at 250° for 40-45 minutes or until set and dry. Turn the oven off; leave meringues in oven for 1½ hours. Remove meringues from parchment paper.

4. In a microwave, melt candy coating; stir until smooth. Dip bottoms of meringues into melted coating, allowing excess to drip off. Place on waxed paper; let stand until set. Store in an airtight container.

YIELD: 6 DOZEN.

lemon pirouettes

When you've had your fill of chocolate, indulge in one of these refreshing and dainty pirouettes. White candy coating and toasted coconut give each cookie an extra special touch.

TASTE OF HOME TEST KITCHEN

4 egg whites

1 cup sugar

1 cup unsalted butter, melted

1 teaspoon grated lemon peel

½ teaspoon vanilla extract

¼ teaspoon lemon extract

1 cup all-purpose flour

8 ounces white candy coating, coarsely chopped

½ cup flaked coconut, toasted

1. Using a pencil, draw three 3-in. circles on a sheet of parchment paper. Place paper, pencil mark down, on a baking sheet; set aside.

2. In a large bowl, beat egg whites on medium speed until soft peaks form. Gradually beat in sugar, 1 tablespoon at a time, on high until stiff peaks form. Beat in the butter, lemon peel and extracts. Gradually beat in flour until smooth.

3. Spread 2 teaspoons of batter over each circle. Bake at 400° for 4-6 minutes or until edges are lightly browned.

4. Working quickly, loosen cookies from parchment paper with a thin spatula and roll up. Repeat with remaining batter.

5. In a microwave, melt candy coating; stir until smooth. Dip each cookie halfway, allowing excess to drip off. Place on waxed paper and sprinkle with coconut. Let stand until set. Store in an airtight container.

YIELD: 5 DOZEN.

tender cherry shortbread cookies

I can't begin to imagine how many dozens of these luscious cookies I have made over the years. The drizzled chocolate catches the eye of anyone who walks past the cookie tray...and prompts them to try one or two.

LORRAINE CALAND | SHUNIAH, ONTARIO

2 cups unsalted butter, softened

1 cup confectioners' sugar

3 cups all-purpose flour

½ cup cornstarch

⅛ teaspoon salt

½ cup dried cherries, finely chopped

2 teaspoons dried lavender flowers, optional

1 cup dark chocolate chips, melted

1 cup white baking chips, melted

1. In a large bowl, cream butter and confectioners' sugar until light and fluffy. Combine the flour, cornstarch and salt; gradually add to the creamed mixture. Stir in cherries and lavender if desired. Divide dough in half.

2. Roll each portion into an 8-in. x 3-in. x 2-in. rectangle. Wrap each in plastic wrap. Refrigerate overnight or until firm. Unwrap and cut into ¼-in. slices. Place 1 in. apart on ungreased baking sheets. Bake at 325° for 15-18 minutes or until edges are lightly browned.

3. Cool for 2 minutes before carefully removing to wire racks to cool completely. Drizzle each with melted dark and white chips. Let stand until set.

YIELD: 4 DOZEN.

EDITOR'S NOTE: *Look for dried lavender flowers in spice shops. If you are using lavender from the garden, make sure it has not been treated with chemicals.*

bake 'n' take fun

It just isn't Christmas without Christmas cookies! Cookie exchanges are a great way to share recipes, baking and have a little fun in the process. Here are six memorable ideas to try with your friends.

1. **TRADITIONAL COOKIE EXCHANGE**

2. **ALL IN THE FAMILY**

3. **GOODWILL COOKIE EXCHANGE**

4. **BAKING BONANZA**

5. **DROP IN & DECORATE**

6. **COOKIE RECIPE BOOKLET**

1. For a **TRADITIONAL COOKIE EXCHANGE**, ask each guest to bring one dozen baked cookies. (You can get away with half a dozen cookies if the guest list is large, around 10 or more people.) At the party, provide containers for guests. These can be as basic as a paper plate and plastic wrap, a disposable food container or a resealable plastic bag, or as fancy as embellished paper boxes or Christmas-themed tins you picked up at your local hobby store.

2. The holidays are all about family traditions. For an **ALL IN THE FAMILY COOKIE EXCHANGE**, ask guests to bring one dozen of their favorite family Christmas cookie and to mail you the story behind the cookie in advance. Then, on the day of the party, give guests a booklet containing the stories behind each cookie.

3. With so many tempting treats, the holidays make it hard to avoid extra calories. But who wants to give up the fun of holiday baking? A **GOODWILL COOKIE EXCHANGE** lets you enjoy the best of both worlds. Have your guests bring a dozen cookies each and then assemble cookie packages to take to nursing homes, homeless shelters, or give as gifts to neighbors and friends.

4. A **BAKING BONANZA** party works best for smaller groups (fewer than five people). Ask each of your guests to bring one recipe and the necessary ingredients for it (alternatively, you can create a master ingredient list and divide it equally among the group). Then crank up the Christmas tunes as you bake your goodies.

5. In lieu of a traditional cookie exchange, invite friends to **DROP IN & DECORATE**. Ask each guest to bring one dozen baked, plain cookies. You supply a variety of decorating items (frostings, gels, dragees, colored sugars, etc.) or guests can bring some of their own. Then, spend the afternoon decorating Christmas cookies just like you did when you were kids.

6. Make your afternoon even more memorable by compiling the recipes you and your friends baked. Ask your guests to send you their cookie recipes in advance, and assemble a **RECIPE BOOKLET** for everyone to take home with their cookies.

The "Nutcracker" ballet... chestnuts roasting on an open fire...pecan pie...for many people, nuts are as traditional to the holiday season as are Santa Claus and his team of flying reindeer.

Centered around pecans, walnuts, almonds, pistachios and other salty, crunchy and buttery favorites, this imaginative and tasty menu offers a feast of flavor, texture and variety.

In addition to some very merry snacks, complementary sides and tempting desserts, you'll discover must-try entrees such as elegant Butternut Ravioli with Bourbon Pecan Sauce and succulent Apple and Walnut Stuffed Pork Tenderloin with Red Currant Sauce.

NUTTY HOLIDAY FARE

Butternut Ravioli with
Bourbon Pecan Sauce (p. 82)

Apple and Walnut Stuffed
Pork Tenderloin with Red Currant Sauce (p. 84)

GO NUTS
FOR CHRISTMAS!

butternut ravioli
with bourbon pecan sauce

(PICTURED ON PAGE 80)

Each year our family receives 25 pounds of pecans from a friend. With that many nuts, it requires some imagination to create different dishes. Making these tender butternut ravioli draped in a rich bourbon pecan sauce is one way I mix things up a bit.

MICHELE CLAYBROOK-LUCAS | MEDIA, PENNSYLVANIA

2   cups cubed peeled butternut squash

1   can (14½ ounces) vegetable broth

⅛   teaspoon ground cloves

1   cup ricotta cheese

¼   cup ground pecans, toasted

½   teaspoon garlic powder

½   teaspoon salt

¼   teaspoon pepper

32   wonton wrappers

BOURBON PECAN SAUCE

2   tablespoons butter

2   tablespoons all-purpose flour

½   teaspoon salt

¼   teaspoon pepper

¾   cup half-and-half cream

⅔   cup 2% milk

½   cup finely chopped pecans, toasted

1   tablespoon bourbon

GARNISH

Minced fresh parsley and additional chopped pecans

1. In a large saucepan, combine squash and broth. Bring to a boil. Reduce heat; cover and simmer for 15-20 minutes or until squash is tender. Drain. Mash squash with cloves. Transfer to a large bowl; cool to room temperature.

2. In a small bowl, combine the ricotta, pecans, garlic powder, salt and pepper; add to squash mixture.

3. Spoon 1 tablespoon squash mixture off center on a wonton wrapper. (Keep wrappers covered with a damp paper towel until ready to use.) Moisten edges with water. Fold wonton over diagonally and seal edges of triangle with a fork. Repeat with remaining wrappers and filling. Refrigerate 5-10 minutes.

4. In a Dutch oven, bring water to a boil. Reduce heat to a gentle simmer. Cook ravioli in batches for 1-2 minutes or until they float. Remove with a slotted spoon; keep warm.

5. Meanwhile, in a small skillet, melt butter. Stir in the flour, salt and pepper until smooth. Gradually stir in cream and milk. Bring to a boil; cook and stir for 2 minutes or until thickened. Stir in pecans and bourbon; heat through. Serve with ravioli. Sprinkle with parsley and additional pecans.

YIELD: 6 SERVINGS.

EDITOR'S NOTE: *To toast nuts, spread in a 15-in. x 10-in. x 1-in. baking pan. Bake at 350° for 5-10 minutes or until lightly browned, stirring occasionally. Or spread in a dry nonstick skillet and heat over low heat until lightly browned, stirring occasionally.*

CUT SQUASH WITH EASE

Here's a method to cut winter squash that doesn't rely just on strength. Use a rubber mallet and a large knife. Cover mallet with a food storage bag and secure to the handle with a rubber band. Insert the knife lengthwise into the middle of the squash. Hold the knife handle with one hand and hit the top of the blade by the handle with the mallet. Continue hitting the knife with the mallet until the squash is cut in half.

chicken sliders on pecan biscuits

Hot-from-the-oven, pecan biscuit "buns" make these mini pecan-chicken burgers extra special.

JEANNE HOLT | MENDOTA HEIGHTS, MINNESOTA

⅓ cup mayonnaise

¼ cup dried cranberries, chopped

2 tablespoons honey Dijon mustard

BURGERS

1 egg

½ cup shredded Swiss cheese

½ cup ground pecans, toasted

⅓ cup soft bread crumbs

2 green onions, finely chopped

2 tablespoons honey Dijon mustard

2 teaspoons minced fresh tarragon

¾ teaspoon salt

¼ teaspoon pepper

1¼ pounds ground chicken

BISCUITS

2 cups all-purpose flour

1 tablespoon baking powder

½ teaspoon salt

½ cup shortening

⅔ cup 2% milk

½ cup shredded Swiss cheese

½ cup finely chopped pecans, toasted

¼ cup canola oil

5 romaine leaves

1. Combine the mayonnaise, cranberries and mustard. Cover; refrigerate.

2. Combine the egg, Swiss cheese, pecans, bread crumbs, onions, mustard, tarragon, salt and pepper. Crumble chicken over mixture and mix well. Shape into 12 patties. Cover and refrigerate.

3. For biscuits, in a small bowl, combine flour, baking powder and salt. Cut in shortening until mixture resembles coarse crumbs. Stir in milk just until moistened. Stir in cheese and pecans. Turn onto a lightly floured surface; knead 8-10 times.

4. Pat or roll out to a 12-in. x 4-in. rectangle; cut into twelve 2-in. square biscuits. Place 2 in. apart on an ungreased baking sheet. Bake at 450° for 8-12 minutes or until golden brown.

5. Meanwhile, in a large skillet, cook chicken patties in oil over medium heat for 2-4 minutes on each side or until a thermometer reads 165° and juices run clear.

6. Slice warm biscuits in half. Spread bottoms with mayonnaise mixture; top with a burger and lettuce. Replace tops.

YIELD: 12 SERVINGS.

apple and walnut stuffed pork tenderloin with red currant sauce

(PICTURED ON PAGE 81)

My roasted pork tenderloin is stuffed with two of our favorite ingredients: walnuts and apples. Needless to say, this entree is my family's most-requested pork dish.

GLORIA BRADLEY | NAPERVILLE, ILLINOIS

1 tablespoon butter

1 cup chopped walnuts

1 medium apple, peeled and finely chopped

3 tablespoons dried cranberries

1 tablespoon minced fresh parsley

1 tablespoon olive oil

1 garlic clove, minced

1 pork tenderloin (1½ pounds)

⅓ cup apple butter

½ teaspoon salt

½ teaspoon ground coriander

SAUCE

1 cup red currant jelly

1 shallot, finely chopped

2 tablespoons cranberry juice

2 tablespoons honey

1 tablespoon dried currants

1 tablespoon cider vinegar

1. In a large heavy skillet, melt butter. Add walnuts; cook and stir over medium heat until toasted, about 2 minutes. Remove ½ cup for serving. Add apple to the remaining walnuts; cook and stir 1 minute longer. Cool slightly.

2. Place the cranberries, parsley, oil, garlic and apple mixture in a food processor; cover and process until finely chopped.

3. Cut a lengthwise slit down the center of the roast to within ½ in. of bottom. Open roast so it lies flat; cover with plastic wrap. Flatten to ½-in. thickness. Remove wrap; spread apple butter on one long side of tenderloin to within ¼ in. of edges. Top with apple mixture. Close meat; tie with kitchen string. Place on a rack in a shallow roasting pan; rub with salt and coriander.

4. Bake at 350° for 55-65 minutes or until a thermometer reads 145°. Let stand for 5 minutes before slicing.

5. Meanwhile, in a small saucepan, combine sauce ingredients; bring to a boil. Reduce heat; simmer, uncovered, for 12-14 minutes or until slightly thickened. Serve with pork; top with reserved walnuts.

YIELD: 6 SERVINGS.

STUFFING A TENDERLOIN... STEP BY STEP

Stuffed tenderloin makes an elegant main dish, and it's easier to prepare than you may think. By following the recipe above and how-to photos to the left, you'll have a special occasion entree that not only tastes wonderful, but looks beautiful on your holiday table.

what-a-nut brittle ice cream

If you think you've tried every kind of ice cream there is, think again! My creation was inspired by my love of nuts and brittle. The crunch of the brittle combined with the creamy goodness of homemade ice cream is the perfect balance of sweet-and-salty decadence.

HANNAH WOLTERS | CULLEOKA, TENNESSEE

- 1   cup whole milk
- ⅔   cup packed brown sugar
- ½   teaspoon salt
- 1   egg
- ⅔   cup creamy peanut butter
- 2   cups heavy whipping cream
- ½   cup vanilla yogurt
- 1   teaspoon vanilla extract
- ½   cup chopped mixed nuts
- ½   cup crushed peanut brittle

1. In a large heavy saucepan, heat the milk, brown sugar and salt until bubbles form around sides of pan. Whisk a small amount of hot mixture into the egg. Return all to the pan, whisking constantly.

2. Cook and stir over low heat until mixture is thickened and coats the back of a spoon. Remove from the heat; whisk in peanut butter. Quickly transfer to a bowl; place in ice water and stir for 2 minutes. Stir in the cream, yogurt and vanilla. Press waxed paper onto surface of custard. Refrigerate for several hours or overnight.

3. Fill cylinder of ice cream freezer two-thirds full; freeze according to the manufacturer's directions, adding nuts and brittle during churning.

4. When ice cream is frozen, transfer to a freezer container; freeze for 2-4 hours before serving.

YIELD: 1¼ QUARTS.

almond pesto crackers

Homemade crackers beat the store-bought variety, and my basil-infused bites are no exception. People love the unique flavor, and the beautiful green color is perfect for the holidays.

SUE BROWN | WEST BEND, WISCONSIN

2 cups loosely packed basil leaves

1½ cups grated Parmesan cheese

3 garlic cloves, minced

⅓ cup unblanched almonds or pine nuts

⅛ teaspoon salt

Dash pepper

5 tablespoons olive oil

CRACKERS

1½ cups unsalted butter, softened

1 cup shredded Parmesan cheese

3¾ cups all-purpose flour

1½ teaspoons pepper

¾ teaspoon salt

2 eggs, lightly beaten

3 tablespoons water

1½ cups chopped almonds

1. Place the basil, cheese and garlic in a food processor; cover and pulse until chopped. Add the almonds, salt and pepper; cover and process until blended. While processing, gradually add oil in a steady stream. Set aside.

2. In a large bowl, cream butter until light and fluffy. Beat in cheese and ⅓ cup pesto mixture. Combine the flour, pepper and salt; gradually add to creamed mixture and mix well. Divide dough into thirds.

3. On a lightly floured surface, shape each portion into a 6-in. log. Whisk eggs and water. Brush over logs; roll in almonds. Wrap logs in plastic wrap. Freeze for at least 30 minutes or until firm.

4. Unwrap logs and cut into ¼-in. slices. Place 1 in. apart on lightly greased baking sheets. Bake at 350° for 12-15 minutes or until bottoms are lightly browned. Remove to wire racks to cool completely.

YIELD: 6 DOZEN.

pistachio granola

After a long search for the perfect granola, I found this recipe and tweaked it just a little for my taste.

CANDY SUMMERHILL | ALEXANDER, ARKANSAS

2 cups old-fashioned oats

⅔ cup packed brown sugar

¼ cup apple cider or unsweetened apple juice

½ teaspoon ground cinnamon

¼ teaspoon salt

⅔ cup Cheerios

⅔ cup pistachios, chopped

⅔ cup dried cherries

½ cup dried apples, chopped

½ cup dried blueberries

½ cup sunflower kernels

1. In a large skillet, toast oats over medium heat until golden brown. Remove and set aside. In the same skillet, cook and stir brown sugar and apple cider over medium-low heat until brown sugar is dissolved, about 1-2 minutes. Add cinnamon and salt; stir to combine.

2. Stir in the cereal, pistachios, fruits, sunflower kernels and reserved oats until coated. Cool. Store in an airtight container.

YIELD: 6 CUPS.

edamame peanut falafel with peanut yogurt sauce

Originally given to me by a friend associated with the Southern Peanut Growers, this meatless entree makes a tasty change of pace. The golden patties get a nice crunch from the peanuts, and the spicy flavor complements the tangy yogurt dressing.

BARBARA MARTIN | TUSCALOOSA, ALABAMA

1   cup (8 ounces) plain yogurt

¼   cup chopped dry roasted peanuts

2   teaspoons lemon juice

1   garlic clove, minced

¼   teaspoon salt

⅛   teaspoon pepper

FALAFEL

2½   cups frozen shelled edamame, thawed

1½   cups dry roasted peanuts

½   cup minced fresh cilantro

2   eggs, lightly beaten

3   tablespoons chopped seeded jalapeno pepper

4   garlic cloves, minced

2   teaspoons baking powder

1   teaspoon salt

    Oil for deep-fat frying

1. In a small bowl, combine the first six ingredients; chill until serving.

2. In a food processor, combine the first eight falafel ingredients; process until finely chopped. Using a ¼ cup measure, shape mixture into patties.

3. In an electric skillet or deep fryer, heat oil to 375°. Fry patties, a few at a time, for 1-2 minutes on each side or until golden brown. Drain on paper towels. Serve with yogurt sauce.

YIELD: 1 DOZEN (1 CUP SAUCE).

pistachio-date cake with chantilly creme

The distinctive taste of dark beer adds a hearty and interesting note to this spiced cake studded with pistachio nuts and chopped dates and accented with a gingered cream topping.

JANICE ELDER | CHARLOTTE, NORTH CAROLINA

1   cup butter, softened

2   cups packed brown sugar

2   eggs

3   cups cake flour

2   teaspoons baking soda

1   teaspoon ground cardamom

1   teaspoon ground ginger

½   teaspoon ground nutmeg

½   teaspoon salt

2   cups dark beer, room temperature

2   cups chopped dates

1½ cups chopped pistachios

1   cup heavy whipping cream

3   tablespoons confectioners' sugar

½   teaspoon vanilla extract

¼   cup finely chopped crystallized ginger

1. In a large bowl, cream butter and brown sugar until light and fluffy, about 5 minutes. Add eggs, one at a time, beating well after each addition. Combine the flour, baking soda, cardamom, ginger, nutmeg and salt; add to the creamed mixture alternately with beer. Beat just until combined. Fold in dates and pistachios.

2. Transfer to a greased and floured 10-in. fluted tube pan. Bake at 300° for 1¼ to 1½ hours or until toothpick inserted near the center comes out clean. Cool for 10 minutes before removing from pan to a wire rack to cool completely.

3. In a large bowl, beat cream until it begins to thicken. Add confectioners' sugar and vanilla; beat until stiff peaks form. Fold in ginger. Serve with cake.

YIELD: 16 SERVINGS.

nutty cranberry rice pilaf

I like to bring healthy foods to the table, especially around the holidays. Most of my meals contain onions or garlic or both. Here is one recipe that can be used as a side dish or as a satisfying meatless main dish.

RENEE HAGENS | PITTSBURGH, PENNSYLVANIA

1   large onion, chopped

3   tablespoons olive oil

2   cups uncooked long grain rice

3   garlic cloves, minced

1   carton (32 ounces) vegetable stock

¼   cup dried cranberries

½   teaspoon salt

½   teaspoon each dried oregano, basil and dill weed

¼   teaspoon pepper

½   cup coarsely chopped cashews

1. In a large saucepan, saute onion in oil until tender. Add rice; cook and stir for 5 minutes or until lightly browned. Add garlic; cook 1 minute longer.

2. Stir in the stock, cranberries and seasonings. Bring to a boil. Reduce heat; cover and simmer for 20-25 minutes or until liquid is absorbed and rice is tender. Remove from the heat. Stir in cashews.

YIELD: 8 SERVINGS.

pine nut dumplings in raspberry sauce

My Italian-inspired dessert reminds me of my grandmother.
Top these warm dumplings and raspberry sauce with vanilla ice cream.

BROOKE SZCZEPANSKI | GLOUCESTER, VIRGINIA

- 4 cups fresh or frozen raspberries
- ¼ cup sugar
- ¼ cup merlot
- ¼ cup honey
- 2 tablespoons lemon juice
- ⅛ teaspoon salt
- 1 cinnamon stick (3 inches)

DUMPLINGS

- ¾ cup all-purpose flour
- ¼ cup sugar
- 1 teaspoon baking powder
- ½ teaspoon minced fresh rosemary or ⅛ teaspoon dried rosemary, crushed
- ¼ teaspoon salt
- 3 tablespoons cold butter
- ¾ cup pine nuts, toasted, divided
- 5 tablespoons buttermilk

1. In large saucepan, combine the first seven ingredients. Bring to a boil over medium heat. Reduce heat to low. Let it simmer, uncovered, while preparing dumplings.

2. In a small bowl, combine flour, sugar, baking powder, rosemary and salt. Cut in the butter until mixture resembles fine crumbs. Add ½ cup of the pine nuts. Stir in the buttermilk just until mixture is moistened.

3. Drop by tablespoonfuls onto simmering raspberry sauce. Cover and simmer for 20 minutes or until a toothpick inserted in a dumpling comes out clean (do not lift the cover while simmering). Discard cinnamon stick.

4. Sprinkle servings with remaining pine nuts. Serve warm.

YIELD: 6 SERVINGS.

EDITOR'S NOTE: *To toast nuts, spread in a 15-in. x 10-in. x 1-in. baking pan. Bake at 350° for 5-10 minutes or until lightly browned, stirring occasionally. Or spread in a dry nonstick skillet and heat over low heat until lightly browned, stirring occasionally.*

macadamia-crusted mahi mahi with coconut "beurre blanc"

Although this mahi mahi specialty tastes like you are splurging, it is really a healthy twist on a decadent favorite. The entree is delicious served with saffron rice or couscous.

KAREN SHELTON | COLLIERVILLE, TENNESSEE

- ⅓ cup orange juice
- 2 tablespoons finely chopped shallot
- 1½ teaspoons minced fresh gingerroot
- 1 small garlic clove, minced
- 1 can (13.66 ounces) light coconut milk
- 1 teaspoon sugar

- ⅛ teaspoon salt
- Dash pepper
- 1 tablespoon butter

MAHI MAHI
- 6 mahi mahi fillets (3 ounces each)
- ¼ teaspoon salt
- ⅛ teaspoon pepper
- 4 teaspoons grated orange peel

- 1 tablespoon orange juice
- 1½ teaspoons minced fresh gingerroot
- 2 teaspoons garlic powder
- 2 teaspoons ground cumin
- ¾ cup panko (Japanese) bread crumbs
- ½ cup chopped macadamia nuts
- 3 tablespoons olive oil

1. In a small saucepan, combine the orange juice, shallot, ginger and garlic. Bring to a boil over medium-high heat. Cook for 3 minutes. Stir in the coconut milk, sugar, salt and pepper. Simmer, stirring occasionally, until mixture is reduced by half, about 20 minutes. Remove from the heat and whisk in butter.

2. Pat fish dry; place on a parchment-lined baking sheet. Sprinkle with salt and pepper.

3. In a small bowl, combine the orange peel, juice, ginger, garlic powder and cumin. Spoon over fish. Let stand for 10 minutes. Combine the bread crumbs, nuts and oil; mound onto each fillet.

4. Bake, uncovered, at 425° for 14-16 minutes or until fish just turns opaque and crumb mixture is golden brown. Cover loosely with foil if crust browns too quickly. Serve with sauce.

YIELD: 6 SERVINGS (1 CUP SAUCE).

a bit nutty boston brown bread

Hazelnuts lend this dense bread a delightfully nutty taste that pairs well with just about anything.

LORRAINE CALAND | SHUNIAH, ONTARIO

- 3 cups whole wheat flour
- 1 cup all-purpose flour
- 2½ teaspoons baking soda
- 1 teaspoon salt
- 2½ cups buttermilk
- 1 cup molasses
- 1 cup golden raisins
- ¾ cup chopped hazelnuts, toasted

1. In a large bowl, combine the flours, baking soda and salt. In a small bowl, whisk buttermilk and molasses. Stir into dry ingredients just until moistened. Fold in raisins and nuts. Transfer to two greased 8-in. x 4-in. loaf pans.

2. Bake at 350° for 45-50 minutes or until a toothpick inserted near the center comes out clean. Cool for 10 minutes before removing from pans to wire racks.

YIELD: 2 LOAVES (12 SLICES EACH).

EDITOR'S NOTE: *To toast nuts, spread in a 15-in. x 10-in. x 1-in. baking pan. Bake at 350° for 5-10 minutes or until lightly browned, stirring occasionally. Or spread in a dry nonstick skillet and heat over low heat until lightly browned, stirring occasionally.*

honey walnut butter

Tired of plain old peanut butter? Try this slightly sweet alternative made from nutritious walnuts. It makes a deliciously different spread for toast, bagels, English muffins and apples.

TASTE OF HOME
TEST KITCHEN

1 cup chopped walnuts, toasted

Pinch salt

3 tablespoons canola oil

2 tablespoons honey

Apple wedges

1. Place walnuts and salt in a food processor. Cover and process until the nuts are finely ground.

2. Add oil and honey; cover and process until mixture forms a smooth paste. Chill until serving. Serve with apple wedges.

YIELD: ¾ CUP.

EDITOR'S NOTE: *To toast nuts, spread in a 15-in. x 10-in. x 1-in. baking pan. Bake at 350° for 5-10 minutes or until lightly browned, stirring occasionally. Or spread in a dry nonstick skillet and heat over low heat until lightly browned, stirring occasionally.*

pecan vinaigrette

Its slight nutty flavor and lip-puckering tartness make this my go-to dressing for salads and steamed vegetables. And if you run out, whisk together another batch in mere minutes!

KATHLEEN SPECHT | CLINTON, MONTANA

½ cup canola oil

¼ cup red wine vinegar

1 shallot, finely chopped

1 teaspoon Dijon mustard

¼ teaspoon salt

⅛ teaspoon pepper

⅓ cup finely chopped pecans, toasted

In a small bowl, whisk the oil, vinegar, shallot, mustard, salt and pepper. Cover and refrigerate. Just before serving, stir in chopped pecans.

YIELD: 1 CUP.

catfish with brown butter-pecan sauce

*I created this recipe for my husband, who is from the Midwest and grew up eating fried catfish.
The rich, toasty pecans and tangy citrus are a perfect complement to any fish.*

TRISHA KRUSE | EAGLE, IDAHO

⅓ cup all-purpose flour

½ teaspoon salt

½ teaspoon cayenne pepper

¼ teaspoon pepper

4 catfish fillets (6 ounces each)

6 tablespoons butter, divided

¾ cup chopped pecans

2 teaspoons grated lemon peel

2 teaspoons lemon juice

Lemon wedges

1. In a large resealable plastic bag, combine the flour, salt, cayenne and pepper. Add catfish, one fillet at a time, and shake to coat. In a large skillet, cook fillets in 2 tablespoons butter over medium-high heat for 2-4 minutes on each side or until fish flakes easily with a fork. Remove fish to a serving platter and keep warm.

2. In the same skillet, melt remaining butter. Add pecans and cook over medium heat until toasted, about 2-3 minutes. Stir in lemon peel and juice. Serve with fish and lemon wedges.

YIELD: 4 SERVINGS.

spicy peanut soup

*After enjoying a unique soup at a little cafe, I knew I had to try and duplicate it at home.
I think my version comes pretty close. It's the best way to chase away winter's chill.*

LISA MEREDITH | EAGAN, MINNESOTA

2 medium carrots, chopped

1 small onion, chopped

2 tablespoons olive oil

2 garlic cloves, minced

1 large sweet potato, peeled and cubed

½ cup chunky peanut butter

2 tablespoons red curry paste

2 cans (14½ ounces each) vegetable broth

1 can (14½ ounces) fire-roasted diced tomatoes, undrained

1 bay leaf

1 fresh thyme sprig

½ teaspoon pepper

½ cup unsalted peanuts

1. In a large saucepan, cook carrots and onion in oil over medium heat for 2 minutes. Add garlic; cook 1 minute longer.

2. Stir in sweet potato; cook 2 minutes longer. Stir in peanut butter and curry paste until blended. Add the broth, tomatoes, bay leaf, thyme and pepper.

3. Bring to a boil. Reduce heat; cover and simmer for 15-20 minutes or until sweet potatoes and carrots are tender. (Soup will appear curdled.) Discard bay leaf and thyme sprig. Stir soup until blended. Sprinkle with peanuts.

YIELD: 7 SERVINGS.

COOKING WITH CURRY

Red curry's spicy—but not too spicy—flavor makes it a popular choice when preparing Thai and Indian dishes. Not to be confused with curry powder, curry paste combines dry spices with ground fresh herbs, garlic, chilies and other ingredients to form a thick paste used in a variety of meat entrees, stews, soups, condiments and more.

pistachio gorgonzola cheesecake

*More than anything, I love having friends over for drinks and appetizers.
My savory cheesecake always makes a grand impression!*

MICHAELA ROSENTHAL | WOODLAND HILLS, CALIFORNIA

- 2 shallots, quartered
- 1 pound crumbled Gorgonzola cheese, divided
- 1 cup unsalted butter, cubed
- 1 package (8 ounces) cream cheese, softened and cubed
- ¼ cup Madeira wine
- 2 tablespoons grated orange peel
- 1 tablespoon heavy whipping cream
- ½ teaspoon white pepper
- ½ teaspoon ground mustard
- 1½ cups pistachios, toasted and chopped, divided
- 8 green onions, thinly sliced
- 2 tablespoons minced fresh basil
- 2 tablespoons minced fresh parsley
- 2 tablespoons oil-packed sun-dried tomatoes, drained and chopped
- Assorted crackers

1. Line the bottom of a 9-in. springform pan with parchment paper; set aside. Place shallots in a food processor; cover and process until chopped. Add 2 cups Gorgonzola, butter, cream cheese, wine, orange peel, cream, pepper and mustard; cover and process until blended. Set aside.

2. In a small bowl, combine 1 cup pistachios, green onions, basil, parsley, tomatoes and remaining Gorgonzola cheese.

3. Spread half of mixture in prepared pan. Top with half of cream cheese mixture. Repeat layers. Pat down. Cover and refrigerate for at least 8 hours or overnight.

4. Remove sides of pan. Carefully unmold onto a serving platter. Remove parchment paper. Finely chop remaining pistachios; press onto sides of cheesecake. Serve with crackers.

YIELD: 24 SERVINGS.

EDITOR'S NOTE: *To toast nuts, spread in a 15-in. x 10-in. x 1-in. baking pan. Bake at 350° for 5-10 minutes or until lightly browned, stirring occasionally. Or spread in a dry nonstick skillet and heat over low heat until lightly browned, stirring occasionally.*

R ing in the Chinese New Year by gathering a group of your friends and serving a buffet of tasty Chinese dishes.

As you and your guests take note of who was born under which animal symbol (and judge whether or not that person matches the description), indulge in a feast of authentic favorites.

Pile plates high with fall-off-the-bone-tender Chinese Barbecued Ribs, moist and flavorful Tea-Smoked Peking Chicken, Asian Sugar-Snap Peas and Cabbage, Mushroom Fried Rice and, of course, Shrimp Spring Rolls and Chinese Hot Mustard. Who knows? Your kitchen might become your favorite Chinese restaurant!

NEW YEAR BUFFET
Tea-Smoked Peking Chicken (p. 104)
Chinese Barbecued Ribs (p. 102)
Asian Sugar Snap Peas and Cabbage (p. 100)
Mushroom Fried Rice (p. 100)
Shrimp Spring Rolls (p. 98)
Chinese Hot Mustard (p. 104)

CHINESE
NEW YEAR CELEBRATION

asian chicken dumplings

(PICTURED AT RIGHT)

To celebrate my two daughters' Chinese heritage, we occasionally make Chinese food, especially around traditional Asian holidays like Chinese New Year. I took a traditional pork dumpling recipe and modified it using ground chicken so we can enjoy it anytime, not just holidays.

JOY OLCOTT | MILLERSVILLE, PENNSYLVANIA

1   pound ground chicken

4   green onions, chopped

½   cup chopped cabbage

¼   cup minced fresh cilantro

2   teaspoons minced fresh gingerroot

1   teaspoon salt

¼   teaspoon Chinese five-spice powder

2   tablespoons water

1   package (10 ounces) pot sticker or gyoza wrappers

     Cabbage leaves

     Reduced-sodium soy sauce

1. Place the first seven ingredients in a food processor; cover and process until finely chopped. Add water; cover and process until blended.

2. Place 1 tablespoon chicken mixture in the center of one wrapper. (Keep remaining wrappers covered with a damp paper towel to prevent them from drying out.) Moisten edges with water. Fold wrapper over filling to form a semicircle; press edges firmly to seal, pleating the front side to form three to five folds.

3. Holding sealed edges, stand each dumpling on an even surface; press to flatten bottom. Repeat with remaining wrappers and filling; cover dumplings with plastic wrap.

4. Line a steamer basket with four cabbage leaves. Arrange dumplings in batches 1 in. apart over cabbage; place in a large saucepan over 1 in. of water. Bring to a boil; cover and steam for 10-12 minutes or until a thermometer reads 165°. Discard cabbage. Repeat. Serve with soy sauce.

YIELD: 2½ DOZEN.

ginger egg drop soup

Egg drop soup is a must when my family eats Chinese food. With my simplified at-home version, my boys can enjoy it whenever they want.

JONA BLESKIN | GREAT FALLS, MONTANA

6   cups chicken broth

¾   teaspoon ground ginger

¾   teaspoon ground mustard

¼   teaspoon ground ancho chili pepper

¼   cup cornstarch

¼   cup cold water

4   eggs

2   tablespoons water

1. In a large saucepan, combine the broth, ginger, mustard and chili pepper. Bring to a boil. Combine cornstarch and cold water until smooth; gradually stir into the pan. Bring to a boil; cook and stir for 2 minutes or until thickened.

2. Whisk eggs and water. Turn off the heat. Drizzle beaten eggs into hot broth, without stirring. Let stand for 2-3 minutes or until eggs are set. Remove from the heat and stir.

YIELD: 6 SERVINGS.

pork lettuce wraps

My husband loves a particular restaurant's lettuce wraps. I changed a few ingredients to make a version we can indulge in at home. He loves them so much I'll make a double batch and serve it as our main course.

BRENDA BUERKLE
RIVERTON, WYOMING

1½ teaspoons cornstarch

3 tablespoons reduced-sodium soy sauce

2 tablespoons oyster sauce

1 tablespoon cold water

1 tablespoon hoisin sauce

1 teaspoon sugar

1 teaspoon canola oil

FILLING

1 pound ground pork

1 cup chopped celery

1 cup sliced fresh shiitake mushrooms

¾ cup sliced water chestnuts, drained and chopped

1 teaspoon canola oil

6 green onions, finely chopped

2 garlic cloves, minced

½ teaspoon crushed red pepper flakes

1 package (8.8 ounces) thin rice noodles

12 large lettuce leaves

1. In a small bowl, combine the first seven ingredients until smooth; set aside.

2. In a large skillet, cook pork over medium heat until no longer pink; drain. Remove and keep warm. In the same pan, stir-fry the celery, mushrooms and water chestnuts in oil until crisp-tender. Add the onions, garlic and pepper flakes; stir-fry 1 minute longer. Add pork; heat through.

3. Meanwhile, cook noodles according to package directions. Rinse under cold water; drain well and set aside.

4. Stir cornstarch mixture; add to pork mixture. Bring to a boil; cook and stir for 2 minutes or until thickened. Divide rice noodles among lettuce leaves; top with pork mixture. Fold lettuce over filling.

YIELD: 12 SERVINGS.

shrimp spring rolls

(PICTURED ON PAGE 95)

I began making these egg rolls in my college food science class, and I have made them countless times since with my own students. For best results, make sure the filling is cool before you put it in the wrappers. The oil should be hot enough so that the rolls sizzle when added.

LAURA BAKKER | OMAHA, NEBRASKA

½ cup packed brown sugar

1 tablespoon cornstarch

¼ teaspoon chicken bouillon granules

½ cup cold water

½ cup red wine vinegar

½ cup finely chopped green pepper

1 jar (2 ounces) diced pimientos, drained

1 tablespoon reduced-sodium soy sauce

2 garlic cloves, minced

½ teaspoon minced fresh gingerroot

SPRING ROLLS

2 teaspoons cornstarch

½ teaspoon sugar

¼ teaspoon salt

2 tablespoons reduced-sodium soy sauce

¾ pound uncooked medium shrimp, peeled, deveined and chopped

2 garlic cloves, minced

4 teaspoons canola oil, divided

2 cups finely shredded cabbage

1 cup finely chopped fresh mushrooms

½ cup finely chopped water chestnuts

½ cup shredded carrot

4 green onions, thinly sliced

12 egg roll or Chinese spring roll wrappers (6-8 inches)

Oil for deep-fat frying

1. In a saucepan, combine brown sugar, cornstarch and bouillon granules. Whisk in water and vinegar until smooth. Add the green pepper, pimientos, soy sauce, garlic and ginger. Bring to a boil. Cook and stir for 2 minutes or until thickened; set aside.

2. In a small bowl, combine the cornstarch, sugar and salt. Stir in soy sauce until smooth; set aside.

3. In a large skillet or wok, stir-fry shrimp and garlic in 1 teaspoon oil until shrimp turns pink. Remove and keep warm.

4. Stir-fry the cabbage, mushrooms, water chestnuts and carrot in remaining oil for 2-3 minutes or until carrot is crisp-tender.

5. Stir cornstarch mixture and add to the pan. Bring to a boil; cook and stir for 1-2 minutes or until thickened. Add shrimp and green onions; set aside to cool.

6. With one corner of egg roll wrapper facing you, place ⅓ cup shrimp mixture just below center of wrapper. Cover remaining wrappers with a damp paper towel until ready to use. Fold bottom corner over filling. Moisten remaining edges of wrapper with water. Fold side corners toward center over filling. Roll spring roll up tightly, pressing at tip to seal. Repeat. In an electric skillet or deep fryer, heat oil to 375°. Fry spring rolls, a few at a time, for 3-5 minutes or until golden brown, turning occasionally. Drain on paper towels. Serve with sauce.

YIELD: 1 DOZEN (1 CUP SAUCE).

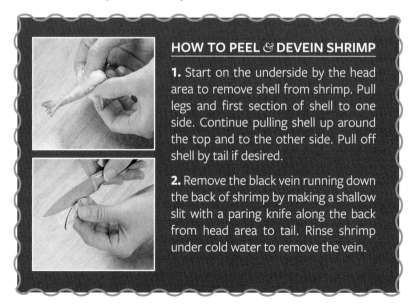

HOW TO PEEL & DEVEIN SHRIMP

1. Start on the underside by the head area to remove shell from shrimp. Pull legs and first section of shell to one side. Continue pulling shell up around the top and to the other side. Pull off shell by tail if desired.

2. Remove the black vein running down the back of shrimp by making a shallow slit with a paring knife along the back from head area to tail. Rinse shrimp under cold water to remove the vein.

chinese scallion pancakes

Unlike true pancakes, cong you bing—*Chinese scallion pancakes—are made from a dough instead of a batter. The tasty appetizers are the perfect "sponge" for mopping up extra sauce and can be made ahead of time for convenience. Just wrap in foil and reheat in the oven.*

TASTE OF HOME TEST KITCHEN

3   cups all-purpose flour

1⅓ cups boiling water

4   teaspoons sesame oil

6   green onions, chopped

1   teaspoon salt

½   cup canola oil

DIPPING SAUCE

3   tablespoons reduced-sodium soy sauce

1   tablespoon brown sugar

2   teaspoons minced fresh gingerroot

2   teaspoons rice vinegar

½   teaspoon sesame oil

⅛   teaspoon crushed red pepper flakes

1. Place flour in a large bowl; stir in boiling water until dough forms a ball. Turn onto a floured surface; knead until smooth and elastic, about 4-6 minutes. Place in a large bowl; cover and let rest for 30 minutes.

2. Divide dough into eight portions; roll each portion into an 8-in. circle. Brush with ½ teaspoon sesame oil; sprinkle with 1 heaping tablespoon of green onion and ⅛ teaspoon salt. Roll up jelly-roll style; holding one end of rope, wrap dough around, forming a coil, pinching to seal. Flatten slightly. Roll each coil to ⅛-in. thickness.

3. In a large skillet, heat 1 tablespoon canola oil. Cook pancakes, one at a time, over medium-high heat for 2-3 minutes on each side or until golden brown.

4. Meanwhile, in a small bowl, combine sauce ingredients. Serve with pancakes.

YIELD: 8 PANCAKES (¼ CUP SAUCE).

asian sugar snap peas and cabbage

(PICTURED ON PAGE 95 & AT RIGHT)

Looking for an attractive, appealing addition to your Chinese New Year buffet?
I recommend this simple salad starring crisp, sweet peas and crunchy cabbage.

CAROLE RESNICK | CLEVELAND, OHIO

1 pound fresh sugar snap peas, trimmed

¼ cup hoisin sauce

¼ cup reduced-sodium soy sauce

2 tablespoons agave nectar

1 tablespoon lime juice

2 teaspoons rice vinegar

2 teaspoons sriracha Asian hot chili sauce or 1 teaspoon hot pepper sauce

8 Chinese or napa cabbage leaves, julienned

1 tablespoon sesame seeds, toasted

1. In a large saucepan, bring 6 cups water to a boil. Add peas; cover and cook for 1-2 minutes. Drain and immediately place peas in ice water. Drain and pat dry.

2. For dressing, in a small bowl, whisk the hoisin sauce, soy sauce, agave nectar, lime juice, vinegar and chili sauce. In a large serving bowl, combine the peas, cabbage and sesame seeds. Add dressing; toss to coat.

YIELD: 8 SERVINGS.

Editor's Note: *Look for sriracha sauce in the Asian foods section of the grocery store or ethnic market.*

mushroom fried rice

(PICTURED ON PAGE 95)

After moving, I couldn't find a Chinese restaurant I liked, so I decided to create my own Chinese dishes.
This is one of my favorites, and can be served as a vegetarian main dish or side dish.

JACOB KITZMAN | SEATTLE, WASHINGTON

1 teaspoon plus 2 tablespoons sesame oil, divided

3 eggs, beaten

2 tablespoons canola oil

2 small onions, finely chopped

6 medium fresh mushrooms, thinly sliced

2 teaspoons minced garlic

1 teaspoon minced fresh gingerroot

4 cups cold cooked rice

1 cup frozen peas, thawed

¼ cup reduced-sodium soy sauce

¼ teaspoon salt

¼ teaspoon pepper

3 green onions, thinly sliced

Optional ingredients: Chinese-style mustard, duck sauce and additional soy sauce

1. In a large skillet, heat 1 teaspoon sesame oil over medium-high heat. Add eggs to skillet. Cook and stir until set. Remove to a plate; set aside.

2. In the same skillet, heat canola oil and remaining sesame oil. Saute onions and mushrooms for 2-3 minutes or until mushrooms are tender. Add garlic and ginger; saute 1-2 minutes longer.

3. Stir in the rice, peas, soy sauce, salt and pepper. Chop egg into small pieces; stir into skillet and heat through. Stir in green onions. Serve with mustard, duck sauce and additional soy sauce if desired.

YIELD: 8 SERVINGS.

pork stir-fry with noodle nests

A tender, flavorful pork and vegetable stir-fry is served on beds of crispy noodle "nests."

LORRAINE CALAND
SHUNIAH, ONTARIO

2   tablespoons mirin (sweet rice wine)
1   tablespoon tamari soy sauce
1½ teaspoons cornstarch
1   pound boneless pork loin chops, thinly sliced
10 ounces fresh or 6 ounces dried Chinese egg noodles

STIR-FRY

1   cup chicken broth
½   cup oyster sauce
¼   cup mirin (sweet rice wine)
2   tablespoons tamari soy sauce
1   tablespoon plus 1½ teaspoons cornstarch
1   tablespoon minced fresh gingerroot
1   garlic clove, minced
2   tablespoons canola oil
1   small Chinese or napa cabbage, shredded
1   can (8¾ ounces) whole baby corn
1   can (8 ounces) sliced water chestnuts, drained
1   can (8 ounces) bamboo shoots, drained
1   cup sliced fresh mushrooms
2   celery ribs, sliced
2   shallots, chopped
2   cups fresh snow peas
    Cooking spray

1. In a large resealable plastic bag, combine mirin, tamari and cornstarch. Add pork; seal bag and turn to coat. Refrigerate for at least 1 hour.

2. Cook noodles according to package directions; drain and rinse in cold water. Spread noodles over a paper towel-lined baking sheet; set aside.

3. Drain and discard marinade from pork. Combine the broth, oyster sauce, mirin, tamari, cornstarch, ginger and garlic.

4. In a large skillet or wok, stir-fry pork in oil for 2 minutes. Add the cabbage, corn, water chestnuts, bamboo shoots, mushrooms, celery and shallots; cook 4-6 minutes longer or until pork is no longer pink and vegetables are crisp-tender.

5. Stir cornstarch mixture and add to pan. Bring to a boil; cook and stir for 2 minutes or until thickened. Stir in snow peas; heat through.

6. Arrange noodles into six nests on a greased baking sheet; spray tops with cooking spray. Broil 4-5 in. from the heat for 7-9 minutes or until tops are golden brown. Serve with stir-fry.

YIELD: 6 SERVINGS.

chinese barbecued ribs

(PICTURED ON PAGE 95)

One bite of these fabulous ribs and you'll understand why my friends and family ask for them time after time. They're based on a recipe from my father-in-law, but I've added my own touches over the years.

ROXANNE CHAN | ALBANY, CALIFORNIA

½ cup char sui sauce

¼ cup rice vinegar

¼ cup sherry or reduced-sodium chicken broth

¼ cup reduced-sodium soy sauce

¼ cup oyster sauce

¼ cup hoisin sauce

4 garlic cloves, minced

2 teaspoons Chinese five-spice powder

2 teaspoons minced fresh gingerroot

4 pounds pork spareribs

Thinly sliced green onions, optional

1. In a small bowl, combine the first nine ingredients. Reserve half of the sauce for basting.

2. Place ribs, bone side down, in a shallow roasting pan lined with foil. Spoon remaining sauce over ribs. Cover and bake at 350° for 1 hour; drain.

3. Bake, uncovered, for 30-40 minutes or until ribs are tender, basting occasionally with reserved sauce. Cut ribs into serving-size pieces. Sprinkle with green onions if desired.

YIELD: 4 SERVINGS.

Editor's Note: *Look for char sui sauce in the Asian foods section of the grocery store or ethnic market.*

sweet and spicy cucumber salad

You can't go wrong adding this crunchy salad to your Chinese buffet. The bright flavors are a perfect combination of sweet, tart and spicy.

TASTE OF HOME TEST KITCHEN

4 English cucumbers

3 tablespoons reduced-sodium soy sauce

2 tablespoons rice vinegar

2½ teaspoons sugar

2 teaspoons sesame oil

1 garlic clove, minced

½ teaspoon salt

½ teaspoon crushed red pepper flakes

1. Slice cucumbers in half lengthwise. With a spoon, remove and discard the seeds; cut into ½-inch slices. Transfer cucumbers to a large bowl.

2. In a small bowl, whisk the remaining ingredients; pour over cucumbers and toss to coat. Serve with a slotted spoon.

YIELD: 6 SERVINGS.

tangerine cream roulade

Now you can make those heavenly cake rolls seen in Chinese bakeries at home! Our refreshing recipe features bright citrus flavors, moist cake and a sweet cream filling.

TASTE OF HOME
TEST KITCHEN

4 eggs, separated

½ teaspoon cream of tartar

⅔ cup sugar, divided

3 tablespoons tangerine juice

2 tablespoons canola oil

1 tablespoon grated tangerine peel

1 teaspoon vanilla extract

1 cup cake flour

1 teaspoon baking powder

¼ teaspoon salt

FILLING

1 cup heavy whipping cream

2 tablespoons confectioners' sugar

2 teaspoons grated tangerine peel

1 tablespoon chopped candied orange peel

Confectioners' sugar

1. Place egg whites in a small bowl; let stand at room temperature for 30 minutes. Line a greased 15-in. x 10-in. x 1-in. baking pan with waxed paper and grease the paper; set aside.

2. In a large bowl, beat egg yolks until lemon-colored. Gradually beat in ⅓ cup sugar. Stir in the juice, oil, tangerine peel and vanilla. Sift the flour, baking powder and salt together twice; gradually add to yolk mixture and mix well.

3. With clean beaters, beat egg whites and cream of tartar on medium speed until soft peaks form. Gradually beat in remaining sugar, 1 tablespoon at a time, on high until stiff peaks form. Gradually fold into batter. Spread into prepared pan.

4. Bake at 375° for 10-12 minutes or until cake springs back when lightly touched. Cool for 5 minutes. Turn cake onto a kitchen towel dusted with confectioners' sugar. Gently peel off waxed paper. Roll up cake in the towel jelly-roll style, starting with a short side. Cool completely on a wire rack.

5. For filling, in a small bowl, whip the cream to soft peaks. Add confectioners' sugar, tangerine peel and candied orange peel. Unroll cake; spread filling over cake to within 1 in. of edges. Roll up again. Place seam side down on a platter.

6. Refrigerate for at least 2 hours. Just before serving, dust with confectioners' sugar. Refrigerate leftovers.

YIELD: 12 SERVINGS.

tea-smoked peking chicken

(PICTURED ON PAGE 94)

This whole chicken is simmered in an aromatic soy-based broth, then smoked. A mixture of rice, tea leaves and brown sugar is used to smoke this traditional chicken dish, giving it irresistible flavor.

MAY DER | SOUTH PASADENA, CALIFORNIA

3 tablespoons whole peppercorns

3 tablespoons salt

1 whole broiler/fryer chicken (4 to 5 pounds)

8 cups water

1 cup reduced-sodium soy sauce

2 green onions, sliced

3 slices fresh gingerroot

2 whole star anise

1 cinnamon stick (3 inches)

1 teaspoon Chinese five-spice powder

½ cup uncooked long grain rice

½ cup loose black tea leaves

½ cup packed brown sugar

1 teaspoon sesame oil

1. Place peppercorns in a spice grinder or a mortar and pestle; grind until coarsely ground. Place peppercorns and salt in a small dry skillet; toast over medium heat for 1-2 minutes or until aromatic, stirring occasionally. Cool completely.

2. Pat chicken dry; rub peppercorn mixture over the outside and inside of chicken. Cover and refrigerate for at least 4 hours or overnight.

3. In a stockpot, combine the water, soy sauce, green onions, ginger, star anise, cinnamon stick and five-spice powder; bring to a boil. Reduce heat; simmer, uncovered, for 10 minutes.

4. Add chicken. Return to a boil. Reduce heat; simmer, covered, for 35-40 minutes or until a thermometer inserted in thigh reads 180°, turning chicken once. Remove chicken; discard cooking liquid.

5. Line bottom of a clean stockpot with a double thickness of foil. Sprinkle rice, tea leaves and brown sugar over foil; place a wire rack over rice mixture. Place chicken on rack breast side up.

6. Cook over low heat until rice mixture begins to smoke. Cover pot tightly with foil; place lid on top. Smoke for 25-30 minutes or until chicken is golden brown.

7. Remove chicken; brush with sesame oil. Let stand 15 minutes before carving. Chicken may also be served cold. To serve cold, cool chicken slightly; cover and refrigerate until chilled.

YIELD: 6 SERVINGS.

Editor's Note: *Look for Szechuan peppercorns in Asian markets or visit* penzeys.com.

chinese hot mustard

(PICTURED ON PAGE 94)

You know that Chinese hot mustard you can't get enough of at restaurants? Good news! It's surprisingly simple to make, and a definite highlight of an authentic Chinese meal.

MATT WARREN | MEQUON, WISCONSIN

¼ cup ground mustard

1 teaspoon sugar

½ teaspoon salt

¼ cup cold water

2 teaspoons canola oil

In a small bowl, combine the mustard, sugar and salt. Stir in water and oil until smooth. Refrigerate until serving.

YIELD: ½ CUP.

what's your sign?

The Chinese Zodiac is made up of 12 animals: Rat, Ox, Tiger, Rabbit, Dragon, Snake, Horse, Goat, Monkey, Rooster, Dog and Pig. Each sign is known for certain qualities. Distribute copies of this chart to your Chinese New Year party guests and have some fun guessing who was born under which sign based on their personality.

RAT
(1936, 1948, 1960, 1972, 1984, 1996, 2008, 2020)

Those born under the sign of the Rat are quick-witted, clever, charming, sharp and funny. They have excellent taste, make good friends and are generous and loyal to those in their pack. Motivated by money, they can be greedy. They are always curious, seeking knowledge and welcoming challenges. Compatible with Dragon or Monkey.

OX
(1937, 1949, 1962, 1973, 1985, 1997, 2009, 2021)

Those born under the sign of the Ox are steadfast, solid, goal-oriented leaders, detail-oriented, hardworking, stubborn, serious and introverted. They can feel lonely and insecure, and take comfort in friends and family. They are reliable, protective and strong companions. Compatible with Snake or Rooster.

TIGER
(1938, 1950, 1962, 1974, 1986, 1998, 2010, 2022)

Those born under the sign of the Tiger are authoritative, self-possessed, have strong leadership qualities, are charming, ambitious, courageous, warm-hearted, highly seductive, moody, intense, and ready to pounce at any time. Compatible with Horse or Dog.

RABBIT
(1939, 1951, 1963, 1975, 1975, 1987, 1999, 2011, 2023)

Those born under the sign of the Rabbit enjoy being surrounded by family and friends. They're popular, compassionate, sincere, and like to avoid conflict. They are sometimes seen as pushovers. Rabbits enjoy home and entertaining at home. Compatible with Goat or Pig.

DRAGON
(1940, 1952, 1964, 1976, 1988, 2000, 2012, 2024)

Those born under the sign of the Dragon are energetic and warm-hearted, charismatic, lucky at love and egotistical. They're natural leaders, good at giving orders and doing what's necessary to remain on top. Compatible with Monkey and Rat.

SNAKE
(1941, 1953, 1977, 1989, 2001, 2013, 2025)

Those born under the sign of the Snake are seductive, gregarious, generous, charming, good with money, analytical, insecure, jealous, slightly dangerous and smart. They rely on gut feelings, are hard-working and intelligent. Compatible with Rooster or Ox.

HORSE
(1942, 1954, 1966, 1978, 1990, 2002, 2014, 2026)

Those born under the sign of the Horse love to roam free. They're energetic, self-reliant, money-wise, and they enjoy traveling and love. They're sharp-witted, impatient and sometimes seen as drifters. Compatible with Dog or Tiger.

GOAT
(1943, 1955, 1967, 1979, 1991, 2003, 2015, 2027)

Those born under the sign of the Goat enjoy being alone in their thoughts. They're creative thinkers, wanderers, unorganized, high-strung and insecure. They need lots of love, support and reassurance. Appearance is important, too. Compatible with Pig or Rabbit.

MONKEY
(1944, 1956, 1968, 1980, 1992, 2004, 2016, 2028)

Those born under the sign of the Monkey thrive on having fun. They're energetic, upbeat and good at listening, but lack self-control. They like being active and enjoy pleasing themselves before pleasing others. Compatible with Rat or Dragon.

ROOSTER
(1945, 1957, 1969, 1981, 1993, 2005, 2017, 2029)

Those born under the sign of the Rooster are practical, resourceful, observant, analytical, straightforward, trusting, honest, perfectionist, neat and conservative. Compatible with Ox or Snake.

DOG
(1946, 1958, 1970, 1982, 1994, 2006, 2018, 2030)

Those born under the sign of the Dog are loyal, faithful, honest, distrustful, prone to mood swings, dogmatic and sensitive. They also excel in business. Compatible with Tiger or Horse.

PIG
(1947, 1959, 1971, 1983, 1995, 2007, 2019, 2031)

Those born under the sign of the Pig are extremely good-mannered and tasteful. They're perfectionists who enjoy the finer things but are not perceived as snobs. They enjoy helping others and are good companions until someone close crosses them. They're intelligent and always seeking more knowledge. Compatible with Rabbit or Goat.

givingthanks

Perhaps it's the simplicity of the holiday—food, friends and a thankful heart—that makes Thanksgiving a favorite with many. This bountiful chapter features everything you need for a gratifying feast—from complete menus to savory breads and tempting desserts. Cooks who want to impress won't want to miss the formal dinner menu featuring Turducken.

Move over turkey! A new breed of bird—make that birds!—has moved onto the menu this Thanksgiving.

Introducing Turducken, quite possibly the ultimate in holiday entrees. It's a chicken stuffed inside a duck stuffed inside a turkey. Each moist, juicy slice contains portions of all three meats, and is separated by an incredibly savory sourdough bread stuffing.

Drape slices of this show stopping main dish with Perfect Gravy—it's brimming with old-fashioned flavor. Then, round out your plates with pretty Roasted Carrots with Dill Weed and a hearty serving of Celeriac & Garlic Mashed Potatoes.

TURDUCKEN & TRIMMINGS

A FORMAL AFFAIR

A FEW WEEKS BEFORE

- Prepare two grocery lists: one for nonperishable items to purchase now and one for perishable items to purchase a few days before Thanksgiving Day.
- Order a deboned duck, chicken and turkey (legs and wings still intact) from your butcher.

TWO DAYS BEFORE

- Buy the remaining grocery items, including the duck, chicken and turkey.

THE DAY BEFORE

- Set the table.
- Clean and cut carrots for Roasted Carrots with Dill Weed.
- For Amazing Spinach Salad, prepare the dressing, cook the pancetta, wash and dry the spinach, and seed the pomegranate. Store in separate containers in the refrigerator.
- Prepare squash mixture for Autumn Squash Tartlets; cover and chill.
- Prepare Spiced Tea Poached Pears. Cover Dutch oven and chill. Make sauce. Place in a covered container; chill.
- Bake cake for Chocolate-Caramel Pumpkin Torte. Wrap cake tightly in plastic wrap.
- Assemble stuffing for Turducken; cover and chill.

THANKSGIVING DAY

- In the morning, peel and cube the potatoes and celery root for the Celeriac & Garlic Mashed Potatoes. Cover with cold water; refrigerate.
- Prepare frostings for Chocolate-Caramel Pumpkin Torte. Assemble cake; refrigerate until serving.
- Assemble and bake Turducken.
- Prepare Celeriac & Garlic Mashed Potatoes.
- Remove the Turducken from the oven. Increase the temperature to 375°. Bake Autumn Squash Tartlets.
- Let the cooked Turducken stand 20 minutes before carving. Meanwhile, make Perfect Gravy.
- Remove Autumn Squash Tartlets from the oven. Increase the temperature to 425°. Bake Roasted Carrots with Dill Weed.
- Assemble Amazing Spinach Salad.
- Reheat Spiced Tea Poached Pears; serve with sauce.

autumn squash tartlets

I use the fall squash from my family's Mississippi pumpkin farm to develop recipes that teach people how to cook with squash. My lovely autumn appetizer can be made with any fall squash.

LESLEE COLSON | MONTGOMERY, ALABAMA

1 package (17.3 ounces) frozen puff pastry, thawed

2½ cups cubed acorn squash

3 tablespoons heavy whipping cream

4 teaspoons dry bread crumbs

1½ teaspoons minced fresh rosemary

1½ teaspoons minced fresh thyme

½ teaspoon salt

⅛ teaspoon pepper

2 ounces fresh goat cheese

1. Unfold the puff pastry; cut out sixteen 2-in. circles from each pastry sheet. Press onto the bottom and up the sides of greased miniature muffin cups.

2. Place squash and cream in a food processor. Cover and process for 1-2 minutes or until smooth. Transfer to a large bowl; stir in the bread crumbs, rosemary, thyme, salt and pepper.

3. Spoon mixture into pastry cups. Bake at 375° for 15-17 minutes or until golden brown. Top with cheese. Broil for 1-2 minutes or until the cheese is melted. Serve tartlets warm.

YIELD: 32 TARTLETS.

celeriac & garlic mashed potatoes

(PICTURED ON PAGE 109)

*My family can't get enough of this comforting fall favorite, especially at Thanksgiving.
I love the addition of the celery root. Its mild flavor pairs well with the garlic and potato.*

LYNELLE MARTINSON | PLOVER, WISCONSIN

3 medium Yukon Gold potatoes, peeled and cubed

1 large celery root, peeled and chopped

3 garlic cloves, peeled

2 tablespoons butter

2 tablespoons 2% milk

½ teaspoon salt

¼ teaspoon pepper

1 tablespoon minced chives

1. Place the potatoes, celery root and garlic in a Dutch oven; cover with water. Bring to a boil. Reduce heat; cover and cook for 15 minutes or just until tender. Drain; cool slightly.

2. In a large bowl, mash vegetables with butter, milk, salt and pepper. Stir in chives.

YIELD: 6 SERVINGS.

perfect gravy

(PICTURED ON PAGE 109)

*My old-fashioned gravy is the finishing touch to my family's holiday meal.
Sliced turkey and mashed potatoes just wouldn't be complete with out this savory topping.*

SHARON ADAMCZYK | WIND LAKE, WISCONSIN

Turkey giblets and neck bone

6 cups reduced-sodium chicken broth

2 large onions, sliced

2 medium carrots, sliced

1 cup white wine or water

½ cup chopped celery leaves

6 garlic cloves

1 bay leaf

¾ cup butter, cubed

¾ cup all-purpose flour

¾ teaspoon salt

½ teaspoon pepper

1. Place the giblets, neck bone, broth, onions, carrots, wine, celery leaves, garlic and bay leaf in a Dutch oven; bring to a boil. Reduce heat; cover and simmer for 1¼ hours.

2. Strain and discard the giblets, neck bone, vegetables and bay leaf. Set cooking juices aside; cool slightly. (Refrigerate if made ahead.)

3. Just before serving, in a large saucepan, melt the butter. Stir in the flour, salt and pepper until smooth; gradually add broth mixture. Bring to a boil; cook and stir for 2 minutes or until thickened.

YIELD: 6 CUPS.

amazing spinach salad

Crunchy, sweet, savory and healthy, this all-in-one salad has everything my family craves. Plus it's easy to assemble—a must at the holidays.

LISA MARGARONE | SAFETY HARBOR, FLORIDA

⅓ cup canola oil

3 tablespoons ketchup

2 tablespoons sugar

2 tablespoons grated onion

2 tablespoons cider vinegar

2 tablespoons olive oil

1½ teaspoons Worcestershire sauce

¼ teaspoon kosher salt

¼ teaspoon coarsely ground pepper

8 ounces sliced pancetta or bacon, cut into ¼ inch strips

2 packages (6 ounces each) fresh baby spinach

2 cups (8 ounces) crumbled Gorgonzola cheese

1 cup grape tomatoes

1 cup pomegranate seeds

1. Place first nine ingredients in a jar with a tight-fitting lid; shake well. Chill until serving.

2. In a skillet, cook pancetta over medium heat until crisp. Remove to paper towels; drain. Arrange spinach on a serving plate. Set the cheese, tomatoes and pancetta over the top.

3. Just before serving, shake the dressing and drizzle over the salad. Sprinkle with the pomegranate seeds.

YIELD: 12 SERVINGS.

turducken

(PICTURED ON PAGE 109)

This is no ordinary holiday bird. A turducken is a dish consisting of a deboned chicken stuffed into a deboned duck, which itself is stuffed into a deboned turkey. It's the ultimate feast!

TASTE OF HOME TEST KITCHEN

1½ cups fresh sage

½ cup packed fresh parsley sprigs

½ cup grated Parmesan cheese

2 garlic cloves

¼ teaspoon salt

½ cup olive oil

STUFFING

1 medium fennel bulb, chopped

1 medium onion, chopped

¾ cup butter, cubed

4 garlic cloves, minced

½ teaspoon salt

¼ teaspoon pepper

12 cups cubed day-old sourdough bread

1 cup chopped peeled ripe pears

¾ cup chopped hazelnuts

1 cup chicken broth

½ cup egg substitute

TURDUCKEN

1 turkey (16 to 18 pounds), skin intact and deboned except legs and wings

1 domestic duck (4 to 5 pounds), deboned

1 broiler/fryer chicken (3 to 4 pounds), deboned

Large needle

Kitchen string

1 tablespoon olive oil

1. For pesto, place the sage, parsley, Parmesan cheese, garlic and salt in a food processor; cover and process until blended. While processing, gradually add oil in a steady stream; set aside.

2. In a large skillet, saute fennel and onion in butter until tender. Add garlic; cook 1 minute longer. Stir in salt and pepper. In a large bowl, combine the bread cubes, pears, hazelnuts, fennel mixture and ½ cup reserved pesto. In another bowl, whisk broth and egg substitute. Pour over bread mixture; stir until moistened. Cover and refrigerate until assembly.

3. Place turkey skin side down on work surface; press 5 cups stuffing mixture over turkey. Layer with duck, skin side down and 4 cups stuffing. Top with chicken skin side down and remaining stuffing. **A**

4. Carefully pull turkey skin over filling. Truss turkey skin at 1-in. intervals with a large needle and kitchen string. **B** Ask a friend to help tuck wings under turkey while you tie the drumsticks together. Place breast side up on a rack in a roasting pan. Brush with oil.

5. Bake, uncovered, at 325° for 5¼ to 5¾ hours or until a thermometer reads 180° in the center of turducken, basting occasionally with pan drippings. Cover loosely with foil if turkey browns too quickly. During the last 30 minutes of cooking, brush remaining pesto over turducken. Cover and let stand for 20 minutes before slicing. **C**

YIELD: 36 SERVINGS.

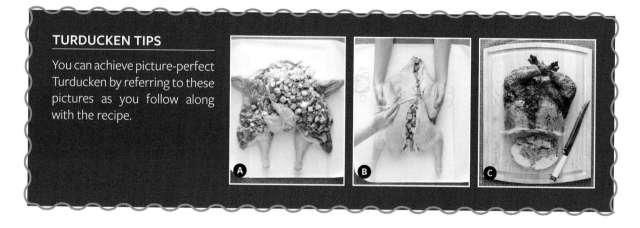

TURDUCKEN TIPS

You can achieve picture-perfect Turducken by referring to these pictures as you follow along with the recipe.

chocolate-caramel pumpkin torte

The key is to this "to-die-for-delicious" cake is to let it cool completely before cutting and assembling with the frostings.

LAUREN BRENNAN
HOOD RIVER, OREGON

½ cup butter, softened

1¼ cups sugar

2 eggs

1 cup canned pumpkin

1 teaspoon vanilla extract

1½ cups all-purpose flour

1½ teaspoons baking powder

1 teaspoon salt

1 teaspoon ground cinnamon

½ teaspoon baking soda

½ teaspoon ground nutmeg

½ cup sour cream

½ cup chopped walnuts, toasted

CARAMEL FROSTING

½ cup butter, softened

½ cup caramel sundae syrup

1 cup confectioners' sugar

1 teaspoon vanilla extract

CHOCOLATE FROSTING

½ cup butter, softened

⅓ cup baking cocoa

1 cup confectioners' sugar

1 tablespoon 2% milk

1 teaspoon vanilla extract

GARNISH

⅓ cup chopped walnuts, toasted

3 tablespoons milk chocolate English toffee bits

1. Line a greased 15-in. x 10-in. x 1-in. baking pan with waxed paper; grease the paper. Set aside.

2. In a large bowl, cream butter and sugar until light and fluffy. Add eggs, one at a time, beating well after each addition. Beat in pumpkin and vanilla (mixture will appear curdled). Combine the flour, baking powder, salt, cinnamon, baking soda and nutmeg; add to the creamed mixture alternately with sour cream, beating well after each addition. Stir in walnuts.

3. Transfer to prepared pan. Bake at 350° for 15-20 minutes or until a toothpick inserted near the center comes out clean. Cool for 10 minutes before inverting onto a wire rack to cool completely. Carefully remove waxed paper.

4. For caramel frosting, in a small bowl, beat butter and sundae syrup until fluffy. Add confectioners' sugar and vanilla; beat until smooth.

5. For chocolate frosting, in a small bowl, beat butter and cocoa until fluffy. Add the confectioners' sugar, milk and vanilla; beat until smooth.

6. Trim cake edges; cut widthwise into fourths. Place one layer on a serving plate; top with half of the chocolate frosting. Top with another cake layer and top with half of the caramel frosting. Repeat layers. Sprinkle with walnuts and toffee bits. Chill until serving.

YIELD: 12 SERVINGS.

roasted carrots with dill weed

(PICTURED ON PAGE 108)

Try my recipe for roasted carrots for an almost effortless side dish that pairs wonderfully with Thanksgiving turkey. Just a handful of ingredients keeps it simple but flavorful.

DONNA NOEL | GRAY, MAINE

2½ pounds medium carrots, halved lengthwise and widthwise

3 tablespoons butter, melted

1 tablespoon snipped fresh dill or 1 teaspoon dill weed

½ teaspoon salt

¼ teaspoon pepper

Place carrots in a greased 15-in. x 10-in. x 1-in. baking pan. Drizzle with butter and sprinkle with dill, salt and pepper; toss to coat. Bake, uncovered, at 425° for 15-18 minutes or until carrots are tender, stirring once.

YIELD: 6 SERVINGS.

spiced tea poached pears

Pears are among my favorite fall fruit—prepared in this lovely dessert, they're especially spectacular. It's easy elegance at its best, and that's important around the holidays.

PETER HALFERTY | CORPUS CHRISTI, TEXAS

7 cups water

1¼ cups packed light brown sugar

½ cup whole-berry cranberry sauce

⅓ cup honey

9 orange-flavored black tea bags

12 medium pears

SAUCE

½ cup creme fraiche or sour cream

1 tablespoon confectioners' sugar

1 tablespoon grated orange peel

1. In a Dutch oven, combine the water, brown sugar, cranberry sauce and honey. Bring to a boil. Remove from the heat; add tea bags. Cover and steep for 5-8 minutes.

2. Meanwhile, core pears from bottom, leaving stems intact. Peel pears; cut a thin slice from bottom to level if necessary. Remove and discard tea bags. Add pears to the pan. Bring to a boil. Reduce heat; cover and simmer for 12-15 minutes or until pears are tender. Remove the pears with a slotted spoon and keep warm.

3. In a small saucepan, bring 2 cups tea mixture to a boil; cook until liquid is reduced to ½ cup, about 20 minutes.

4. In a small bowl, combine the creme fraiche, confectioners' sugar and orange peel. Place pears on dessert plates. Drizzle with syrup and serve with sauce.

YIELD: 12 SERVINGS.

a tree of thanks

Repurposed glass soda bottles create a whimsical display for the many things you're thankful for this holiday season. As friends and family arrive, ask them to add their own "thankful notes" to the branches.

- ☐ glass soda bottles (cleaned and dried)
- ☐ spray paint
- ☐ vinyl letters
- ☐ branches or sticks
- ☐ assorted scrapbook papers
- ☐ permanent marker
- ☐ ribbon, cut in 6-in. lengths

1. Following manufacturer's instructions, apply as many coats of spray paint as needed to each bottle's exterior for complete coverage. Let dry.

2. Adhere one vinyl letter centered on side of each bottle to spell "thanks" and arrange bottles in letter order.

3. Arrange the branches in each finished bottle.

4. Cut several leaf shapes from the assorted scrapbook paper. Write, or ask guests to write, one thing for which they are thankful on each leaf.

5. Using a hole punch, punch a hole at the top of the leaf. String a ribbon through the hole and attach the paper leaves to the branches.

CRAFTER'S NOTE: *We used Krylon's Satin Brushed Metallic in Caramel Latte. The vinyl letters were purchased online at E.A.D Designs (http://stencilwords.com)*

Sure, the holidays are about traditions, but every now and then it's worth bending the rules a bit. Especially if it's to make room for Barbecued Turkey. Its crispy skin, sassy flavor and moist meat will ensure that no one will miss the usual roasted bird.

In fact, this entire menu takes traditional Turkey Day fare from "tired" to "ta da!" Who knew that a splash of rum and the addition of raisins could take plain old cranberries to new heights? And why mash only potatoes when you can mix in turnips, parsnips and pumpkin, too?

The versatility of Roasted Sweet Potato Salad with Chili Lime Dressing and Blue Cheese Apple Slaw makes these sides a great addition to your Thanksgiving Day menu or any fall potluck.

NEW HARVEST FLAVORS

GRILLED TURKEY FEAST

giving*thanks* | **GRILLED TURKEY** FEAST

A FEW WEEKS BEFORE

- Prepare two grocery lists: one for nonperishable items to purchase now and one for perishable items to purchase a few days before Thanksgiving Day.
- Bake the Cranberry Muffins with Walnut-Thyme Streusel. Cool; place in a resealable plastic bag and freeze.
- Order a fresh turkey or buy and freeze a frozen turkey.

FOUR TO THREE DAYS BEFORE

- Thaw the frozen turkey in a pan in the refrigerator. (Allow 24 hours of thawing for every 5 pounds. A thawed turkey can be refrigerated for 1 to 2 days.)
- Buy the remaining grocery items, including the fresh turkey if ordered.

THE DAY BEFORE

- Set the table.
- For Southern Green Beans with Apricots, clean and trim green beans; refrigerate in a resealable plastic bag.
- Make Pumpkin Pie Cups; cover and chill.
- Prepare sauce for Barbecued Turkey. Store in a covered container; chill.
- Make Cranberry Rum-Raisin Relish. Store in a covered container; chill.
- For Glazed Walnut-Pear Salad, prepare pears and vinaigrette; store separately.
- Prepare dressing for Roasted Sweet Potato Salad with Chili Lime Dressing; cover and chill.

THANKSGIVING DAY

- In the morning, peel and cube the potatoes, turnips and parsnips for the Autumn Harvest Mashed Potatoes. Cover with cold water; refrigerate.
- In the morning, prepare Roasted Sweet Potato Salad with Chili Lime Dressing and Blue Cheese Apple Slaw; cover and chill.
- Bake Apple Pie Bundles; drizzle with glaze.
- Thaw Cranberry Muffins with Walnut-Thyme Streusel at room temperature. Wrap the muffins in foil and reheat at 350°; for 10 minutes.
- Grill the Barbecued Turkey. Reheat sauce; baste and continue grilling as directed.
- Let the cooked turkey stand for 20 minutes before carving.
- Prepare Autumn Harvest Mashed Potatoes.
- Roast Maple-Chipotle Roasted Squash.
- Prepare Southern Green Beans with Apricots.
- Assemble Glazed Walnut-Pear Salad.

glazed walnut-pear salad

The taste and presentation of this salad will fool guests into thinking it took a long time to prepare. While it's a favorite during the holidays, the fresh-tasting salad is also a frequent request during the summer.

BARB ALBERT-YOCKEY | TRAFALGAR, INDIANA

6 tablespoons maple syrup

1½ teaspoons ground ginger

4 large pears, quartered

2 tablespoons cider vinegar

2 tablespoons olive oil

¼ teaspoon salt

1 bunch romaine, torn

1 bunch red leaf lettuce, torn

1 medium red onion, halved and thinly sliced

½ cup glazed walnuts or pecans

½ cup dried cherries

¼ cup dried cranberries

1. In a small bowl, combine syrup and ginger. Set aside 2 tablespoons for dressing. Toss pears with remaining syrup mixture. Place pears in a foil-lined 15-in. x 10-in. x 1-in. baking pan. Bake at 425° for 15 minutes. Carefully turn pears over; bake 5-10 minutes longer or until lightly browned and tender. Cool pears; chop and set aside.

2. In a small bowl, whisk vinegar, oil, salt and reserved syrup mixture. In a large bowl, combine the romaine, leaf lettuce, onion, walnuts, cherries and cranberries. Add vinaigrette; toss to coat. Top with pears.

YIELD: 12 SERVINGS (1 CUP EACH).

barbecued turkey

(PICTURED ON PAGE 119)

I don't remember where my sister found this recipe, but it quickly became a family favorite. From the zesty, flavorful sauce and crispy skin to the juicy meat, it's the best Thanksgiving turkey I've ever tried.

VALERIE DELANO | CASCADE, MONTANA

2 large onions, chopped

2 garlic cloves, minced

¼ cup plus 2 tablespoons canola oil, divided

2 cups ketchup

½ cup water

½ cup maple syrup

¼ cup cider vinegar

¼ cup molasses

¼ cup Dijon mustard

¼ cup Worcestershire sauce

1 teaspoon celery seed

1 teaspoon crushed red pepper flakes

4 teaspoons pepper, divided

½ teaspoon ground ginger

1 turkey (12 to 14 pounds)

1 tablespoon salt

1. In a large saucepan, saute onions and garlic in ¼ cup oil until tender. Stir in the ketchup, water, syrup, vinegar, molasses, mustard, Worcestershire sauce, celery seed, pepper flakes, 1 teaspoon pepper and ginger. Bring to a boil. Reduce heat; simmer, uncovered, for 30 minutes or until slightly thickened. Set aside 1½ cups for serving.

2. Remove giblets from turkey (discard or save for another use). Using long-handled tongs, moisten a paper towel with cooking oil and lightly coat grill rack. Prepare grill for indirect heat, using a drip pan. Skewer turkey openings; tie drumsticks together. Rub remaining oil over skin of turkey. Sprinkle salt and remaining pepper over turkey and inside cavity.

3. Place turkey over drip pan; grill, covered, over indirect medium heat for 1 hour. Brush with some of the sauce mixture. Grill 1½ to 2 hours longer or until a thermometer reads 180°, basting frequently with remaining sauce. Cover and let stand for 20 minutes before carving. Serve with reserved sauce.

YIELD: 12 SERVINGS (1½ CUPS SAUCE).

autumn harvest mashed potatoes

(PICTURED ON PAGE 119)

I first made these potatoes as a surprise for my daughter during her freshman year of college. Canned pumpkin and a medley of root vegetables take mashed potatoes from ordinary to extraordinary.

SUSAN SUTPHIN | SEVIERVILLE, TENNESSEE

4 large red potatoes, cubed

3 medium turnips, cubed

2 medium parsnips, peeled and cubed

⅓ cup butter, cubed

1 can (15 ounces) solid-pack pumpkin

1 teaspoon garlic salt with parsley

¾ teaspoon salt

½ teaspoon pepper

⅛ teaspoon ground nutmeg

1. Place the potatoes, turnips and parsnips in a large saucepan and cover with water. Bring to a boil. Reduce heat; cover and simmer for 15-20 minutes or until tender. Drain.

2. Mash vegetables with butter; stir in the pumpkin, garlic salt, salt, pepper and nutmeg. Transfer to a serving bowl.

YIELD: 10 SERVINGS.

apple pie bundles

These cute bundles taste like an apple pie but without all of the work—no fork needed! The ingredients can easily be doubled for when you're expecting a crowd.

AMY WOOD
WICHITA, KANSAS

1¼ cups chopped peeled tart apples

1 tablespoon plus 2 teaspoons apple butter

1 tablespoon sugar

½ teaspoon apple pie spice

¼ teaspoon ground cinnamon

1 sheet refrigerated pie pastry

2 tablespoons butter, melted

½ cup confectioners' sugar

2 to 3 teaspoons water

1. In a small bowl, combine apples, apple butter, sugar, apple pie spice and cinnamon.

2. On a lightly floured surface, roll out pastry to a 12-in. circle. Cut out 18 circles with a floured 3-in. round cutter, rerolling scraps if necessary. Press pastry onto the bottoms and up the sides of greased miniature muffin cups.

3. Spoon apple filling into each cup. Bring pastry edges over filling and twist; pinch seams to seal. Brush tops with butter.

4. Bake at 375° for 18-20 minutes or until golden brown. Cool for 5 minutes before removing from pans to wire racks.

5. Combine confectioners' sugar and enough water to achieve a drizzling consistency. Spoon over bundles. Serve warm.

YIELD: 1½ DOZEN.

EDITOR'S NOTE: *This recipe was tested with commercially prepared apple butter.*

maple-chipotle roasted squash

I always seem to grow more squash than I can use, so I decided to come up with a recipe that could be used as a side dish. The smokiness from the chipotle peppers and subtle sweetness from the maple syrup make this recipe worth sharing.

YVONNE STARLIN | HERMITAGE, TENNESSEE

1   large acorn squash, cut into ½-inch slices

¼   cup finely chopped onion

1   tablespoon butter

3   tablespoons maple syrup

2   chipotle peppers in adobo sauce, seeded and finely chopped

¼   teaspoon salt

¼   teaspoon curry powder

1. Place squash in a large bowl; set aside.

2. In a small skillet, saute onion in butter until tender. Add the syrup, chipotle peppers, salt and curry powder; heat through. Pour over squash and toss to coat. Transfer to a greased 15-in. x 10-in. x 1-in. baking pan. Bake, uncovered, at 425° for 20-25 minutes or until tender.

YIELD: 4 SERVINGS.

roasted sweet potato salad with chili lime dressing

(PICTURED ON PAGE 118)

When I made this dish for a school event, the entire staff went wild over it. It's delicious, beautiful and easy to make.

SUE MILLER | KIRKLAND, WASHINGTON

2   pounds large sweet potatoes, peeled and cubed

2   tablespoons olive oil

1   large sweet red pepper, cut into ½-inch pieces

8   green onions, chopped

½   cup minced fresh parsley

¼   cup minced fresh cilantro

DRESSING

⅓   cup olive oil

¼   cup lime juice

4   teaspoons chili powder

¾   teaspoon salt

¾   teaspoon ground cumin

½   teaspoon pepper

⅛   teaspoon cayenne pepper, optional

1. In a large bowl, toss sweet potatoes with oil. Transfer to a greased 15-in. x 10-in. x 1-in. baking pan. Bake at 400° for 30-40 minutes or until potatoes are tender, stirring twice. Cool for 10 minutes. In a large bowl, combine the red pepper, onions, parsley, cilantro and sweet potatoes.

2. In a small bowl, whisk the oil, lime juice, chili powder, salt, cumin, pepper and cayenne if desired. Drizzle over salad; toss to coat. Serve warm or cold.

YIELD: 7 SERVINGS.

FLAME KISSED SWEET POTATOES

Since you have the grill fired up already, why not grill some sweet potatoes, too? Just peel and wash them, then cut into 1/2-inch slices. Cook them on the grill, brushing each side with butter several times and turning them often until tender.

cranberry muffins with walnut-thyme streusel

A friend gave me a great recipe for blueberry muffins. I wanted to make a batch, but I didn't have any blueberries. So I substituted dried cranberries and played around with the other ingredients until I came up with these tender bites.

BRIDGET KLUSMAN | OTSEGO, MICHIGAN

2½ cups all-purpose flour

2 cups old-fashioned oats

½ cup packed brown sugar

3 teaspoons baking powder

1 teaspoon baking soda

¼ teaspoon salt

1 egg

2 cups (16 ounces) plain yogurt

½ cup butter, melted

3 teaspoons vanilla extract

1⅓ cups dried cranberries

STREUSEL

¼ cup all-purpose flour

¼ cup old-fashioned oats

¼ cup brown sugar

¼ cup finely chopped walnuts, toasted

¼ teaspoon dried thyme

¼ cup cold butter

1. In a large bowl, combine first six ingredients. In another bowl, combine egg, yogurt, butter and vanilla. Stir into dry ingredients just until moistened. Fold in cranberries. Fill greased muffin cups three-fourths full.

2. Combine the flour, oats, brown sugar, walnuts and thyme; cut in butter until crumbly. Sprinkle over tops.

3. Bake at 400° for 18-20 minutes or until a toothpick inserted into muffin comes out clean. Cool for 5 minutes before removing from pans to wire racks. Serve warm.

YIELD: 2 DOZEN.

cranberry rum-raisin relish

(PICTURED ON PAGE 118)

Break away from tradition and serve this tasty alternative to plain ol' cranberry sauce. The rum and clove give it a homey, warm flavor that pairs well with traditional Thanksgiving dishes.

AMY NUTONI | LA CRESCENT, MINNESOTA

8   whole cloves

1   large navel orange

1   package (15 ounces) golden raisins

1   package (12 ounces) fresh or frozen cranberries

2   cups sugar

½   cup water

½   cup rum

1   cinnamon stick (3 inches)

1. Place cloves on a double thickness of cheesecloth; bring up corners of cloth and tie with string to form a bag. Set aside.

2. Using a citrus zester, remove zest from orange in narrow strips; set aside. Peel and chop the orange.

3. In a small saucepan, combine the raisins, cranberries, sugar, water, rum, cinnamon, spice bag and chopped orange. Cook over medium heat until berries pop, about 15 minutes.

4. Remove from the heat; discard spice bag and cinnamon stick. Stir in orange zest. Transfer to a small bowl; cool slightly. Refrigerate until chilled.

YIELD: 4 CUPS.

blue cheese apple slaw

(PICTURED ON PAGE 118)

The holidays are busy. That's why I appreciate this no-fuss recipe that can be made ahead and chilled until you are ready to eat. If you want your dish to have more color, just add more carrot.

LIBBY WALP | CHICAGO, ILLINOIS

½   cup mayonnaise

½   cup sour cream

¼   cup cider vinegar

2   tablespoons lemon juice

1   tablespoon stone-ground mustard

2   teaspoons sugar

½   teaspoon salt

½   teaspoon pepper

1   medium head cabbage, shredded

1   medium tart apple, shredded

1   medium carrot, shredded

½   cup crumbled blue cheese

1. In a small bowl, whisk the first eight ingredients.

2. In a large bowl, combine the cabbage, apple, carrot and cheese. Pour dressing over salad; toss to coat. Cover and refrigerate until serving.

YIELD: 9 SERVINGS.

SHREDDING CABBAGE BY HAND

To shred cabbage by hand, cut cabbage into wedges. Place cut side down on a cutting board. With a large sharp knife, cut into thin slices.

acorn napkin rings

Bring a touch of nature indoors with these rustic yet chic napkin rings.
Use artificial acorns purchased at a craft store or go on a hunt in your own backyard.

- ☐ miniature (2-inch diameter) grapevine wreaths (enough for each place setting)
- ☐ assorted artificial flowers and/or greenery
- ☐ hot glue gun
- ☐ acorns

1. While holding the wreath in one hand, use the other hand to wrap the artificial greenery or tuck artificial flowers around the wreath.

2. Secure greenery and/or flowers to the wreath using hot glue.

3. Attach acorns to the top of the wreath using hot glue. Press and hold acorns to the wreath until acorns are securely attached to wreath.

4. Slip the finished wreath over a napkin and place at each place setting.

I t's the littlest things in life that can bring some of the biggest blessings...like the aroma of freshly baked bread. Because cooler weather tends to bring out the baker in all of us, you won't want to miss the heavenly collection of home-baked treats gathered here.

Morning sweet rolls will start the day on an extra special note, while savory selections are perfect for pairing with the Thanksgiving meal. (We highly suggest Onion-Garlic Herb Rosettes!)

Whether you are looking for a traditional loaf or something slightly more inventive, this bounty of breads, rolls, muffins and more will be sure to make your family feast a memorable occasion.

BAKERY STYLE FAVORITES
Onion-Garlic Herb Rosettes (p. 130)

A CORNUCOPIA
OF BREADS

onion-garlic herb rosettes

(PICTURED ON PAGE 128)

Flood your kitchen with the heavenly aroma of these special rolls baking in the oven. I initially created this recipe for a traditional loaf pan, but find people really enjoy the individual rosettes.

RYAN GARDNER | RICHMOND, VIRGINIA

1 package (¼ ounce) active dry yeast

2 cups warm water (110° to 115°)

1 cup old-fashioned oats

¼ cup canola oil

6 garlic cloves, minced

2 tablespoons minced fresh parsley

2 tablespoons minced fresh rosemary

1 tablespoon sugar

2 teaspoons salt

2 cups whole wheat flour

2½ to 3 cups all-purpose flour

2 cups (8 ounces) shredded cheddar cheese

1 large onion, chopped

EGG WASH

1 egg

1 tablespoon water

1. In a large bowl, dissolve yeast in warm water. Add the oats, oil, garlic, parsley, rosemary, sugar, salt and whole wheat flour. Beat on medium speed for 3 minutes or until smooth. Stir in enough all-purpose flour to form a firm dough. Stir in cheese and onion.

2. Turn onto a floured surface; knead until smooth and elastic, about 6-8 minutes. Place in a greased bowl, turning once to grease the top. Cover with plastic wrap and let rise in a warm place until doubled, about 1 hour.

3. Punch dough down. Divide dough into 48 balls. Roll each into a 12-in. rope; tie into a loose knot. Bring bottom end up and tuck into center of roll; wrap top end around and tuck under roll. Place 2 in. apart on greased baking sheets. Cover and let rise in a warm place until doubled, about 30 minutes.

4. In a small bowl, combine egg and water. Brush over rolls. Bake at 350° for 10-15 minutes or until golden brown. Remove from pans to wire racks to cool.

YIELD: 4 DOZEN.

"KNEAD" TO KNOW BAKING TIP

The trick to making tender homemade rolls and bread is proper kneading and rising. Follow these simple steps to achieve perfectly baked creations every time.

1) Turn dough onto a lightly floured surface; shape into a ball. Fold top of dough toward you. With palms, push with a rolling motion away from you. Turn dough a quarter turn; repeat motion until dough is smooth and elastic. 2) Press two fingers 1/2 in. into the dough. If the dents remain, the dough is doubled in size and ready to punch down.

pear and poppy seed loaf

Hands down, this slightly sweet loaf is my husband's and children's favorite. Instead of butter, I top slices with plain yogurt.

SHERRY FLAQUEL | CUTLER BAY, FLORIDA

2¼ cups all-purpose flour

⅔ cup sugar

3 tablespoons poppy seeds

1½ teaspoons baking powder

1 teaspoon baking soda

¼ teaspoon salt

⅛ teaspoon ground cardamom

1 egg, beaten

1 cup buttermilk

¼ cup honey

2 tablespoons butter, melted

1 teaspoon vanilla extract

1 cup finely chopped peeled ripe pears

1. In a large bowl, combine the first seven ingredients. In a small bowl, combine the egg, buttermilk, honey, butter and vanilla. Stir into dry ingredients just until moistened. Fold in pears.

2. Transfer to a greased 8-in. x 4-in. loaf pan. Bake at 350° for 55-65 minutes or until a toothpick inserted near the center comes out clean. Cool loaf for 10 minutes before removing from pan to a wire rack to cool completely.

YIELD: 1 LOAF (12 SLICES).

sage-apple cider bread

Who knew sage and apple cider would create such a fantastic bread?
This versatile loaf with just a hint of sweetness makes wonderful sandwiches or stuffing.

CHRISTINE WENDLAND | BROWNS MILLS, NEW JERSEY

1 package (¼ ounce) active
dry yeast

1¼ cups warm apple cider or
juice (110° - 115°)

2 cups bread flour

⅓ cup butter, melted

2 tablespoons sugar

1 egg

¼ cup fresh sage, thinly sliced

¾ teaspoon salt

1¼ to 1¾ cups all-purpose flour

2 teaspoons 2% milk

1. In a large bowl, dissolve yeast in warm cider. Add bread flour, butter, sugar, egg, sage and salt. Beat on medium speed for 3 minutes. Stir in enough all-purpose flour to form a firm dough.

2. Turn onto a floured surface; knead until smooth and elastic, about 6-8 minutes. Place in a greased bowl, turning once to grease the top. Cover and let rise in a warm place until doubled, about 1 hour.

3. Punch dough down. Turn onto a lightly floured surface. Shape into a loaf. Place in a greased 9-in. x 5-in. loaf pan. Cover and let rise until doubled, about 40 minutes. Brush with milk.

4. Bake at 375° for 30-40 minutes or until golden brown. Remove from pan to a wire rack to cool.

YIELD: 1 LOAF (16 SLICES).

two-cheese corn muffins

Savory muffins are my favorite, and these fit the bill. They're cheesy and flavorful,
yet still light and fluffy. I can whip them up in no time, which is a definite plus
when I'm trying to prepare the rest of the Thanksgiving meal.

KC QUARETTI | NORTH VENICE, FLORIDA

2 cups all-purpose flour

2 tablespoons fresh sage,
chopped

1½ teaspoons baking powder

1 teaspoon salt

1 teaspoon garlic powder

½ teaspoon baking soda

2 eggs

1 cup buttermilk

¼ cup butter, melted

1 cup fresh or frozen corn

¾ cup shredded part-skim
mozzarella cheese

½ cup shredded cheddar
cheese

1. In a large bowl, combine the flour, sage, baking powder, salt, garlic powder and baking soda. In small bowl, combine the eggs, buttermilk and butter. Stir into dry ingredients just until moistened. Fold in corn and cheeses.

2. Fill greased muffin cups three-fourths full. Bake at 400° for 15-20 minutes or until a toothpick inserted in muffin comes out clean. Cool for 5 minutes before removing from pan to wire rack. Serve warm.

YIELD: 1 DOZEN.

OUT OF BUTTERMILK?

There are a number of substitutes for buttermilk in baking. For each cup of buttermilk, use 1 tablespoon of white vinegar or lemon juice plus enough milk to measure 1 cup. Stir, then let stand for 5 minutes. You can also use 1 cup of plain yogurt or 1-3/4 teaspoons cream of tartar plus 1 cup milk.

cinnamon roll biscuits

*When my grandchildren visit, this is their favorite "breakfast at Grammy's house" treat.
If you're not a nut lover, these biscuits are also delicious without the pecans.*

JOYCE CONWAY | WESTERVILLE, OHIO

2   cups all-purpose flour

3   teaspoons baking powder

1   teaspoon salt

¼   teaspoon baking soda

1   cup buttermilk

¼   cup canola oil

1   teaspoon vanilla extract

½   cup butter, softened

½   cup sugar

¾   teaspoon ground cinnamon

¼   teaspoon ground cardamom

½   cup chopped pecans,
    optional

GLAZE

1   cup confectioners' sugar

1   teaspoon vanilla extract

3   to 4 teaspoons 2% milk

1. In a large bowl, combine flour, baking powder, salt and baking soda. Combine the buttermilk, canola oil and vanilla; stir into dry ingredients just until moistened (dough will be sticky).

2. Turn onto a well-floured surface; knead 8-10 times. Roll out dough into a 15-in. x 9-in. rectangle. Spread butter to within ½ in. of edges. Combine sugar, cinnamon, cardamom and pecans, if desired; sprinkle over butter. Roll up jelly-roll style, starting with a long side; pinch seam to seal. Cut into 1½-in. slices.

3. Place 1 in. apart on a parchment paper-lined baking sheet. Bake at 400° for 20-25 minutes until lightly browned.

4. Meanwhile, in small bowl, combine the confectioners' sugar, vanilla and enough milk to achieve a drizzling consistency. Drizzle over warm biscuits. Serve immediately.

YIELD: 14 BISCUITS.

sweet potato pan rolls

Spiced with cinnamon and nutmeg, these different but wonderful rolls are great alongside a variety of dishes—from chicken to a bowl of steaming chili.

CARLY CURTIN | ELLICOTT CITY, MARYLAND

1 package (¼ ounce) active dry yeast

½ cup warm water (110° to 115°)

½ cup mashed sweet potato

¼ cup butter, melted

3 tablespoons honey

2 tablespoons canola oil

1 egg

1 teaspoon salt

½ teaspoon sugar

¼ teaspoon ground cinnamon

Dash ground nutmeg

3½ to 4 cups bread flour

1. In a large bowl, dissolve yeast in warm water. Add the sweet potato, butter, honey, oil, egg, salt, sugar, cinnamon, nutmeg and 1 cup flour. Beat on medium speed until smooth. Stir in enough remaining flour to form a soft dough (dough will be sticky).

2. Turn onto a floured surface; knead until smooth and elastic, about 6-8 minutes. Place in a greased bowl, turning once to grease the top. Cover and let rise in a warm place until doubled, about 1 hour.

3. Punch dough down. Turn onto a lightly floured surface; divide into 16 pieces. Shape each piece into a ball. Place in two greased 9-in. round baking pans. Cover and let rise for 30 minutes or until doubled.

4. Bake at 375° for 20-25 minutes or until golden brown.

YIELD: 16 ROLLS

pumpkin apple bread

My grandsons think this seasonal loaf is pretty special—they took it with them to college when they knew they wouldn't be home for the holidays. It's destined to become a family tradition in your home, too.

VICTORIA COOKLIN | MASSILLON, OHIO

3 cups all-purpose flour

2 teaspoons baking soda

1½ teaspoons ground cinnamon

1 teaspoon ground cloves

1 teaspoon ground nutmeg

¾ teaspoon salt

¼ teaspoon ground allspice

4 eggs

2¼ cups sugar

1 can (15 ounces) solid-pack pumpkin

¾ cup canola oil

2 cups chopped peeled tart apples

1 cup golden raisins

TOPPING

½ cup sugar

⅓ cup all-purpose flour

1 teaspoon ground cinnamon

¼ cup cold butter

1. In a large bowl, combine the first seven ingredients. In another large bowl, whisk the eggs, sugar, pumpkin and oil. Stir into dry ingredients just until moistened. Fold in apples and raisins. Transfer to two greased 9-in. x 5-in. loaf pans.

2. For topping, in a small bowl, combine the sugar, flour and cinnamon. Cut in butter until mixture resembles coarse crumbs; sprinkle over each loaf.

3. Bake at 350° for 50-60 minutes or until a toothpick inserted near the center comes out clean. Cool for 10 minutes before removing from pans to wire racks.

YIELD: 2 LOAVES (16 SLICES EACH).

rustic swedish rye bread

My great-grandmother gets all the credit for this hearty loaf that she brought over from Sweden when she came to live in America. It's one of those all-purpose breads that goes well with almost any meal.

HEATHER COOK | MALTA, MONTANA

5 orange peel strips (1 to 3 inches)

½ cup plus 2 tablespoons water, divided

2 tablespoons honey

BREAD

1 package (¼ ounce) active dry yeast

¼ cup warm water (110° to 115°)

2 cups warm 2% milk (110° to 115°)

½ cup packed brown sugar

1 egg

1 tablespoon dark corn syrup

1 tablespoon molasses

1 tablespoon shortening

1½ teaspoons salt

½ teaspoon aniseed

½ teaspoon fennel seed

1½ cups rye flour

4 to 4¼ cups all-purpose flour

1. In a small saucepan, combine orange peel strips and ½ cup water. Bring to a boil. Reduce heat to medium-low; cook, uncovered, for 10 minutes or until softened. Drain; set strips aside.

2. In the same saucepan, combine honey and remaining water. Bring to a boil; return strips to pan. Reduce heat to medium-low; cook, uncovered, for 3-5 minutes or until almost all of the syrup is absorbed, stirring occasionally (watch carefully to prevent scorching). Cool strips on waxed paper coated with cooking spray.

3. In a large bowl, dissolve yeast in warm water. Add the milk, brown sugar, egg, corn syrup, molasses, shortening, salt, aniseed, fennel seed, rye flour and 2 cups all-purpose flour. Beat on medium speed for 3 minutes.

4. Chop candied orange strips; add to dough. Stir in enough remaining flour to form a soft dough (dough will be sticky). Turn onto a floured surface; knead until smooth and elastic, about 6-8 minutes.

5. Place in a greased bowl, turning once to grease the top. Cover and let rise in a warm place until doubled, about 1 hour. Divide dough in half. Shape each into a 6-inch round loaf. Place on a greased baking sheet. Cover and let rise until doubled, about 45 minutes.

6. Bake at 400° for 20-25 minutes or until golden brown. Remove to wire racks to cool.

YIELD: 2 LOAVES (8 SLICES EACH).

I s it the oh-so smooth, velvety texture or is it the seemingly endless combination of rich flavors, delicate crusts and delightful toppings that never fail to make cheesecake one of the most irresistible desserts?

Whatever your reason for saying "yes" to a slice of pure heaven, you will not be disappointed with this sinful selection of autumn-inspired dessert decadence.

Try a slice of Salted Butterscotch Cheesecake—the buttery pretzel crust complemented by a luscious filling truly creates a sweet-and-salty combination that is simply divine! It is perfect for any celebration where a memorable finale is needed.

CHEERS FOR CHEESECAKE
Salted Butterscotch Cheesecake (p. 138)

AUTUMN CHEESECAKES

salted butterscotch cheesecake

(PICTURED ON PAGE 136)

Salted butterscotch is everywhere—in candy, ice cream and now...cheesecake! Silky cheesecake is dressed with a sweet butterscotch sauce that really stands out next to the salty pretzel crust.

TASTE OF HOME TEST KITCHEN

1¼ cups finely crushed pretzels

½ cup butter, melted

¼ cup sugar

FILLING

1 can (14 ounces) sweetened condensed milk

¾ cup 2% milk

1 package (3.4 ounces) instant butterscotch pudding mix

3 packages (8 ounces each) cream cheese, softened

1 teaspoon vanilla extract

3 eggs, lightly beaten

BUTTERSCOTCH SAUCE

¼ cup butter, cubed

1 cup packed dark brown sugar

¾ cup heavy whipping cream

3 teaspoons vanilla extract

½ teaspoon salt

TOPPING

1 carton (8 ounces) mascarpone cheese, softened

Sea salt

1. Place a greased 9-in. springform pan on a double thickness of heavy-duty foil (about 18 in. square). Securely wrap foil around pan.

2. In a small bowl, combine the pretzels, butter and sugar. Press onto the bottom of prepared pan. Place pan on a baking sheet. Bake at 350° for 10 minutes. Cool on a wire rack.

3. In a small bowl, whisk the condensed milk, milk and pudding mix for 2 minutes. Let stand for 2 minutes or until pudding is soft-set.

4. Meanwhile, in a large bowl, beat cream cheese until smooth. Beat in pudding mixture and vanilla. Add eggs; beat on low speed just until combined. Pour over crust. Place springform pan in a large baking pan; add 1 in. of hot water to larger pan.

5. Bake at 325° for 55-65 minutes or until center is almost set and top appears dull. Remove springform pan from water bath. Cool on a wire rack for 10 minutes. Carefully run a knife around edge of pan to loosen; cool 1 hour longer.

6. In a small saucepan, melt butter. Stir in brown sugar and cream. Bring to a boil, stirring constantly. Remove from the heat; stir in vanilla and salt.

7. In a small bowl, combine mascarpone cheese and ⅓ cup sauce until smooth. Spread over cooled cheesecake; refrigerate overnight. Cover and refrigerate remaining sauce.

8. Remove sides of pan. Just before serving, sprinkle cheesecake with sea salt; drizzle with butterscotch sauce.

YIELD: 12 SERVINGS.

REMOVING CHEESECAKE FROM THE PAN

If you prefer to remove the bottom of the pan before serving, ask someone to lend an extra hand. Take a large knife or metal spatula and carefully run it under the bottom of the cheesecake that's been chilled overnight to loosen it. Then use two or three large pancake turners to carefully lift the cake over to the platter.

holiday sweet potato cheesecake

Guests can't get enough of this deliciously different cheesecake that combines my two favorite desserts— sweet potato pie and cheesecake.

MELANIE BAUDER
MANLIUS, NEW YORK

1¾ cups graham cracker crumbs

⅓ cup butter, melted

¼ cup sugar

FILLING

2 packages (8 ounces each) cream cheese, softened

½ cup sugar

1 teaspoon vanilla extract

2 eggs, lightly beaten

SWEET POTATO FILLING

1 cup mashed sweet potatoes (about ¾ pound)

½ cup sugar

½ cup evaporated milk

¼ cup butter, melted

1 egg

½ teaspoon vanilla extract

⅛ teaspoon each ground cinnamon, cloves and nutmeg

⅛ teaspoon salt

TOPPING

¾ cup sour cream

3 tablespoons sugar

1½ teaspoons vanilla extract

Glazed chopped pecans, optional

1. Place a greased 9-in. springform pan on a double thickness of foil (about 18 in. square). Securely wrap foil around pan.

2. In a small bowl, combine the cracker crumbs, butter and sugar. Press onto the bottom and 1½ in. up the sides of prepared pan. Place pan on a baking sheet. Bake at 325° for 10 minutes. Cool on a wire rack.

3. In a large bowl, beat cream cheese and sugar until smooth. Beat in vanilla. Add eggs; beat on low speed just until combined. Pour into crust.

4. In a large bowl, combine sweet potatoes with sugar, evaporated milk, butter, egg, vanilla, spices and salt. Spoon over cheesecake batter. Place springform pan in a large baking pan; add 1 in. of hot water to larger pan. Bake at 325° for 50-55 minutes or until center is just set and top appears dull.

5. Combine sour cream, sugar and vanilla. Spread over cheesecake. Bake 5-10 minutes longer or just until set. Remove pan from water bath. Cool on a wire rack for 10 minutes.

6. Carefully run a knife around edge of pan to loosen; cool 1 hour longer. Refrigerate overnight. Remove sides of pan. Sprinkle cheesecake with pecans if desired.

YIELD: 12 SERVINGS.

blissful peanut butter-chocolate cheesecake

(PICTURED AT RIGHT)

When I think of this specialty cheesecake, three words come to mind: "decadent," "fun" and "delicious."

JULIE RUBLE | CHARLOTTE, NORTH CAROLINA

32 Nutter Butter cookies

⅓ cup butter, melted

4 packages (8 ounces each) cream cheese, softened

1 cup sugar

3 ounces semisweet chocolate, melted

3 ounces bittersweet chocolate, melted

1 teaspoon vanilla extract

4 eggs, lightly beaten

PEANUT BUTTER MOUSSE

1½ teaspoons unflavored gelatin

2 tablespoons cold water

1 cup heavy whipping cream

3 tablespoons creamy peanut butter

2 tablespoons sugar

2 egg yolks

GARNISH

3 ounces semisweet chocolate, chopped

Chocolate curls and sweetened whipped cream, optional

1. Place a greased 9-in. springform pan on a double thickness of heavy-duty foil (about 18 in. square). Securely wrap foil around pan.

2. Place cookies in a food processor; cover and process until fine crumbs. Stir in butter. Press onto the bottom and 2 in. up the sides of prepared pan; set aside.

3. In a bowl, beat cream cheese and sugar until smooth. Beat in the melted chocolates and vanilla. Add eggs; beat on low speed just until combined. Pour into crust. Place springform pan in a large baking pan; add 1 in. of hot water to larger pan.

4. Bake at 325° for 60-65 minutes or until center is just set and top appears dull. Remove springform pan from water bath. Cool on a wire rack for 10 minutes. Carefully run a knife around edge of pan to loosen; cool 1 hour longer.

5. For peanut butter mousse, sprinkle gelatin over cold water; let stand for 1 minute. Microwave on high for 20-30 seconds. Stir and let stand for 1 minute or until gelatin is dissolved.

6. Meanwhile, in a small heavy saucepan, heat the cream, peanut butter and sugar until bubbles form around sides of pan. Whisk a small amount of hot mixture into the egg yolks. Return all to the pan, whisking constantly.

7. Cook and stir over low heat until mixture is thickened and coats the back of a spoon. Stir in gelatin mixture. Quickly transfer to a bowl; place in ice water and stir for 15 minutes or until cold and thickened. Pour over cheesecake. Refrigerate overnight. Remove sides of pan.

8. For garnish, in a microwave, melt chocolate. Drizzle over cheesecake. Add chocolate curls and whipped cream if desired.

YIELD: 12 SERVINGS.

amaretto cheesecake

Sometimes the best-loved recipes are the most basic. Just ask my family; they rave over this classic!

BARBARA CAINE | SUSSEX, NEW JERSEY

- 2 cups graham cracker crumbs
- ½ cup butter, melted
- ¼ cup sugar

FILLING
- 4 packages (8 ounces each) cream cheese, softened

- 1½ cups sugar
- 2 tablespoons amaretto
- 1 teaspoon vanilla extract
- 1 teaspoon almond extract
- ⅛ teaspoon salt
- 4 eggs, lightly beaten

TOPPING
- 2 cups (8 ounces each) sour cream
- ¼ cup sugar
- 1 teaspoon almond extract

1. Combine the cracker crumbs, butter and sugar. Press onto the bottom and 1 in. up the sides of a greased 9-in. springform pan.

2. Beat cream cheese and sugar until smooth. Beat in the amaretto, extracts and salt. Add eggs; beat on low speed just until combined. Pour into crust. Place pan on a baking sheet. Bake at 325° for 55-60 minutes. Let stand for 5 minutes. Combine sour cream, sugar and almond extract; spread over top of cheesecake. Bake 5 minutes longer.

3. Cool on a wire rack for 10 minutes. Carefully run a knife around edge of pan to loosen; cool 1 hour longer. Refrigerate overnight. Remove sides of pan.

YIELD: 12 SERVINGS.

turtle pumpkin cheesecake

I can never decide which one I like best: pumpkin pie or cheesecake? So, I decided to combine the two.

YVONNE STARLIN | HERMITAGE, TENNESSEE

- 1½ cups crushed gingersnap cookies (about 30 cookies)
- ¼ cup butter, melted

FILLING
- 4 packages (8 ounces each) cream cheese, softened
- 1 cup packed brown sugar

- ⅔ cup sugar
- 1 can (15 ounces) solid-pack pumpkin
- 2 tablespoons all-purpose flour
- 2 teaspoons pumpkin pie spice
- 4 eggs, lightly beaten

TOPPING
- ½ cup chopped pecans, toasted
- 4 ounces bittersweet chocolate, chopped
- 2 tablespoons butter
- ½ cup caramel sundae syrup

1. Combine cookie crumbs and butter. Press onto bottom and 1 in. up sides of a greased 10-in. springform pan. Place pan on a baking sheet. Bake at 325° for 8-10 minutes. Cool on a wire rack.

2. In a large bowl, beat cream cheese and sugars until smooth. Beat in pumpkin, flour and pie spice. Add eggs; beat on low speed just until combined. Pour into crust. Return pan to baking sheet. Bake for 55-65 minutes or until center is almost set.

3. Cool on a wire rack for 10 minutes. Carefully run a knife around edge of pan to loosen; cool 1 hour longer. Refrigerate overnight. Remove sides of pan. Just before serving, sprinkle pecans over cheesecake; press down lightly. In a microwave, melt chocolate and butter until smooth. Cut cheesecake into slices; drizzle with chocolate mixture and caramel syrup.

YIELD: 16 SERVINGS.

pear-topped caramel cheesecake

Sweet pears and rich caramel never tasted better than they do in this pleasing fall cheesecake. The arrangement of sliced pears on top of the dessert is sure to make a stunning impression.

FAY BROWN | WICHITA FALLS, TEXAS

1½ cups crushed gingersnap cookies (about 30 cookies)

3 tablespoons butter, melted

4 packages (8 ounces each) cream cheese, softened

1 cup packed brown sugar

¾ cup sour cream

¾ cup dulce de leche

2 tablespoons cornstarch

4 eggs, lightly beaten

2 medium pears, peeled and cut into ¼-inch slices

1 teaspoon ground ginger

1. In a small bowl, combine cookie crumbs and butter; press onto the bottom of a greased 9-in. springform pan. Place pan on a baking sheet. Bake at 375° for 8 minutes. Cool on a wire rack. Reduce heat to 325°.

2. In a large bowl, beat cream cheese and brown sugar until smooth. Beat in the sour cream, dulce de leche and cornstarch. Add eggs; beat on low speed just until combined. Pour over crust. Arrange pears over top; sprinkle with ginger.

3. Bake at 325° for 65-75 minutes or until center is just set and top of cheesecake appears dull. Cool on a wire rack for 10 minutes. Carefully run a knife around edge of pan to loosen; cool 1 hour longer. Refrigerate overnight. Remove sides of pan.

YIELD: 12 SERVINGS.

EDITOR'S NOTE: *This recipe was tested with Nestle dulce de leche. Look for it in the international foods section.*

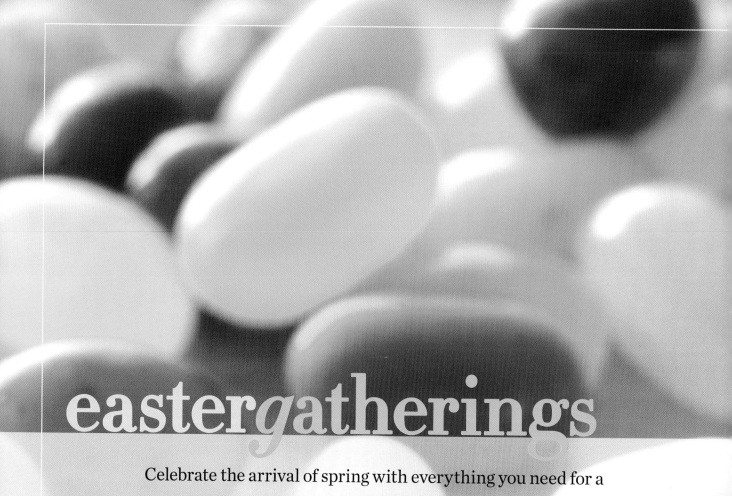

eastergatherings

Celebrate the arrival of spring with everything you need for a
memorable holiday. Our vintage Easter dinner not only gives
you an excuse to use Grandma's good china but will bring back
fond memories of Easters past. And don't miss the "way cool"
Spring Break chapter. It's filled with all sorts of tasty treats
and fun activities to keeps kids—and parents—entertained.

S erve a taste of nostalgia with this pretty vintage-inspired Easter dinner. It's the perfect excuse to dust off Grandma's good china, dye some Easter eggs and create a meal that is pleasing to the eyes and the palate.

No Easter is complete without a juicy baked ham. Pineapple-Glazed Ham takes center stage in this menu, conjuring up memories of Easter dinners past.

Serve with Scalloped Potatoes and Parsnips, slices of freshly baked Garlic Fontina Bread spread with Basil Flavored Butter, Asparagus with Creamy Garlic Mustard Sauce and refreshing Radish, Cucumber and Grapefruit Salad. It will be an Easter meal your loved ones won't soon forget.

VINTAGE-INSPIRED EASTER

Pineapple-Glazed Ham (p. 150)
Scalloped Potatoes and Parsnips (p. 150)
Basil Flavored Butter (p. 149)
Garlic Fontina Bread (p. 152)
Radish, Cucumber and Grapefruit Salad (p. 153)
Asparagus with
Creamy Garlic Mustard Sauce (p. 152)

VINTAGE CHARM

eastergatherings | VINTAGE CHARM

A FEW WEEKS BEFORE

- Prepare two grocery lists: one for nonperishable items to purchase now and one for perishable items to purchase a few days before Easter.
- Order a fully cooked bone-in ham (7 to 9 pounds).
- Bake Garlic Fontina Bread. Let cool, place in a heavy-duty resealable plastic bag and freeze.

TWO DAYS BEFORE

- Buy remaining grocery items.
- Make the Basil Flavored Butter; refrigerate.

THE DAY BEFORE

- Set the table.
- Prepare glaze for Pineapple-Glazed Ham; cover and chill.
- For Asparagus with Creamy Garlic Mustard Sauce, clean and trim the asparagus; refrigerate in a resealable plastic bag. Combine the sauce ingredients; store in a covered container in the refrigerator.
- Section grapefruit and slice radishes for Radish, Cucumber and Grapefruit Salad. Prepare dressing. Place separately in covered containers; chill.
- Assemble Coconut Croissant Bread Pudding. Cover; refrigerate overnight.

EASTER DAY

- In the morning, peel and slice potatoes and parsnips for Scalloped Potatoes and Parsnips. Cover with cold water; refrigerate.
- Thaw Garlic Fontina Bread at room temperature.
- Bake Pineapple-Glazed Ham. Reheat glaze; baste and continue baking as directed.
- Assemble Scalloped Potatoes and Parsnips.
- Remove ham from oven. Increase temperature to 375º. Bake Scalloped Potatoes and Parsnips.
- Cook asparagus for Asparagus with Creamy Garlic Mustard Sauce; heat sauce on stovetop.
- If desired, wrap Garlic Fontina Bread in foil and reheat in oven.
- Assemble Radish, Cucumber and Grapefruit Salad.
- Prepare Basil Onion Cream Soup.
- Remove Coconut Crunch Croissant Bread Pudding from the refrigerator 30 minutes before baking according to recipe directions.

basil-onion cream soup

My father-in-law introduced me to this rich soup. It is surprisingly simple to make, yet looks so elegant when served in a shallow soup bowl with a side of crusty bread. Use it to dress up any meal, or when you are making a special dinner for friends or family.

MELISSA KOEHLER
WAUSAU, WISCONSIN

- 2 medium onions, chopped
- ¼ cup butter
- 2 tablespoons canola oil
- 6 tablespoons all-purpose flour
- 6 cups chicken broth
- 1 cup heavy whipping cream
- ⅓ cup minced fresh basil or 2 tablespoons dried basil
- Salt and pepper to taste

1. In a large saucepan, saute onions in butter and oil. Stir in the flour until blended; gradually add broth.

2. Bring to a boil; cook and stir for 2 minutes or until thickened. Stir in the cream and the basil. Season with salt and pepper. Heat through.

YIELD: 6 SERVINGS.

basil flavored butter

(PICTURED ON PAGE 147)

During the summer we have a bountiful supply of fresh basil. I make up several batches of this basil butter at one time, and freeze them for use throughout the year. Use it on vegetables, fish, corn, bread...the possibilities for this tasty butter never end.

DONNA NOECKER | PLANO, TEXAS

- ½ cup unsalted butter, softened
- ⅓ cup minced fresh basil
- 1 garlic clove, minced
- 1 teaspoon lemon juice

In a small bowl, combine all ingredients until well blended. Transfer to a sheet of plastic wrap; roll into a 1-in. diameter log. Refrigerate until firm.

YIELD: ½ CUP.

pineapple-glazed ham

(PICTURED ON PAGE 146)

Think of Easter dinner and your mind probably wanders to juicy baked ham. Here is a main dish that's destined to become a tradition as time honored as dying Easter eggs. The sweet pineapple glaze is irresistible.

TASTE OF HOME TEST KITCHEN

1 fully cooked bone-in ham (7 to 9 pounds)

1 cup packed brown sugar

1 cup unsweetened pineapple juice

¼ cup lemon juice

¼ cup maraschino cherry juice

1 tablespoon Dijon mustard

¼ teaspoon ground cloves

1. Place ham on a rack in a shallow roasting pan. Score the surface of the ham, making diamond shapes ½ in. deep. Bake at 325° for 1½ hours.

2. In a large saucepan, combine remaining ingredients. Bring to a boil; cook until liquid is reduced by half, about 20 minutes.

3. Brush ham with some of the glaze; bake 30-60 minutes longer or until a thermometer reads 140°, brushing occasionally with remaining glaze.

YIELD: 15 SERVINGS.

scalloped potatoes and parsnips

(PICTURED ON PAGE 146)

Cheese makes any dish better, in my opinion, and this gooey, comforting potato and parsnip casserole is no exception. Even those who turn up their noses at vegetables will dig into this dish.

CORINNA PLATT | BELLINGHAM, WASHINGTON

6 large Yukon Gold potatoes, peeled and thinly sliced

3 medium parsnips, peeled and thinly sliced

4 garlic cloves, thinly sliced

1 medium leek (white portion only), thinly sliced

3 tablespoons butter

3 tablespoons all-purpose flour

1 teaspoon salt

¼ teaspoon pepper

Pinch cayenne pepper

Pinch ground nutmeg

4 cups heavy whipping cream

1 cup (4 ounces) shredded white cheddar cheese

½ cup shredded fontina cheese

½ cup shredded Monterey Jack cheese

1 tablespoon minced fresh thyme

⅛ teaspoon Worcestershire sauce

1. Place the potatoes, parsnips and garlic in a large saucepan and cover with water. Bring to a boil. Reduce heat; cover and simmer for 15-20 minutes or until tender. Drain and set aside.

2. Meanwhile, in a small saucepan, cook leek in butter over medium heat for 3-4 minutes or until tender. Stir in the flour, salt, pepper, cayenne and nutmeg until blended. Gradually add cream. Bring to a boil. Cook and stir for 2 minutes or until thickened. Stir in the cheeses, thyme and Worcestershire sauce just until cheese is melted. Remove from the heat; stir into potato mixture.

3. Transfer to a greased 13-in. x 9-in. baking dish. Bake, uncovered, at 375° for 30-35 minutes or until bubbly and lightly browned.

YIELD: 12 SERVINGS.

coconut croissant bread pudding

I'm a fan of coconut and bread pudding, so I thought, "Why not combine them?" I was thrilled with the outcome. The recipe is especially good for holidays and gatherings because it travels well and is delicious at room temperature.

DEVON DELANEY
WESTPORT, CONNECTICUT

1 tablespoon butter, softened

12 miniature croissants, split

½ cup chopped dried apricots

½ cup flaked coconut

2 cups cream of coconut

1⅓ cups whole milk

4 eggs, lightly beaten

1 teaspoon vanilla extract

½ cup chopped macadamia nuts

1. Grease the bottom and sides of a 13-in. x 9-in. baking dish with softened butter. Arrange croissant bottoms in the dish; sprinkle with half of the apricots and coconut. Layer with croissant tops and the remaining apricots and flaked coconut.

2. In a saucepan, combine cream of coconut and milk. Cook over medium heat until bubbles form around sides of the pan.

3. Whisk a small amount of hot milk mixture into eggs; return all to the pan, stirring constantly. Remove from the heat and stir in vanilla.

4. Slowly ladle egg mixture over coconut. Let stand for 10-15 minutes or until croissants are softened.

5. Cover and bake at 350° for 30 minutes. Uncover; sprinkle with nuts. Bake 5-10 minutes longer or until a knife comes out clean. Serve warm.

YIELD: 12 SERVINGS.

garlic fontina bread

(PICTURED ON PAGE 146)

*With its golden brown color and soft texture, this bread is a must at any family meal.
It's a modified version of a traditional white bread recipe my brother gave me.
Try it as garlic bread toast, on grilled sandwiches or enjoy as is.*

CINDY RYAN | ST. JOHNS, MICHIGAN

2 packages (¼ ounce each) active dry yeast

2 cups warm water (110° to 115°)

3 tablespoons sugar

2 tablespoons shortening

1 tablespoon garlic powder

2 teaspoons salt

5 to 5½ cups all-purpose flour

1½ cups plus 2 tablespoons shredded fontina cheese, divided

1½ teaspoons canola oil

1. In a large bowl, dissolve yeast in warm water. Add the sugar, shortening, garlic powder, salt and 3 cups flour. Beat until smooth. Stir in enough remaining flour to form a firm dough. Stir in 1½ cups cheese.

2. Turn onto a floured surface; knead until smooth and elastic, about 6-8 minutes. Place in a greased bowl, turning once to grease the top. Cover and let rise in a warm place until doubled, about 1 hour.

3. Punch dough down. Shape into two loaves. Place in two greased 9-in. x 5-in. loaf pans. Cover and let rise in a warm place until doubled, about 30 minutes. Brush with oil and sprinkle with remaining cheese.

4. Bake at 375° for 30-35 minutes or until golden brown. Cool on a wire rack.

YIELD: 2 LOAVES (16 SLICES EACH).

asparagus with creamy garlic mustard sauce

(PICTURED ON PAGE 147)

My favorite recipes are those that are special enough for company, yet easy to make. My second favorite recipes are those that are healthy, yet taste great. This tender asparagus dish fits both categories!

COLEEN MCCREA KATZ | HAVERTOWN, PENNSYLVANIA

3 pounds fresh asparagus, trimmed

½ cup sour cream

½ cup mayonnaise

¼ cup lemon juice

2 tablespoons Dijon mustard

2 tablespoons minced fresh basil

2 tablespoons snipped fresh dill

1½ teaspoons coarsely ground pepper

½ teaspoon garlic powder

¼ teaspoon salt

1. In a large skillet, bring 4 cups water to a boil. Add asparagus; cover and cook for 2 to 2½ minutes. Drain and immediately place asparagus in ice water. Drain and pat dry.

2. In a small saucepan, combine the sour cream, mayonnaise, lemon juice, mustard, basil, dill, pepper, garlic powder and salt. Cook and stir over low heat just until heated through. Serve with asparagus.

YIELD: 12 SERVINGS.

radish, cucumber and grapefruit salad

(PICTURED BELOW & PAGE 147)

Looking for a light and refreshing way to round out your meal? Tart grapefruit complements spicy radishes and crunchy cucumbers perfectly in this spring salad. It's a quick and healthy addition to your holiday menu.

CONNIE BOLL | CHILTON, WISCONSIN

2   large red grapefruit

1   pound radishes, thinly sliced

1   English cucumber, thinly sliced

4   green onions, thinly sliced

2   tablespoons snipped fresh dill

DRESSING

⅓   cup ruby red grapefruit juice

2   tablespoons honey

1   tablespoon canola oil

¼   teaspoon salt

⅛   teaspoon pepper

      Sunflower kernels, optional

1. Cut each grapefruit in half horizontally. With a sharp knife, cut around each section to loosen fruit; place in a large bowl. Add the radishes, cucumber, onions and dill.

2. In a small bowl, whisk the grapefruit juice, honey, oil, salt and pepper. Pour over grapefruit mixture; toss to coat. Sprinkle with sunflower kernels if desired. Serve with a slotted spoon.

YIELD: 10 SERVINGS.

EASTER EGGS WITH A VINTAGE TWIST

Dying Easter eggs is as traditional to the holiday as the Easter Bunny himself! Give this year's batch a creative twist with this fun and colorful tie-dyed technique that makes use of old silk ties.

1. Cut the stitching on the back of each silk tie.

2. Remove the inner lining.

3. Next cut the tie into pieces large enough to wrap around an egg or about 5-6 in. square.

4. On a flat surface, place an egg centered on one side of a silk square right side up (the dyed pattern print should be touching the egg). Roll the egg so that the silk fabric fits tightly around its surface. Fold the ends over twisting slightly to temporarily secure in place. Repeat wrapping technique for each egg.

5 . Then put the silk covered egg into a knee-high nylon stocking. Stretch the stocking until it presses the silk firmly against the egg. Knot the end.

"tie" dyed easter eggs

Now that you've cut your ties and wrapped your eggs, you're ready for the fun part! After completing the steps outlined on page 154, follow the steps here to give the eggs a swirly, whimsical appearance.

- ☐ 100% silk ties
- ☐ knee-high nylon stockings
- ☐ non-aluminum cooking pot with lid (not for food)
- ☐ vinegar
- ☐ measuring cup
- ☐ colander (not for food)
- ☐ towel

1. Put the silk-covered eggs into a non-aluminum cooking pot. Cover with water until immersed about an inch. Add one cup of vinegar and gently mix so as not to disturb the eggs. Bring water to a rapid boil.

2. Cover, letting the eggs simmer for about 30 minutes. Be careful not to overcook eggs, causing them to crack.

3. Gently remove eggs from pot and let cool in a colander until warm to the touch.

4. Carefully cut off nylon stockings, unwrapping each egg. Place eggs on a towel to dry. Store the finished eggs in the original egg carton in your refrigerator until ready to display.

CRAFTER'S NOTE: *Each knee-high nylon stocking can be used a few times by tying the end after cutting. Each silk tie square can also be used 2-3 times before the dye is exhausted.*

ood things do come in small packages! Just take a look at the fun-sized versions of classic pies and tarts featured here.

From sweet, just-picked fruit encased in a flaky crust (Ginger Peach Pie, anyone?) to creamy custard atop a buttery graham cracker base, these pint-sized treats pack in all the luscious flavor of their high-yield counterparts in a dessert that requires a single fork.

So let them eat cake! These petite sweets are portable and adorable, and sure to satisfy any hankering for a home-baked treat.

CUTIE PIES (AND TARTS)
Ginger Peach Pies (p. 158)

MINI PIES & TARTS

ginger peach pies

(PICTURED ON PAGE 156)

I love ginger in any form, so I always look for ways to include it in my recipes, especially desserts. The sweetness of fresh peaches and subtle spiciness of ginger make every bite of these mini pies divine!

RAE ENDICOTT | BRANSON, MISSOURI

3¾ cups all-purpose flour

¾ teaspoon salt

1 cup cold butter, cubed

9 tablespoons shortening, cubed

6 to 9 tablespoons ice water

FILLING

5 cups sliced peeled peaches

1 tablespoon lemon juice

¾ cup sugar

2 tablespoons cornstarch

¼ cup crystallized ginger, chopped

½ teaspoon salt

2 tablespoons butter, cubed

OPTIONAL TOPPING

½ cup crystallized ginger

¼ cup coarse sugar

1. In a large bowl, combine flour and salt; cut in butter and shortening until crumbly. Gradually add water, tossing with a fork, until dough forms a ball. Divide dough into seven portions; wrap each in plastic wrap. Refrigerate for about 1 hour or until easy to handle.

2. On a lightly floured surface, roll out five portions of dough to fit a 5-in. pie plate. Transfer pastry to pie plates and trim to ½ in. beyond edge of plates; flute edges.

3. In a large bowl, toss peaches with lemon juice. Combine the sugar, cornstarch, ginger and salt. Add to peaches and toss to coat. Transfer to pie shells. Dot with butter. Transfer pies to a baking sheet.

4. If a streusel topping is desired, combine remaining pastry with crystallized ginger and coarse sugar; sprinkle over pies. Bake at 375° for 35-40 minutes or until golden brown and filling is bubbly. Cool on a wire rack.

YIELD: 5 MINI PIES.

PRETTY PASTRY TECHINIQUES

RUFFLE TRIM: Trim pastry to 1/2 in. beyond the rim of the plate. Position thumb and index finger about 1 in. apart on the edge of the pastry, pointing out. Position index finger on the other hand between thumb and index finger; gently push pastry toward the center in an upward motion. Continue around edge.

LEAF TRIM: Trim pastry of the bottom crust even with the plate's edge. Roll out remaining dough to 1/8-in. thickness. Cut out leaf shapes, using cookie cutters. With a sharp knife, score dough to create leaf vines. Brush bottom of each leaf with water and place around pasty edge. Press lightly to secure.

key lime marshmallow meringue tarts

After spending time last winter in Key West, my husband and I became obsessed with Key lime pie. This is my petite version of one we tried. Marshmallow creme lends an extra-special touch.

BARBARA HAHN | PARK HILLS, MISSOURI

1¼ cups graham cracker crumbs

½ cup almond paste

⅓ cup unsalted butter, melted

2 tablespoons brown sugar

FILLING

2 cans (14 ounces each) sweetened condensed milk

¾ cup plus 2 tablespoons Key lime juice

MERINGUE

2 egg whites

¼ teaspoon cream of tartar

1 jar (7 ounces) marshmallow creme

1. In a large bowl, combine cracker crumbs, almond paste, butter and sugar; press onto bottom and up sides of eight ungreased 4-in. fluted tart pans with removable bottoms. Place on baking sheets. Bake at 350° for 7-9 minutes or until lightly browned. Cool on wire racks.

2. In large bowl, whisk the milk and lime juice. Pour into crusts.

3. In a large bowl with clean beaters, beat egg whites and cream of tartar on medium speed until soft peaks form. Add marshmallow creme, a tablespoon at a time, beating on high until stiff peaks form. Spread the meringue over filling. Return tarts to baking sheets.

4. Bake at 325° for 15-20 minutes or until meringue is lightly browned. Cool completely on wire racks. Refrigerate for at least 4 hours before serving.

YIELD: 8 TARTS.

pina colada macadamia pies

Refreshing, light and different, these personalized tarts offer a taste of the tropics.

JONI HILTON | ROCKLIN, CALIFORNIA

35 vanilla wafers

½ cup macadamia nuts, toasted

½ cup flaked coconut

¼ cup butter, melted

FILLING

2 teaspoons unflavored gelatin

2 tablespoons cold water

½ cup unsweetened pineapple juice

1 can (15 ounces) cream of coconut

¾ cup pina colada yogurt

TOPPING

¾ cup heavy whipping cream

2 tablespoons confectioners' sugar

⅓ cup macadamia nuts, toasted

Fresh pineapple wedges

1. Place wafers and nuts in a food processor. Cover; pulse until fine crumbs form. Add coconut and butter; cover and pulse until blended. Press onto the bottom and up the sides of five greased 5-in. pie pans. Refrigerate for 30 minutes.

2. Transfer pie pans to a baking sheet. Bake at 350° for 10-12 minutes or until lightly browned. Cool on a wire rack.

3. In a small saucepan, sprinkle gelatin over cold water; let stand for 1 minute. Add pineapple juice. Heat over low heat, stirring until gelatin is completely dissolved. Remove from the heat. In a large bowl, stir cream of coconut until blended. Stir in yogurt; add gelatin mixture. Pour into crusts. Refrigerate for 8 hours.

4. In a small bowl, beat cream until it begins to thicken. Add confectioners' sugar; beat until soft peaks form. Spread over filling. Sprinkle with nuts and garnish with pineapple.

YIELD: 5 MINI PIES.

banana cream pies

This luscious pared-down version of a classic lets you enjoy your favorite treat without wasteful leftovers.

CAROL MAERTZ | SPRUCE GROVE, ALBERTA

1½ cups graham cracker crumbs

¼ cup sugar

⅓ cup butter, melted

FILLING

⅔ cup sugar

⅓ cup cornstarch

½ teaspoon salt

1 can (12 ounces) evaporated milk

1 cup water

3 egg yolks, lightly beaten

1 teaspoon vanilla extract

1 cup heavy whipping cream

2 tablespoons confectioners' sugar

2 large firm bananas

1. Combine cracker crumbs, sugar and butter; press onto bottom and up sides of five 5-in. pie plates. Place on a baking sheet. Bake at 375° for 8-10 minutes. Cool on a wire rack.

2. In a small saucepan, combine sugar, cornstarch and salt. Stir in milk and water until smooth. Cook and stir over medium-high heat until thickened and bubbly. Reduce heat; cook and stir 2 minutes longer. Remove from heat. Stir a small amount of hot filling into egg yolks; return all to pan, stirring constantly. Bring to a gentle boil; cook and stir 2 minutes longer. Remove from heat. Stir in vanilla. Press plastic wrap onto surface of custard. Cover; refrigerate for 30 minutes.

3. In a small bowl, beat cream until it thickens. Add confectioners' sugar; beat until stiff peaks form. Slice bananas into crusts; spoon custard over. Top with whipped cream. Refrigerate for at least 3 hours before serving.

YIELD: 5 MINI PIES.

raspberry ricotta pies

My grandmother recalls enjoying ricotta pie on Easter when she was little. Now, I've taken her recipe and created a downsized version!

STEPHEN DEBENEDICTIS
WAKEFIELD, MASSACHUSETTS

3   cups all-purpose flour

1   cup plus 2 tablespoons butter

3   egg yolks

3   tablespoons cold water

RASPBERRY LAYER

1½ cups fresh or frozen raspberries, thawed

¼   cup sugar

2   tablespoons cornstarch

1   cup semisweet chocolate chips

FILLING

1½ cups ricotta cheese

2   tablespoons all-purpose flour

1½ teaspoons vanilla extract

2   eggs

½   cup sugar

FINISHING

1   egg white

2   tablespoons coarse sugar

1. Place the flour in a large bowl; cut in the butter until crumbly. In a small bowl, whisk the egg yolks and water; gradually add to flour mixture, tossing with a fork until dough forms a ball. Divide dough in half so that one portion is slightly larger than the other. Wrap the smaller portion of dough in plastic wrap; refrigerate.

2. Divide remaining dough into six portions. Roll out each to fit a 5-in. pie plate; transfer pastry to pie plates. Set aside.

3. Press raspberries through a sieve; discard seeds. In a small saucepan, combine sugar and cornstarch. Stir in raspberry puree. Bring to a boil; cook and stir for 2 minutes or until thickened. Remove from heat. Spread over the bottom of each crust. Sprinkle with chocolate chips.

4. In a large bowl, beat the ricotta cheese, flour and vanilla until blended. In a small bowl, beat eggs on high speed for 3 minutes. Gradually add sugar, beating until mixture becomes thick and lemon-colored. Fold into ricotta mixture. Spread into pastry shells.

5. Roll out remaining pastry; make lattice crusts. Trim, seal and flute edges. Whisk egg white; brush over lattice tops. Sprinkle with coarse sugar.

6. Transfer pies to a baking sheet. Bake at 350° for 30-35 minutes or until crust is golden and filling is set. Cool on a wire rack. Refrigerate until serving.

YIELD: 6 MINI PIES.

pecan french silk pies

Individual-sized tarts keep me from overindulging in my favorite dessert—French silk pie.

TERRY SHAW | TYLER, TEXAS

Pastry for double-crust pie (9 inches)

⅔ cup coarsely chopped pecans

⅔ cup corn syrup

5 eggs

1½ cups sugar, divided

¼ cup butter, melted

¼ teaspoon salt

3 ounces unsweetened chocolate, coarsely chopped

1½ teaspoons vanilla extract

¾ cup butter, softened

Whipped cream

1. Divide pastry into five portions. Roll each portion to fit a 4-in. fluted tart pan with removable bottom. Transfer pastry to tart pans; trim even with edges. Place on a baking sheet.

2. Sprinkle pecans into pastry shells. Combine corn syrup, 2 eggs, ½ cup sugar, melted butter and salt; pour over pecans. Bake at 375° for 25-30 minutes or until a knife inserted near the center comes out clean. Cool on a wire rack for 15 minutes.

3. In a small saucepan, combine remaining sugar and eggs. Cook and stir over low heat, until mixture reaches 160° and coats the back of a metal spoon. Remove from the heat; stir in chocolate and vanilla until smooth. Cool to lukewarm (90°), stirring occasionally.

4. In a large bowl, beat softened butter until smooth. Add cooled chocolate mixture; beat on high speed until light and fluffy. Spread over tarts. Cover and refrigerate for at least 6 hours or overnight. Garnish with whipped cream.

YIELD: 5 TARTS.

mini carrot cake tarts

When you crave carrot cake, try these tarts for the same wonderful flavors in a unique presentation.

LAURA MAJCHRZAK | HUNT VALLEY, MARYLAND

1 package (14.1 ounces) refrigerated pie pastry

1 cup packed brown sugar

⅓ cup corn syrup

¼ cup unsalted butter, melted

2 eggs

⅓ cup all-purpose flour

1 teaspoon ground cinnamon

½ teaspoon baking soda

½ teaspoon salt

1½ cups finely shredded carrots

⅓ cup raisins

⅓ cup chopped pecans, toasted

TOPPING

4 ounces cream cheese, softened

½ cup packed brown sugar

⅔ cup heavy whipping cream

3 tablespoons chopped pecans, toasted

1. Cut each pastry sheet into three portions. Roll each into a 5-in. circle. Transfer to six 4-in. fluted tart pans with removable bottoms; trim pastry even with edges. Line unpricked pastry shells with a double thickness of foil. Fill with pie weights. Place on a baking sheet. Bake at 450° for 7 minutes. Remove foil and weights; bake 3 minutes longer. Cool on a wire rack.

2. In a large bowl, beat brown sugar, corn syrup and butter until blended. Add eggs, one at a time, beating well after each addition. Combine flour, cinnamon, baking soda and salt; stir into egg mixture. Fold in carrots, raisins and pecans. Pour into crusts. Bake at 350° for 12-15 minutes or until golden brown. Cool on a wire rack. Beat cream cheese and brown sugar until smooth. Gradually add whipping cream; beat until soft peaks form. Fold in pecans. Serve with tarts.

YIELD: 6 TARTS.

peanut butter mousse tarts

My family loves the flavors of chocolate and peanut butter. Our favorite single-serving tarts give us the best of both worlds in one standout dessert.

SUSAN MARSHALL
COLORADO SPRINGS, COLORADO

¼ cup butter, melted

2 tablespoons creamy peanut butter

1½ cups all-purpose flour

¼ cup packed brown sugar

½ teaspoon salt

¼ teaspoon baking powder

3 tablespoons cold water

½ teaspoon vanilla extract

½ cup miniature semisweet chocolate chips

2 teaspoons shortening

FILLING

1 package (8 ounces) reduced-fat cream cheese

½ cup creamy peanut butter

¼ cup sugar

1 teaspoon vanilla extract

TOPPING

½ cup plus 2 tablespoons miniature semisweet chocolate chips, divided

3 tablespoons lightly salted dry roasted peanuts, chopped

1. In a small bowl, combine butter and peanut butter. In a food processor, combine the flour, brown sugar, salt and baking powder; cover and process until blended. Add butter mixture; cover and pulse until mixture resembles coarse crumbs.

2. While processing, gradually add water and vanilla just until moist crumbs form. Press onto the bottom and up the sides of six ungreased 4-in. fluted tart pans with removable bottoms. Place on a baking sheet. Bake at 350° for 8-10 minutes or until lightly browned. Cool on a wire rack.

3. In a microwave, melt chocolate chips and shortening; stir until smooth. Spread over the bottoms of crusts. Refrigerate.

4. In a small bowl, beat the cream cheese, peanut butter, sugar and vanilla until fluffy. Spread into crusts.

5. For topping, in a microwave, melt ½ cup chocolate chips; stir until smooth. Drizzle over tarts. Sprinkle remaining chocolate chips and peanuts over tops. Refrigerate for at least 2 hours before serving.

YIELD: 6 TARTS.

ooray for spring break! The kiddos are home for the week, and you're scrambling for ideas to keep them entertained and fed while keeping your sanity intact. Never fear! We've packed this chapter full of family-friendly, kid-approved food and fun.

When spring showers dampen outdoor play, call little bakers into the kitchen to prepare this funny and sunny Spring Garden Cookie Puzzle. Refrigerated cookie dough makes it a snap to bake up, while the colorful frosting and assorted colored sugars make it fun for all ages to "paint."

What is the best part of this simply spring art lesson? You get to eat your masterpiece!

KID-FRIENDLY GOODIES!
Spring Garden Cookie Puzzle (p. 166)

SPRING BREAK FUN

spring garden cookie puzzle

(PICTURED ON PAGE 164)

Ready to roll out the cookie dough and create an edible masterpiece? Kids of all ages will love making this fun-to-paint, even-more-fun-to-eat cookie puzzle. Who said it's bad manners to play with your food?

TASTE OF HOME TEST KITCHEN

1 tube (16½ ounces) refrigerated sugar cookie dough

½ cup all-purpose flour

Blanched almonds

2½ cups confectioners' sugar

1 teaspoon vanilla extract

4 to 5 tablespoons 2% milk

Assorted colored sugars and food coloring of your choice

1. Let the cookie dough stand at room temperature for 5-10 minutes to soften. In a large bowl, beat cookie dough and flour until blended. On a parchment paper-lined surface, roll dough into a 14-in. x 11-in. rectangle. With cookie cutters, cut out puzzle shapes. Slide a baking sheet under the parchment paper and dough. Chill for 10 minutes.

2. Remove shapes and place on an ungreased baking sheet. Place an almond on its side into the center of each shape for a handle. Bake shapes at 350° for 7-10 minutes or until edges are golden brown. While still warm, recut shapes with the same cookie cutters to form neat edges. (If cookies cool too quickly, warm in oven to soften.) Remove to wire racks; cool completely.

3. Bake large rectangular puzzle on a parchment paper-lined baking sheet for 12-16 minutes or until edges are golden brown. Immediately recut the shapes inside the puzzle to form neat edges. Cool completely on a wire rack.

4. In a small bowl, combine the confectioners' sugar, vanilla and enough milk to achieve desired consistency. Frost puzzle and shapes with some of the frosting; decorate with sugars. Tint remaining frosting; pipe as desired. Place puzzle shapes inside puzzle.

YIELD: 1 COOKIE PUZZLE.

favorite deep-dish pizza

My kids love to get pizza delivered. But it is not very healthy, plus it's expensive. I came up with a one-bowl pizza that is nutritious and allows the kids to add the toppings of their choice.

SARA LAFOUNTAIN | ROCKVILLE, MARYLAND

1¾ cups whole wheat flour

1¾ cups all-purpose flour

2 packages (¼ ounce each) quick-rise yeast

4 teaspoons sugar

1 teaspoon salt

1½ cups warm water (120° to 130°)

¼ cup olive oil

1 can (8 ounces) pizza sauce

8 ounces fresh mozzarella cheese, sliced

2 cups (8 ounces) shredded Italian cheese blend

½ teaspoon dried oregano

½ teaspoon Italian seasoning

1. In a large bowl, combine wheat flour, 1 cup all-purpose flour, yeast, sugar and salt. Add water and oil; beat until smooth. Stir in enough remaining flour to form a soft dough. Press dough onto the bottom and up the sides of a greased 13-in. x 9-in. baking dish.

2. Top with pizza sauce. Place mozzarella slices over sauce. Sprinkle with shredded cheese blend, oregano and Italian seasoning. Bake, uncovered, at 400° for 20-25 minutes or until golden brown.

YIELD: 8 SERVINGS.

apple and peanut butter stackers

The best way to get kids interested in cooking and eating right is to let them help. Sliced apple "sandwiches" are one fun way to pique their interest and kitchen creativity.

SHIRLEY WARREN
THIENSVILLE, WISCONSIN

2   medium apples

⅓   cup chunky peanut butter

Optional fillings: granola, miniature semisweet chocolate chips and M&M's miniature baking bits

Core apples. Cut each apple crosswise into six slices. Spread peanut butter over 6 slices; sprinkle with fillings of your choice. Top with the remaining apple slices.

YIELD: 6 SERVINGS.

dirt ball pops

Like the popular dessert cup, our "dirt ball" pops add another fun spin on a treat kids adore.

TASTE OF HOME TEST KITCHEN

½   cup almond butter

½   cup honey

½   teaspoon ground cinnamon

½   teaspoon vanilla extract

2   cups Rice Krispies, crushed

½   cup finely shredded unsweetened coconut

20   gummy worms

1   cup Oreo cookie crumbs

Lollipop sticks

1. In a large bowl, combine the almond butter, honey, cinnamon and vanilla. Stir in cereal and coconut.

2. With wet hands, shape mixture into 1-in. balls, inserting gummy worms into balls. Roll in cookie crumbs. Place on a waxed paper-lined baking sheet; insert lollipop stick into balls. Refrigerate for at least 2 hours or until firm. Store truffles in the refrigerator.

YIELD: 20 TRUFFLES.

EDITOR'S NOTE: *Look for unsweetened coconut in the baking or health food section.*

hearty ham mac and cheese

Little tykes can't seem to get enough of macaroni and cheese. In fact, I created this recipe for my friend's family when she was ill. The addition of ham makes it a satisfying one-dish meal.

JENNIFER NYSTROM | MORROW, OHIO

6 slices white bread

3 tablespoons cold butter, cubed

1 package (16 ounces) uncooked elbow macaroni

6 tablespoons butter, cubed

1 garlic clove, minced

1 teaspoon water

1 teaspoon ground mustard

¼ teaspoon cayenne pepper

6 tablespoons all-purpose flour

1 can (14½ ounces) reduced-sodium chicken broth

2 cans (12 ounces each) evaporated milk

1 cup 2% milk

4 cups (16 ounces) shredded Colby cheese

2 cups (8 ounces) shredded cheddar cheese

½ teaspoon salt

⅛ teaspoon coarsely ground pepper

3 cups cubed fully cooked ham (½-in. cubes)

1. Grease a 13-in. x 9-in. baking dish; set aside.

2. For bread crumbs, pulse bread and cold butter in a food processor until crumbs are fine, about 20-25 pulses; set aside.

3. Cook pasta according to package directions. Meanwhile, in a Dutch oven, melt butter over medium heat. Whisk in the garlic, water, mustard and cayenne for 30 seconds. Stir in flour until blended; cook and stir for 2-3 minutes or until golden brown. Gradually whisk in broth and milks. Cook and stir 4-5 minutes longer or until mixture begins to thicken.

4. Remove from the heat; stir in the cheeses, salt and pepper. Drain pasta; add to cheese mixture. Fold in ham. Pour into prepared baking dish; sprinkle with bread crumbs.

5. Bake, uncovered, at 375° for 20-25 minutes or until crumbs are golden brown. Let stand for 5 minutes before serving.

YIELD: 10 SERVINGS.

butterfly pasta

Kids love pasta, especially when it is shaped like fun "butterflies." The lemon and basil pair with Parmesan cheese to transform plain pasta into something totally unique and kid-approved!

LAUREN REIFF | EAST EARL, PENNSYLVANIA

3 cups uncooked bow tie pasta

1 garlic clove, minced

1 tablespoon olive oil

1 tablespoon lemon juice

1 teaspoon dried basil

½ teaspoon salt

¼ teaspoon pepper

½ cup grated Parmesan cheese

1. In a large saucepan, cook pasta according to package directions. Drain pasta and set aside.

2. In the same saucepan, saute garlic in oil for 1 minute. Stir in the lemon juice, basil, salt and pepper. Return pasta to the pan. Add cheese and toss to coat.

YIELD: 4 SERVINGS.

rainbow spritzer

Layers of colorful fruit submerged in a fizzy, sweet beverage make this a kid-friendly sipper that gets two thumbs up.

TASTE OF HOME
TEST KITCHEN

½ cup fresh blueberries

½ cup chopped peeled kiwifruit

½ cup chopped fresh pineapple

½ cup mandarin oranges, drained and chopped

½ cup sliced fresh strawberries or fresh raspberries

1 cup ginger ale, chilled

½ cup lemonade, chilled

½ cup unsweetened pineapple juice, chilled

1. In each of four tall glasses, layer the blueberries, kiwi, pineapple, mandarin oranges and strawberries.

2. In a small bowl, combine the ginger ale, lemonade and pineapple juice. Pour mixture over fruits.

YIELD: 4 SERVINGS.

A-PEELING KITCHEN TIP

There is a quick and simple way to peel kiwifruit: Just use a teaspoon! This method works best with fruit that is ripe but not too soft. First, cut off both ends of a kiwi. Then slip a teaspoon just under the skin, matching the spoon's curve to the curve of the fruit. Now slide the spoon around the kiwi to separate the fruit from the skin, being careful not to dig the spoon into the flesh. Once the spoon has been completely run around the fruit, it will easily slip out of the skin in one smooth piece!

waffled soft pretzels

Classic soft pretzels are transformed into "waffles" that are crispy outside and chewy inside.

KATIE JOHNSON | INMAN, SOUTH CAROLINA

2 teaspoons active dry yeast

1⅓ cups warm water (110° to 115°)

⅓ cup packed brown sugar

¼ teaspoon kosher salt

3½ to 4 cups bread flour

6 cups water

¼ cup baking soda

2 tablespoons butter, melted

Additional kosher salt

1. In a large bowl, dissolve yeast in warm water. Add the brown sugar, salt and 2 cups flour; beat until smooth. Stir in enough remaining flour to form a soft dough.

2. Turn onto a floured surface; knead until smooth and elastic, about 4-6 minutes. Place in a greased bowl, turning once to grease top. Cover and let rise in a warm place until doubled, about 45 minutes.

3. Punch dough down; divide into 12 portions. Roll each into an 18-in. rope; twist into pretzel shapes. Cover; let rest for 10 minutes.

4. In a large saucepan, bring water and baking soda to a boil. Place pretzels into boiling water, one at a time, for 30 seconds. Remove with a slotted spoon and drain on paper towels.

5. Place pretzels onto a preheated waffle iron coated with cooking spray. Cook for 1 to 1½ minutes or until golden brown. Carefully remove to wire racks. Immediately brush with butter and sprinkle with additional salt. Serve warm.

YIELD: 1 DOZEN.

FOR BAKED PRETZELS: *Place on parchment-lined baking sheets. Brush with butter and sprinkle with additional salt. Bake at 475° for 7-9 minutes or until golden brown. Remove from pans to wire racks. Serve warm.*

crumb-topped banana bread

When spring showers keep you and the kids indoors, turn to this rainy day favorite.

TASTE OF HOME TEST KITCHEN

1¾ cups all-purpose flour

1 teaspoon baking powder

1 teaspoon baking soda

¾ teaspoon salt

3 medium bananas, mashed

1 cup sugar

2 eggs, lightly beaten

½ cup butter, melted

1 teaspoon vanilla extract

CRUMB TOPPING

⅓ cup packed brown sugar

3 tablespoons all-purpose flour

3 tablespoons sugar

¼ teaspoon ground cinnamon

2 tablespoons cold butter

1. In a large bowl, combine the flour, baking powder, baking soda and salt. In a small bowl, whisk the bananas, sugar, eggs, butter and vanilla. Stir into dry ingredients just until moistened. Transfer to a greased 9-in. x 5-in. loaf pan.

2. For topping, in a bowl, combine the brown sugar, flour, sugar and cinnamon; cut in butter until crumbly. Sprinkle over batter. Bake at 350° for 50-55 minutes or until a toothpick inserted near the center comes out clean. Cool for 10 minutes before removing from pan to a wire rack.

YIELD: 1 LOAF (16 SLICES).

rainbow pasta

With so many interesting shapes, it's no wonder pasta tops the list of a kid-friendly foods. Create even more mealtime magic by serving colorful rainbow pasta made with food coloring.

- ☐ assorted pasta (i.e. bow tie, wagon wheel, etc.)
- ☐ food coloring
- ☐ assorted toppings: Parmesan cheese, frozen meatballs, shredded mozzarella cheese, mini shrimp

1. In a large saucepan, bring water and 20 drops of food coloring to a boil. If mixing colors, use 10 drops of each color (i.e. 10 drops each of red and blue for purple, 10 drops each of yellow and blue for green and 10 drops each of yellow and red for orange). To have pasta in multiple colors, boil several pots of water at once, or repeat the process after each color.

2. Add the pasta; cook the pasta according to package directions.

3. Drain pasta. If more color is desired, place pasta in a pot or bowl of warm water and add additional food coloring; stir. Continue to add more food coloring and stir until desired color or brightness is achieved.

4. Drain pasta; rinse in cold water. Enjoy with an assortment of fun toppings. We suggest shredded Parmesan cheese, meatballs with shredded mozzarella cheese or mini shrimp.

specialcelebrations

Every day is a celebration with this inspiring collection of
food and fun at your fingertips. Turn your trip to the farmers
market or strawberry farm into a party...treat Mom to a
scrumptious family-style brunch...transform your backyard
into a haunted fairy tale forest...each chapter is loaded with
tasty recipes and creative party themes.

alentine's Day isn't just about tables for two and candlelit dinners. It is about celebrating everyone you hold near and dear. So this February 14, share the love by inviting a few friends over for a truly succulent meal you prepared especially for them.

The impressive centerpiece of this elegant surf-and-turf menu is Grilled Lobster Tails. You'll find that the dinner's melt-in-your-mouth richness pairs wonderfully with tender Rustic Ribeyes dressed with White Wine Mushrooms and a side of earthy Spinach with Pine Nuts and Raisins.

So raise your glass of Pomegranate Champagne Cocktail and dedicate this splendid feast to good friends and great food.

SURF 'N' TURF SPLENDOR
Grilled Lobster Tails (p. 176)
Spinach with Pine Nuts and Raisins (p. 176)
Rustic Ribeyes (p. 178)
White Wine Mushrooms (p. 178)
Pomegranate Champagne Cocktail (p. 180)

DINNER WITH FRIENDS

grilled lobster tails

(PICTURED ON PAGE 174)

I never made lobster at home until I tried this convenient and deliciously different grilled recipe.
It turned out amazing and has left me with little reason to order lobster at a restaurant again.

KATIE RUSH | KANSAS CITY, MISSOURI

6 frozen lobster tails (8 to 10 ounces each), thawed

¾ cup olive oil

3 tablespoons minced fresh chives

3 garlic cloves, minced

½ teaspoon salt

½ teaspoon pepper

1. Using scissors, cut top of lobster shell lengthwise down the center, leaving tail fin intact. Loosen meat from shell, keeping the fin end attached; lift meat and lay over shell. With a knife, cut a slit, ½ inch deep, down center of meat.

2. In a small bowl, combine the remaining ingredients; spoon over lobster meat. Cover and refrigerate for 20 minutes.

3. Place lobster tails, meat side up, on grill rack. Grill, covered, over medium heat for 10-12 minutes or until meat is opaque.

YIELD: 6 SERVINGS.

spinach with pine nuts and raisins

(PICTURED ON PAGE 174)

A nice side for winter meat entrees, this bright and flavorful dish
is a delicious way to get your greens. The simple list of ingredients makes it easy to prepare.

GRETCHEN WHELAN | SAN FRANCISCO, CALIFORNIA

⅓ cup golden raisins

⅓ cup pine nuts

3 garlic cloves, minced

¼ cup olive oil

2 packages (10 ounces each) fresh spinach, torn

¼ teaspoon salt

⅛ teaspoon pepper

1. Place raisins in a small bowl. Cover with boiling water; let stand for 5 minutes. Drain and set aside.

2. In a Dutch oven, cook pine nuts and garlic in oil over medium heat for 2 minutes. Stir in raisins; cook 1 minute longer. Stir in the spinach, salt and pepper; cook for 4-5 minutes or just until tender. Serve with a slotted spoon.

YIELD: 6 SERVINGS.

GET PRIMED ON PINE NUTS

Also known as pignolia or pinon, the pine nut is the small seed from one of several pine tree varieties. They are small, elongated, ivory-colored nuts and have a soft texture and buttery flavor. Frequently used in Italian dishes and sauces such as pesto, pine nuts are often toasted to enhance their flavor.

favorite french onion soup

My ideal restaurant treat is French onion soup, so I came up with a rich version that's easy enough to whip up on a work night or serve as an elegant first course.

JENNIFER MILLER | SMYRNA, TENNESSEE

1   large sweet onion, cut into ½-inch rings

1   large Spanish onion, cut into ½-inch rings

1   large red onion, cut into ½-inch rings

2   tablespoons sugar

1   tablespoon minced fresh thyme or 1 teaspoon dried thyme

2   teaspoons herbes de Provence

¾   teaspoon salt

¼   teaspoon pepper

3   tablespoons olive oil

¼   cup sherry or beef broth

¼   cup dry red wine or beef broth

1   carton (32 ounces) beef broth

6   slices French bread baguette (½ inch thick)

2   cups (8 ounces) shredded Gruyere or Swiss cheese

1. In a Dutch oven, saute the onions, sugar, thyme, herbes de Provence, salt and pepper in oil; cook mixture over medium heat for 15-20 minutes or until it's lightly browned, stirring frequently.

2. Add sherry and wine, stirring to loosen browned bits from pan. Gradually stir in broth. Bring to a boil. Reduce heat; cover and simmer for 10 minutes, stirring occasionally.

3. Place bread slices on an ungreased baking sheet. Broil 3-4 in. from the heat for 1-2 minutes on each side or until lightly browned.

4. Ladle soup into ovenproof bowls. Top each with a slice of toast; sprinkle with cheese. Place bowls on a baking sheet. Broil 2-3 minutes longer or until cheese is golden.

YIELD: 6 SERVINGS.

EDITOR'S NOTE: *Look for herbes de Provence in the spice aisle.*

rustic ribeyes

(PICTURED ON PAGE 174)

*Since I usually have the ingredients on hand, these succulent ribeyes are
a "regular" from my kitchen. But the tender meat also makes a lovely entree
for more significant occasions or when I'm entertaining guests.*

MARY SHIVERS | ADA, OKLAHOMA

¾ cup Worcestershire sauce

3 tablespoons lime juice

1 tablespoon brown sugar

1 tablespoon instant coffee granules

¾ teaspoon ground mustard

½ to ¾ teaspoon crushed red pepper flakes

¼ teaspoon smoked sweet paprika

3 beef ribeye steaks (1-inch thick and 1 pound each)

2 tablespoons canola oil

6 tablespoons unsalted butter

1. In a small bowl, combine the first seven ingredients. Set aside ¼ cup for sauce. Pour remaining marinade into a 2-gallon resealable plastic bag. Add beef; seal bag and turn to coat. Refrigerate for up to 8 hours. Drain and discard marinade.

2. In a large nonstick skillet over medium-high heat, brown beef in oil in batches. Transfer to a greased 15-in. x 10-in. x 1-in. baking pan. Bake, uncovered, at 375° for 4-6 minutes or until meat reaches desired doneness (for medium-rare, a thermometer should read 145°; medium, 160°; well-done, 170°).

3. Meanwhile, in the same skillet, add butter and reserved marinade. Cook and stir over low heat until combined. Serve with steaks.

YIELD: 6 SERVINGS.

white wine mushrooms

(PICTURED ON PAGE 174)

*A handful of ingredients is all you need to create a truly elegant
and robustly flavored dish that can act as a side or a lovely topping for succulent steak.*

TASTE OF HOME TEST KITCHEN

5 garlic cloves, minced

½ cup butter, divided

¾ cup white wine

2 pounds halved baby portobello mushrooms

¼ teaspoon salt

¼ teaspoon coarsely ground pepper

In a large skillet, cook garlic in ¼ cup butter for 1-2 minutes. Stir in wine; add mushrooms. Bring to a boil. Reduce heat; simmer, uncovered, for 15-20 minutes or until liquid is almost evaporated. Stir in salt, pepper and remaining butter; cook until butter is melted.

YIELD: 6 SERVINGS.

mozzarella strawberry salad with chocolate vinaigrette

A chocolate salad dressing? It's the only way to dress a salad on Valentine's Day!
Don't let the unusual name and flavor combination confuse you—the salty prosciutto and mellow
mozzarella are beautifully balanced with the sweet-tart chocolate balsamic vinegar dressing.

TASTE OF HOME TEST KITCHEN

- 6 thin slices prosciutto or deli ham, chopped
- 1 package (5 ounces) spring mix salad greens
- 1½ cups watercress
- 1 carton (8 ounces) fresh mozzarella cheese pearls
- 1½ cups sliced fresh strawberries
- ¼ cup dark chocolate chips
- ¼ cup balsamic vinegar
- ¼ cup olive oil
- 1½ teaspoons honey
- ¼ teaspoon salt
- ⅛ teaspoon pepper

1. In a small skillet, cook prosciutto over medium heat until crisp. Remove to paper towels with a slotted spoon; drain and set aside.

2. Divide the salad greens and watercress among six salad plates. Arrange cheese, strawberries and prosciutto over greens.

3. In a microwave-safe bowl, melt chocolate; stir until smooth. Whisk in vinegar, oil, honey, salt and pepper. Drizzle over salads.

YIELD: 6 SERVINGS.

pomegranate champagne cocktail

(PICTURED ON PAGE 174)

Toast the one your heart adores with this slightly tart and different sparkling pomegranate cocktail. The pomegranate seeds make a fun and colorful garnish.

TASTE OF HOME TEST KITCHEN

1   sugar cube or 1 teaspoon sugar

2   to 4 dashes bitters, optional

1   ounce pomegranate juice

½   ounce brandy

½   ounce pomegranate liqueur

⅓   cup Champagne

GARNISH

Pomegranate seeds

Place sugar in a champagne flute; sprinkle with bitters if desired. Pour the juice, brandy and liqueur into the glass. Top with Champagne. Garnish with pomegranate seeds.

YIELD: 1 SERVING.

olive focaccia

After adding my own special touches to a basic focaccia recipe, including sun-dried tomatoes, olives and roasted sweet red peppers, the results were simply delectable. The flavorful, chewy loaf makes a wonderful accompaniment to nearly any meal.

DEE FROEMEL | HAYWARD, WISCONSIN

1⅛   teaspoons active dry yeast

½   cup warm water (110° to 115°)

1   tablespoon sugar

1   tablespoon Italian seasoning

¼   teaspoon salt

¼   teaspoon pepper

1⅓ to 1⅔ cups all-purpose flour

2   tablespoons oil-packed sun-dried tomatoes, chopped

2   tablespoons roasted sweet red peppers, drained and chopped

2   tablespoons sliced ripe olives, drained

5   Greek olives, sliced

5   sliced green olives with pimientos, drained

2   tablespoons minced fresh parsley

1   tablespoon olive oil

1   teaspoon kosher salt

1   teaspoon shredded Parmesan cheese

1   teaspoon shredded Romano cheese

1. In a large bowl, dissolve yeast in warm water. Add the sugar, Italian seasoning, salt, pepper and 1 cup flour. Beat until smooth. Stir in enough remaining flour to form a firm dough. Stir in tomatoes, peppers, olives and parsley.

2. Turn onto a floured surface; knead until smooth and elastic, about 6-8 minutes. Place in a greased bowl, turning once to grease the top. Cover and let rise in a warm place until doubled, about 50 minutes.

3. Punch dough down. Shape into a 9-in. circle on a greased baking sheet. Cover and let rise in a warm place until doubled, about 25 minutes. With fingertips, make several dimples over top of dough. Brush with oil. Sprinkle with kosher salt and cheeses.

4. Bake at 400° for 14-18 minutes or until golden brown. Remove to a wire rack.

YIELD: 1 LOAF (8 WEDGES).

red raspberry creme brulee

A "berry" enticing twist on traditional creme brulee, my rich, creamy dessert makes the perfect ending to a romantic meal or special occasion.

BARBARA HAHN
PARK HILLS, MISSOURI

1 can (21 ounces) raspberry pie filling

1½ cups heavy whipping cream

6 egg yolks

6 tablespoons sugar

¼ cup coarse sugar

1. Coat six 6-oz. ramekins or custard cups with cooking spray. Spoon a scant 3 tablespoons pie filling into the bottom of each ramekin; set aside.

2. In a small saucepan, heat cream until bubbles form around sides of pan. In a small bowl, whisk egg yolks and 6 tablespoons of sugar. Remove cream from heat; stir a small amount into egg mixture. Return all to the pan, stirring constantly.

3. Pour into the six prepared ramekins. Place in a baking pan; add 1 in. of boiling water to pan. Bake, uncovered, at 325° for 30-35 minutes or until centers are just set (mixture will jiggle). Remove ramekins from water bath; cool for 10 minutes.

4. Spoon remaining pie filling over tops. Cover and refrigerate for at least 4 hours.

5. If using a creme brulee torch, sprinkle each custard with coarse sugar. Heat sugar with the torch until caramelized. Serve immediately.

6. If broiling, place ramekins on a baking sheet; let stand at room temperature for 15 minutes. Sprinkle each custard with coarse sugar. Broil 8 in. from the heat for 4-7 minutes or until sugar is caramelized. Refrigerate for 1-2 hours or until firm.

YIELD: 6 SERVINGS.

From reading bedtime stories and kissing boo-boos when you were little to offering advice and a shoulder to lean on as you grew older, Mom has always been there for you. If you could give her the world, you would. What you can give her is a memorable Mother's Day that begins with a delicious family-style brunch.

Raise a frosty glass of refreshing Creamsicle Mimosa to the special lady in your life. The classic orange and vanilla flavor is sure to bring back fond childhood memories. Then, feast on mouthwatering fare that features the absolute freshest spring ingredients. Chicken and Asparagus Crepes, Spinach Hash Brown Frittata, Sweet Potato Hash and Cherry Almond Streusel Scones are among the sumptuous dishes that make the perfect "thank you" for all that Mom has done over these many wonderful years.

A CELEBRATION FOR MOM

MOTHER'S DAY
FAMILY BRUNCH

chicken and asparagus crepes

(PICTURED ON PAGE 182)

The crepes used in this recipe come from my mom's special collection.
To save time, I make them a day ahead, refrigerate and assemble the next day.

MARY SLOAN | BRIGHTON, MICHIGAN

3 eggs

1½ cups 2% milk

2 tablespoons butter, melted

1 cup all-purpose flour

¼ teaspoon salt

FILLING

1½ cups cut fresh asparagus (1-inch pieces)

1 small onion, chopped

1 teaspoon canola oil

2½ cups sliced fresh mushrooms

3 cups cubed rotisserie chicken

SAUCE

¼ cup butter, cubed

¼ cup all-purpose flour

¼ teaspoon salt

⅛ teaspoon pepper

1½ cups 2% milk

6 slices Swiss cheese, halved

⅔ cup shredded part-skim mozzarella cheese

1. In a large bowl, whisk the eggs, milk and butter. Combine flour and salt; add to egg mixture and mix well. Refrigerate for 1 hour.

2. Heat a lightly greased 8-in. nonstick skillet over medium heat; pour ¼ cup batter into center of skillet. Lift and tilt pan to coat bottom evenly. Cook until top appears dry; turn and cook 15-20 seconds longer. Remove to a wire rack. Repeat with remaining batter, greasing skillet as needed. When cool, stack crepes with waxed paper or paper towels in between.

3. Saute asparagus and onion in oil until tender. Add mushrooms and cook 2 minutes longer. Remove from the heat and stir in chicken. Set aside.

4. For sauce, in a small saucepan, melt butter over medium heat. Stir in flour, salt and pepper until smooth; gradually add milk. Bring to a boil; cook and stir for 2 minutes or until thickened.

5. Spread about ½ cup filling down the center of each crepe; top with 2 tablespoons sauce and 1 piece of Swiss cheese. Roll up and place seam side down in each of two greased 11-in. x 7-in. baking dishes. Sprinkle with mozzarella cheese.

6. Bake, uncovered, at 350° for 20-25 minutes or until bubbly.

YIELD: 12 SERVINGS.

creamsicle mimosa

(PICTURED ON PAGE 182)

Give a toast to your mom with this fizzy breakfast beverage. It tastes like a "grown-up" creamsicle!

DEIRDRE DEE COX | MILWAUKEE, WISCONSIN

2½ cups orange juice

1 cup half-and-half cream

¾ cup superfine sugar

4 teaspoons grated orange peel

2 bottles (750 milliliters each) Champagne or other sparkling wine

Fresh strawberries

1. Place the orange juice, cream, sugar and orange peel in a blender; cover and process until sugar is dissolved. Transfer to an 8-in. square dish. Freeze for 6 hours or overnight.

2. For each serving, scoop ¼ cup mix into a champagne glass; top with Champagne. Garnish with a strawberry and serve immediately.

YIELD: 16 SERVINGS (4 CUPS MIX).

For non-alcoholic version: *Substitute 2 bottles (750 milliliters each) of sparkling apple cider for the Champagne.*

berry breakfast parfaits

Hosting brunch but short on time? My quick, delicious and beautiful parfaits are the perfect solution. Feel free to mix and match your favorite berries.

LISA SPEER
PALM BEACH, FLORIDA

6½ cups frozen unsweetened raspberries

¼ cup packed brown sugar

¼ cup orange juice

2 tablespoons cornstarch

½ teaspoon grated orange peel

2 cups fresh blueberries

2 cups fresh blackberries

2 cups granola

4 cups vanilla Greek yogurt

Additional brown sugar, optional

1. Place the raspberries and the brown sugar in a blender; cover and process until pureed. Press through a sieve; discard seeds.

2. In a small saucepan, combine the raspberry puree, orange juice, cornstarch and orange peel. Cook and stir over medium heat until thickened and bubbly. Reduce heat to low; cook and stir 2 minutes longer. Remove from the heat; cool.

3. In eight parfait glasses, layer half of the raspberry sauce, berries, granola and yogurt. Repeat layers. Sprinkle with additional brown sugar if desired. Serve immediately.

YIELD: 8 SERVINGS.

cherry almond streusel scones

(PICTURED ON PAGE 183)

My kids and I love to mix the ingredients together and turn out these delicious scones.
They're tender, filled with the flavor of tart cherries and topped with a brown sugar-and-almond streusel.

TERESA RALSTON | NEW ALBANY, OHIO

2 cups all-purpose flour

6 tablespoons sugar

2 teaspoons baking powder

¼ teaspoon salt

6 tablespoons cold butter, cubed

¾ cup heavy whipping cream

1 egg, lightly beaten

½ teaspoon almond extract

¾ cup dried cherries

STREUSEL

2 tablespoons all-purpose flour

2 tablespoons brown sugar

¼ teaspoon ground cinnamon

Pinch salt

1 tablespoon cold butter

2 tablespoons sliced almonds

1. In a large bowl, combine the flour, sugar, baking powder and salt. Cut in butter until mixture resembles coarse crumbs. Whisk the cream, egg and extract; stir into crumb mixture just until moistened. Stir in cherries.

2. Transfer to a greased baking sheet. Pat into an 8-in. circle. Cut into eight wedges, but do not separate.

3. For streusel, combine the flour, brown sugar, cinnamon and salt: cut in the butter until crumbly. Stir in almonds. Sprinkle over dough.

4. Bake at 400° for 20-25 minutes or until golden brown. Serve scones warm.

YIELD: 8 SCONES.

MAKE BAKERY-PERFECT SCONES AT HOME

Most scone recipes suggest patting the dough into a circle. For proper baking, be sure the circle meets the dimensions noted in the recipe. Cut the dough into wedges with a dough scraper or knife. It may be helpful to flour the utensil's edge between cuts to prevent the dough from sticking to it.

blue cheese-apple strudels

It wouldn't be a family gathering at our house without this favorite strudel. The sweetness from the apples and the sharpness from the cheese create a heavenly combo wrapped in a buttery, flaky phyllo dough crust.

PATRICIA NIEH
PORTOLA VALLY, CALIFORNIA

- 3 medium tart apples, peeled and finely chopped
- 3 tablespoons lemon juice
- 1 teaspoon dried thyme
- ¼ teaspoon ground nutmeg
- ⅛ teaspoon coarsely ground pepper
- 2 cups (8 ounces) crumbled blue cheese
- ¼ cup chopped walnuts, toasted
- 12 sheets phyllo dough (14 inches x 9 inches)
- ¾ cup unsalted butter, melted
- 1 cup plus 2 tablespoons dry bread crumbs

1. In a large bowl, combine apples, lemon juice, thyme, nutmeg and pepper. Toss to coat. Add cheese and walnuts; set aside.

2. Carefully place one sheet of phyllo dough on a work surface. Brush sheet with butter and sprinkle with 2 tablespoons bread crumbs. Layer with two more sheets of phyllo, brushing each sheet with butter and sprinkling with bread crumbs. Layer with another sheet of phyllo. (Keep remaining phyllo dough covered with plastic wrap and a damp towel to prevent it from drying out.)

3. Spoon 1½ cups apple mixture along the long end of phyllo to within 2 in. of edges. Fold long sides 2 in. over filling. Roll up jelly-roll style, starting with a long side. Repeat, making two more strudels.

4. Transfer strudels to a parchment paper-lined 15-in. x 10-in. x 1-in. baking pan. With a sharp knife, cut slits in the top of each strudel. Brush with remaining butter. Bake at 375° for 20-25 minutes or until golden brown. Serve warm.

YIELD: 3 STRUDELS (8 SLICES EACH).

vanilla bean cake
with white chocolate ganache

For a distinctive dessert with unforgettable flavor, I recommend this stunning cake.
Feel free to substitute your favorite jam to lend your own touch to this signature treat.

LISA BOGAR | COVENTRY, VERMONT

6 eggs

1 cup unsalted butter, softened

1¾ cups sugar, divided

2 teaspoons vanilla extract

1 vanilla bean

3 cups cake flour

3 teaspoons baking powder

½ teaspoon salt

1 cup whole milk

WHITE CHOCOLATE GANACHE

12 ounces white baking chocolate, finely chopped

½ cup heavy whipping cream

SWISS BUTTERCREAM

1 cup sugar

½ teaspoon cream of tartar

4 egg whites

1 cup unsalted butter, softened

7 tablespoons shortening

1 teaspoon vanilla extract

FILLING

⅓ cup apricot preserves

1 cup sliced fresh strawberries

GARNISH

Additional sliced fresh strawberries

1. Line two greased 9-in. round baking pans with parchment paper and grease the paper; set aside. Separate eggs; let eggs stand at room temperature for 30 minutes.

2. In a large bowl, cream butter and 1 cup sugar until light and fluffy. Add egg yolks, one at a time, beating well after each addition. Beat in vanilla. Split vanilla bean and scrape seeds into creamed mixture; discard bean. Combine the flour, baking powder and salt; add to the creamed mixture alternately with milk, beating well after each addition.

3. In a small bowl, beat egg whites on medium speed until soft peaks form. Gradually add remaining sugar, about 2 tablespoons at a time, beating on high until stiff peaks form. Fold a fourth of egg whites into the batter, then fold in remaining whites. Transfer to prepared baking pans.

4. Bake at 350° for 35-40 minutes or until a toothpick inserted near the center comes out clean. Cool for 10 minutes before removing from pans to wire racks to cool completely.

5. Place chocolate in a small bowl. In a small saucepan, bring cream just to a boil. Pour over chocolate; whisk until smooth. Cool, stirring occasionally, to room temperature, about 30 minutes. Beat with an electric mixer until ganache is double in volume, about 2 minutes.

6. For buttercream, in a small bowl, combine sugar and cream of tartar. Place egg whites in a double boiler or metal bowl over simmering water; stir in the sugar mixture.

7. Constantly whisk egg mixture until mixture reaches 120-130°. (Do not overheat.) Stirring gently, keep the egg white mixture at 120-130° for 2 minutes. Immediately transfer to a mixing bowl. With a whisk attachment, beat egg white mixture on high speed for 5 minutes. Reduce speed; beat 5 minutes longer or until cool and stiff. Transfer to a large bowl.

8. In the same mixing bowl with whisk attachment, beat the butter, the shortening and vanilla until light and fluffy. With a spatula, stir a fourth of the egg white mixture into creamed mixture until no white streaks remain. Fold in the remaining egg white mixture until combined. If the frosting is not completely smooth, attach paddle beater to mixer and beat on low speed for about 1 minute.

9. Cut each cake horizontally into two layers. Place bottom layer on a serving plate; spread with half of ganache. Top with another cake layer. Carefully spread with the apricot preserves; top with sliced strawberries. Place the third cake layer on the top; spread with the remaining ganache. Top with remaining cake layer.

10. Spread the buttercream frosting over top and sides of the cake. Top frosted cake with the additional sliced fresh strawberries.

YIELD: 16 SERVINGS.

DRESS IT UP OR DOWN!

From simple to spectacular, Vanilla Bean Cake with White Chocolate Ganache makes a statement. To achieve the eye-catching ruffle design shown on the cover, we used the La Girolle ruffle maker tool from Albert Uster Imports (www.auiswisscatalogue.com/501019/2-RUFF.html).

spinach hash brown frittata

(PICTURED ON PAGE 183)

Mornings are always busy around my house, so I appreciate this recipe for its ease. Make it the night before, cover with plastic wrap, pop it in the refrigerator and bake the next morning!

GILDA LESTER | MILLSBORO, DELAWARE

1 large onion, finely chopped

1 tablespoon olive oil

2 garlic cloves, minced

1 package (10 ounces) frozen chopped spinach, thawed and squeezed dry

¼ teaspoon salt

¼ teaspoon pepper

2 ounces pancetta or bacon strips, finely chopped

3 cups frozen shredded hash brown potatoes, thawed

8 eggs, lightly beaten

1 cup 2% milk

1 cup (4 ounces) fontina cheese, divided

1 cup (4 ounces) shredded cheddar cheese, divided

¼ cup minced fresh parsley

1 tablespoon Worcestershire sauce

1 teaspoon ground mustard

¼ teaspoon ground nutmeg

1. In a large skillet, saute onion in oil until tender. Add garlic; cook 1 minute longer. Stir in the spinach, salt and pepper. Remove from the heat.

2. In another skillet, cook pancetta over medium heat until crisp. Remove to paper towels with a slotted spoon; drain.

3. In a greased 11-in. x 7-in. baking dish, layer the hash browns, spinach mixture and pancetta. In a large bowl, whisk the eggs, milk, ½ cup fontina cheese, ½ cup cheddar cheese, parsley, Worcestershire sauce, mustard and nutmeg; pour over top. Sprinkle with remaining cheeses.

4. Bake, uncovered, at 350° for 35-40 minutes or until a knife inserted near the center comes out clean. Let stand for 10 minutes before cutting.

YIELD: 8 SERVINGS.

sweet potato hash

(PICTURED ON PAGE 183)

Forget traditional hash with plain, ol' potatoes. Add color, flavor and extra nutrition with sweet potatoes!

KEN KINGERY | MOSCOW, IDAHO

1 tablespoon brown sugar

2 teaspoons kosher salt

2 teaspoons smoked paprika

1 teaspoon garlic powder

1 teaspoon chili powder

¼ teaspoon dried rosemary, crushed

4 medium sweet potatoes, peeled and cubed

2 tablespoons olive oil

2 medium red and/or yellow sweet peppers, chopped

½ large sweet onion, thinly sliced

3 garlic cloves, minced

2 fully cooked chicken sausage links, chopped

2 tablespoons minced fresh thyme

1. In a small bowl, combine the first six ingredients; set aside.

2. In a large skillet, saute sweet potatoes in oil in batches until lightly browned. Add the peppers, onion and garlic; saute until vegetables are tender. Stir in the sausage, thyme and spice mixture. Cook 5 minutes longer or until heated through.

YIELD: 8 SERVINGS.

mother's day doodle cake

*Edible "ink" lets kids write—or draw—a sweet Mother's Day message to Mom.
The fun-to-use markers work great on frosted cookies, sandwich bread and bagels too!*

☐ Prepared 13-in. x 9-in. box cake mix, cooled and turned out onto serving tray

☐ 1 sheet white or vanilla fondant

☐ Wilton Food Writer™ edible color markers

1. Roll out the fondant to a size that is just slightly larger than the cake.

2. To transfer the fondant onto the cake, drape as much as you are able to over and around the rolling pin, and with your other hand carry the excess portion of the fondant; lay it over the cake.

3. Smooth over the edges and cut off any excess pieces.

4. Using edible color markers, write or draw on the fondant. (Tip: Do not push down with the marker or it might indent or even tear the fondant.)

Vive la France! You don't have to be French to enjoy the region's rich and flavorful cuisine. In fact, hosting a La Fête Nationale, or Bastille Day, party is the perfect excuse for indulging in your favorite French fare.

From a few decadent desserts to sophisticated (yet very achievable) entrees and everything in between, the recipes showcased here make it easier than ever to bring the flavors of faraway France to your very own backyard soiree.

A bite of Gruyere & Caramelized Onion Tarts, fresh Mini Tomato Sandwiches and impressive Seared Tuna with Nicoise Potato Salad, and your taste buds will declare independence from boring flavors and ordinary party foods.

CELEBRATE ALFRESCO!
Seared Tuna with Nicoise Potato Salad (p. 196)
Mini Tomato Sandwiches (p. 194)
Gruyere & Caramelized Onion Tarts (p. 194)

BASTILLE DAY FÊTE

gruyere & caramelized onion tarts

(PICTURED ON PAGE 193)

Garlic and onion is a match made in heaven in my opinion, so I love creating new recipes to showcase the pair. Gruyere cheese adds impeccable flavor to my eye-catching starter.

LISA SPEER | PALM BEACH, FLORIDA

1   large sweet onion, thinly sliced

2   tablespoons olive oil

1   tablespoon butter

3   garlic cloves, minced

¼   teaspoon salt

¼   teaspoon pepper

1   package (17.3 ounces) frozen puff pastry, thawed

1   cup (4 ounces) shredded Gruyere or Swiss cheese

¼   cup grated Parmesan cheese

2   tablespoons minced fresh thyme or 2 teaspoons dried thyme

1. In a large skillet, saute onion in oil and butter until softened. Reduce heat to medium-low; cook, uncovered, for 40 minutes or until deep golden brown, stirring occasionally. Add garlic; cook 1 minute longer. Stir in salt and pepper.

2. Unfold each puff pastry sheet onto an ungreased baking sheet. Using a knife, score decorative lines around the edges of each pastry. Spread onion mixture to within ½ in. of edges. Sprinkle with cheeses and thyme.

3. Bake at 400° for 12-15 minutes or until golden brown. Cut each tart into 12 pieces. Serve warm.

YIELD: 2 DOZEN.

mini tomato sandwiches

(PICTURED ON PAGE 193)

I grew up enjoying tomato sandwiches and think this slightly upscale version is a tasty choice when dining "alfresco."

SHANNON AVRA | LITTLE ROCK, ARKANSAS

1   package (3 ounces) cream cheese, softened

¼   cup mayonnaise

2   teaspoons minced fresh basil

¼   teaspoon salt, divided

¼   teaspoon pepper, divided

1   French bread baguette (10½ ounces)

8   ounces Brie cheese, thinly sliced

4   plum tomatoes, sliced

1. In a small bowl, combine the cream cheese, mayonnaise, basil and ⅛ teaspoon each salt and pepper. Cover and refrigerate for at least 4 hours.

2. Cut baguette in half horizontally. Spread cream cheese mixture over baguette bottom. Layer with Brie cheese and tomato slices. Sprinkle with remaining salt and pepper. Replace top. Cut into four slices.

YIELD: 4 SERVINGS.

summer bounty ratatouille

The name says it all! Make use of your garden's surplus with this comforting dish. I highly recommend accompanying it with some freshly baked bread or serving it over cooked pasta.

PHYLLIS JACQUES
VENICE, FLORIDA

- 1 large eggplant, peeled and cut into 1-inch cubes
- 1 teaspoon kosher salt
- 2 medium onions, peeled and chopped
- 2 medium sweet red peppers, cut into ½ inch strips
- 3 tablespoons olive oil
- 4 garlic cloves, minced
- 4 medium zucchini, quartered and cut into ½-inch slices
- 3 cans (14½ ounces each) diced tomatoes, undrained
- 1½ cups water
- ¼ cup tomato paste
- 1 tablespoon herbes de Provence
- ½ teaspoon salt
- ½ teaspoon pepper
- ¼ cup chopped fresh basil
- 2 tablespoons minced fresh rosemary
- 2 tablespoons minced fresh parsley
- 2 French bread baguettes (10½ ounces each), cubed and toasted

1. Place eggplant in a colander over a plate; sprinkle with kosher salt and toss. Let eggplant stand for 30 minutes. Rinse and drain well.

2. In a Dutch oven, saute onion and peppers in oil until tender. Add garlic; cook 1 minute longer. Stir in the zucchini, tomatoes, water, tomato paste, herbes de Provence, salt and pepper. Bring to a boil. Reduce heat; simmer, uncovered, for 40-45 minutes or until zucchini is tender. Stir in the basil, rosemary and parsley. Serve over baguette cubes.

YIELD: 13 SERVINGS.

EDITOR'S NOTE: *Look for herbes de Provence in the spice aisle.*

easy french iced coffee

(PICTURED AT RIGHT)

I love to serve this icy, Parisian-inspired beverage when I entertain.
It's delicious, unique and the request of all my guests.

JENNIFER MARTIN | MYERSTOWN, PENNSYLVANIA

3 cups strong brewed hot coffee

1½ cups sugar

4 cups 2% milk

2 cups half-and-half cream

2 teaspoons vanilla extract

1. In a large bowl, whisk coffee and sugar until the sugar is dissolved. Cool. Stir in the milk, cream and vanilla. Freeze in a 3-qt. freezer container for 8 hours or overnight. Transfer to the refrigerator 4 hours before serving. Stir until slushy. Serve immediately.

YIELD: 10 SERVINGS.

seared tuna with nicoise potato salad

(PICTURED ON PAGE 192)

My husband and I traveled to Europe where we had the best Nicoise salad with freshly caught tuna.
This is my take on that fabulous meal. All you need to complete it is a fork and a piece of crusty baguette!

CHERYL WOODSON | LIBERTY, MISSOURI

¾ pound fingerling potatoes, cut into 1-inch pieces

2 tablespoons olive oil

2 medium heirloom tomatoes, seeded and chopped

2 plum tomatoes, seeded and chopped

1 small red onion, chopped

½ cup pickled dill green beans, cut into ½-inch pieces

½ cup pitted Greek olives, chopped

2 hard-cooked eggs, chopped

1 tablespoon capers, drained

DRESSING

¼ cup olive oil

¼ cup lemon juice

1 garlic clove, minced

1 teaspoon grated lemon peel

1 teaspoon anchovy paste

¼ teaspoon pepper

TUNA:

4 tuna steaks (4 ounces each)

2 tablespoons olive oil

½ teaspoon salt

¼ teaspoon pepper

French bread baguette slices and minced fresh basil, optional

1. Place potatoes on a greased 15-in. x 10-in. x 1-in. baking pan. Drizzle with oil; toss to coat.

2. Bake, uncovered, at 425° for 30-35 minutes or until tender, stirring every 10 minutes. Cool.

3. In a large bowl, combine the potatoes, tomatoes, onion, beans, olives, eggs and capers. In a small bowl, whisk dressing ingredients. Drizzle over salad and toss to coat.

4. Brush steaks with oil; sprinkle with salt and pepper. In a large skillet, cook tuna over medium-high heat for 2-3 minutes on each side for medium-rare or until slightly pink in the center. Cut into ½-in. slices. Divide potato salad among four plates. Top with tuna. Serve with baguette and sprinkle with basil if desired.

YIELD: 4 SERVINGS.

chocolate-hazelnut banana crepes

A favorite French specialty, crepes can be served with a variety of fillings. I enjoy them stuffed with a creamy chocolate-hazelnut spread and bananas lightly sauteed in brown sugar and butter. It tastes so special but requires very little effort.

CATHY HALL
PHOENIX, ARIZONA

- 2   eggs
- 2   egg whites
- ¾   cup water
- ½   cup 2% milk
- 1   tablespoon canola oil
- 1   cup all-purpose flour
- 1   tablespoon sugar
- ½   teaspoon salt
- 2   tablespoons butter
- 2   tablespoons brown sugar
- 4   medium bananas, peeled and sliced
- ⅓   cup Nutella

1. In a large bowl, whisk the eggs, egg whites, water, milk and oil. Combine flour, sugar and salt; add to egg mixture and mix well. Refrigerate for 1 hour.

2. Heat a lightly greased 8-in. nonstick skillet over medium heat; pour ¼ cup batter into center of skillet. Lift and tilt pan to coat bottom evenly. Cook until top appears dry; turn and cook 15-20 seconds longer. Remove to a wire rack. Repeat with remaining batter, greasing skillet as needed. When cool, stack crepes with waxed paper or paper towels in between.

3. In a large skillet, melt butter over medium-low heat. Stir in brown sugar until blended. Add bananas; cook for 2-3 minutes or until bananas are glazed and slightly softened, stirring gently. Remove from the heat.

4. Spread Nutella over each crepe; top with bananas. Roll up and serve.

YIELD: 10 SERVINGS.

pine-nut parmesan chicken with rosemary beurre blanc

Pine nuts lend fantastic flavor and rich texture to this company-worthy dish. The sophisticated entree is incredibly doable, yet adds plenty of French flair.

JULIE OHNSTAD | MARIETTA, GEORGIA

4 boneless skinless chicken breast halves (4 ounces each)

½ cup dry bread crumbs

2 tablespoons grated Parmesan cheese

4½ teaspoons pine nuts

1 garlic clove

½ teaspoon minced fresh rosemary

½ teaspoon Italian seasoning

¼ teaspoon kosher salt

1 egg, beaten

4½ teaspoons butter

1 tablespoon olive oil

ROSEMARY BEURRE BLANC

½ cup white wine or chicken broth

2 shallots, chopped

3 tablespoons white wine vinegar

2 tablespoons lemon juice

3 garlic cloves, minced

¼ teaspoon salt

½ cup heavy whipping cream

½ cup butter

2 teaspoons minced fresh rosemary

¼ cup pine nuts, toasted

1. Flatten chicken to ¼-in. thickness; set aside. Place the bread crumbs, cheese, pine nuts, garlic, rosemary, Italian seasoning and salt in a food processor; cover and process until blended. Transfer to a shallow bowl. Place egg in another shallow bowl. Dip chicken breast halves in egg, then coat with bread crumb mixture.

2. In a large skillet, brown chicken in butter and olive oil. Transfer to a greased 11-in. x 7-in. baking dish. Bake, uncovered, at 375° for 10-15 minutes or until a thermometer reads 170°.

3. In a small saucepan, combine the wine, shallots, vinegar, lemon juice, garlic and salt. Bring to a boil; cook until liquid is reduced by three-fourths.

4. Reduce heat to low; stir in cream. Gradually whisk in butter, 1 tablespoon at a time, allowing butter to melt between additions. Remove from the heat; stir in rosemary. Drizzle over chicken and sprinkle with pine nuts.

YIELD: 4 SERVINGS.

A LITTLE BACKGROUND ON BASTILLE DAY

Similar in spirit to the American Independence Day or Canada's Canada Day celebrations, Bastille Day is a festive event that boasts spectacular fireworks and patriotic processions across the country. It commemorates the 1789 destruction of the Bastille prison in central Paris, a symbol of France's first steps toward democracy.

set the stage for your soiree

Some extra fabric creates a chic and effortless backdrop for your Bastille Day buffet.
Clip vintage postcards and Parisian signs over the fabric for an "ooh-la-la" finishing touch.

☐ fabric shears

☐ assorted fabric

☐ twine or clothesline cut to desired length

☐ vintage French postcards, pictures or postcard-size artwork

☐ wire clips or wooden clothespins

1. Using the fabric shears, cut the assorted fabric into strips that measure approximately 1-1/2 inches wide and 9 inches long.

2. Loop a strip of fabric around clothesline, starting in the center. Secure the fabric to the clothesline by tying a knot. Continue adding strips of fabric to both ends of clothesline (strips should be spaced close together). Leave 6 inches of clothesline on either end.

3. Evenly space and secure vintage postcards over the fabric with wire clips or wooden clothespins.

F armers markets, bustling with activity, are a sure sign that spring has sprung. They're also a great excuse for inviting family and friends for a meal that is fresh and healthy. What a terrifc reason to celebrate fresh produce and your local community of farmers!

After arriving home with your resusable bag brimming with garden-fresh produce and fragrant herbs, you won't want to wait another minute to whip up this market-fresh feast.

While you prepare Mushroom Scallop Primavera and Spring Essence Soup with Pistou, why not sip a glass of refreshing Kiwi-Mint Sparkling Water and nibble on Parmesan-Stuffed Artichokes? One bite and you'll understand why locally grown food is always the talk of the town.

FARM-FRESH FARE

FARMERS MARKET
SPRING FEAST

mushroom scallop primavera

(PICTURED ON PAGE 200)

*Although hunting morels in the spring was the inspiration for this delicious pasta dish,
I often purchase the mushrooms at my local farmers market. This is a light and healthy lunch.*

LIZA WALLNER | MILWAUKEE, WISCONSIN

8 ounces uncooked fettuccine

12 large fresh morel mushrooms

8 ounces sliced fresh shiitake mushrooms

4 tablespoons olive oil, divided

2 tablespoons butter

1 medium zucchini, cut into ¼-inch slices

¾ pound fresh peas, shelled (about ¾ cup)

12 sea scallops (about 1 pound)

½ teaspoon salt, divided

¼ teaspoon pepper, divided

2 green onions, thinly sliced

2 tablespoons lemon juice

1 teaspoon grated lemon peel

1. Cook fettuccine according to package directions. Meanwhile, in a large skillet, saute mushrooms in 1 tablespoon oil and 1 tablespoon butter in batches until tender; remove and keep warm. In the same skillet, saute zucchini and peas in 1 tablespoon oil until crisp-tender; remove and set aside.

2. Pat scallops dry with paper towels; sprinkle with ¼ teaspoon salt and ⅛ teaspoon pepper. In the same skillet, heat remaining oil over medium-high heat. Add scallops; cook for 1-2 minutes on each side or until golden brown and firm. Remove and keep warm.

3. Drain fettuccine; return to skillet. Add the vegetable mixture, green onions, lemon juice, peel, and remaining salt and pepper; heat through. Serve with scallops.

YIELD: 4 SERVINGS.

kiwi-mint sparkling water

(PICTURED ON PAGE 201)

*Why buy expensive fruit-flavored sparkling waters when you can create your own?
The Taste of Home Test Kitchen staff used kiwi, lemon and fresh mint,
but feel free to use the fruits and herbs you like best or happen to have on hand.*

TASTE OF HOME TEST KITCHEN

2 bottles (1 liter each) carbonated water, chilled, divided

2 medium kiwifruit, peeled and thinly sliced

1 medium lemon, thinly sliced

½ cup fresh mint leaves

Ice cubes

1. In a large pitcher, combine 1 bottle carbonated water, kiwi, lemon and mint. Refrigerate for at least 30 minutes.

2. Just before serving, stir in remaining carbonated water. Serve over ice.

YIELD: 8 SERVINGS (1 CUP EACH).

farmers market corn salad

I love fresh sweet corn—especially grilled—so I am always looking for innovative ways to serve it. This recipe uses corn right from the cob and combines it with fresh basil.

HARAS CINDIE | JUPITER, FLORIDA

6   medium ears sweet corn

3   tablespoons butter, melted

½   cup chopped cucumber

½   cup fresh or frozen shelled edamame, thawed

½   cup julienned radishes

¼   cup fresh basil leaves, thinly sliced

DRESSING

¼   cup olive oil

3   tablespoons sherry vinegar

1   tablespoon white balsamic vinegar

½   teaspoon salt

Dash pepper

1. Brush corn with butter. Grill corn, covered, over medium heat for 10-12 minutes or until lightly browned, turning and basting occasionally.

2. Cut corn from cobs; transfer to a large bowl. Add vegetables and basil. In a small bowl, whisk dressing ingredients. Pour over vegetables; toss to coat.

YIELD: 6 SERVINGS.

parmesan-stuffed artichokes

(PICTURED ON PAGE 200)

*Because artichokes have been part of my Italian heritage for many years,
I try to cook with them as often as I can. While they can be a little
time-consuming to prepare, the flavorful result is well worth the effort.*

SUE BROWN | WEST BEND, WISCONSIN

2 tablespoons lemon juice

9 baby artichokes

¼ cup butter

2 green onions, chopped

1 garlic clove, minced

1½ cups soft bread crumbs

2 medium tomatoes, seeded and chopped

½ cup plus 2 tablespoons grated Romano cheese, divided

¼ cup minced fresh parsley

¼ teaspoon salt

¼ teaspoon pepper

1. In a large bowl, combine 8 cups water and lemon juice. Remove and discard outer leaves of artichokes. Using a vegetable peeler, peel the stem of an artichoke. Cut off ½-in. from the top; cut in half lengthwise. With a spoon, carefully remove fuzzy center and discard. Place in lemon water and repeat with remaining artichokes.

2. Drain artichokes and place in a Dutch oven; add 1 in. of water. Bring to a boil. Reduce heat; cover and simmer for 10-15 minutes or until tender. Drain.

3. In a large skillet, saute onions and garlic in butter until tender. Remove from the heat; stir in the bread crumbs, tomatoes, ½ cup cheese, parsley, salt and pepper.

4. Spoon heaping tablespoonfuls of crumb mixture into each artichoke half; sprinkle with remaining cheese. Transfer to a greased 15-in. x 10-in. x 1-in. baking pan. Bake at 375° for 20-25 minutes or until golden brown.

YIELD: 1½ DOZEN.

pea shoot salad with lemon vinaigrette

*Pea shoots are the tips of the vines and the top set of leaves of the pea plant.
The tender, crispy shoots make lovely edible garnishes, but they're also tasty in salads
such as this springtime specialty dressed in a lemon vinaigrette created by our Test Kitchen.*

TASTE OF HOME TEST KITCHEN

2 medium lemons, halved and seeded

2 teaspoons plus ¼ cup olive oil, divided

6 cups spring mix salad greens

3 cups torn pea shoots or watercress

½ cup sliced radishes

1¼ teaspoons sugar

1 teaspoon Dijon mustard

¼ teaspoon salt

⅛ teaspoon pepper

1. Rub lemons with 2 teaspoons oil; place in a greased 9-in. square baking dish. Bake, uncovered, at 425° for 15-20 minutes or until tender.

2. Meanwhile, in a large bowl, combine the salad greens, pea shoots and radishes.

3. Cool lemons slightly. Squeeze juice into a small bowl. Finely grate ½ teaspoon lemon peel; add to the bowl. Whisk in the sugar, mustard, salt, pepper and remaining oil. Drizzle over salad; toss to coat.

YIELD: 4 SERVINGS.

rhubarb tart with shortbread crust

Rhubarb is one of the things I most look forward to every spring. So I was especially pleased with how my recipe for rhubarb tart turned out. I'm not sure if it's the creamy texture, pretty color or buttery crust, but it's a hit whenever I serve it.

EMILY SEEFELDT
RED WING, MINNESOTA

3¾ cups chopped fresh rhubarb (about 1¼ pounds)

¼ cup sugar

2 tablespoons water

CRUST

1 cup all-purpose flour

½ cup ground pecans

½ cup cold butter, cubed

⅓ cup confectioners' sugar

¼ teaspoon salt

CURD

6 egg yolks

½ cup sugar

1 tablespoon lemon juice

1½ teaspoons grated lemon peel

5 tablespoons butter, cubed

4 drops red food coloring, optional

Additional confectioners' sugar

1. In a large saucepan, bring rhubarb, sugar and water to a boil. Reduce heat; cook and stir until thickened and rhubarb is tender. Cool slightly. Transfer to a food processor; cover and process until mixture is smooth; set aside.

2. For crust, place the flour, pecans, butter, confectioners' sugar and salt in a food processor; cover and process until crumbly. Press onto the bottom and up the sides of an ungreased 9-in. tart pan with removable bottom. Bake crust at 350° for 18-20 minutes or until lightly browned.

3. Meanwhile, in a small heavy saucepan over medium heat, whisk the egg yolks, sugar, lemon juice, peel and rhubarb mixture until blended. Add butter; cook until butter is melted, whisking constantly. Stir in food coloring if desired; pour into prepared crust.

4. Bake at 350° 12-15 minutes longer or until center is almost set. Cool completely on a wire rack. Refrigerate for at least 1 hour. Just before serving, dust with confectioners' sugar.

YIELD: 12 SERVINGS.

spring essence soup with pistou

(PICTURED ON PAGE 201)

*To create this soup, I went out to my garden and picked what
I had available. I found oregano, leeks, asparagus and rhubarb.*

LAURIE BOCK | LYNDEN, WASHINGTON

- 1 medium leek (white portion only), cut into ¼-inch slices
- 1 large carrot, chopped
- 1 small sweet red pepper, chopped
- 1 tablespoon olive oil
- 2 garlic cloves, minced
- 4 cups chicken stock

- 10 small new potatoes, quartered
- 6 fresh asparagus spears, cut into 1-inch pieces
- 1 cup chopped fresh rhubarb
- 1 teaspoon sugar
- ½ teaspoon salt
- ¼ teaspoon pepper

PISTOU
- ½ cup loosely packed fresh oregano
- 2 tablespoons chopped hazelnuts, toasted
- 1½ teaspoons olive oil
- ½ teaspoon minced garlic
- ⅛ teaspoon salt

1. In a large saucepan, saute the leek, carrot and red pepper in oil until crisp-tender. Add garlic; cook 1 minute longer. Stir in stock and potatoes. Bring to a boil. Reduce heat; cover and simmer for 5 minutes. Stir in the asparagus, rhubarb, sugar, salt and pepper; cover and simmer 4-6 minutes longer or until vegetables are tender.

2. Meanwhile, place the oregano, hazelnuts, oil, garlic and salt in a food processor; cover and pulse until blended. Serve with soup.

YIELD: 6 SERVINGS.

EDITOR'S NOTE: Pistou is an olive oil-based sauce that originated in the south of France and is very similar to its Italian "cousin," pesto.

shaved asparagus salad

I love cooking with garden-fresh ingredients because the end result is usually tasty and healthy. Shaving the asparagus stalks into thin strips, using a vegetable peeler, creates visual appeal for this spring favorite.

CHRIS MIRELL | EL DORADO HILLS, CALIFORNIA

- 1 pound fresh asparagus
- 1 small carrot
- ½ cup shaved Parmesan cheese
- 2 tablespoons lemon juice
- 2 tablespoons olive oil
- ¼ teaspoon kosher salt
- ⅛ teaspoon pepper

1. Using a vegetable peeler, cut asparagus and carrot into very thin lengthwise strips; transfer to a small bowl.

2. In a small bowl, whisk the remaining ingredients; pour over salad and toss to coat. Serve immediately.

YIELD: 6 SERVINGS.

resusable plastic tote

Turn plastic shopping bags into a cute reusable plastic tote.

- ☐ 10-16 plastic shopping bags
- ☐ parchment paper
- ☐ iron and ironing board
- ☐ standard sewing supplies
- ☐ craft knife
- ☐ 1-1/2-in. wide grosgrain ribbon
- ☐ duct tape or sheets (optional)
- ☐ tacky glue (optional)

1. Turn bag inside out and lay flat on a level surface. Cut straight across the top and bottom eliminating handles and opening bag bottom. Flatten cut bag forming two layers of plastic. Trim 5-8 bags in all. Stack cut bags with edges matching and printing on interior.

2. Line ironing board with parchment paper. Place stacked bags on top of parchment paper. Cover top of bags with more parchment paper.

3. Set iron to medium heat. Iron on top of parchment paper for a few minutes. Then flip stacked bags over and iron on top of parchment paper again for a few more minutes. Continue flipping stacked bags and ironing a few minutes at a time on each side. Be sure to iron on top of the parchment paper and never directly on bags. When bags start to fuse, they will wrinkle slightly and shrink around the edges. When completely fused, remove parchment paper. Set fused plastic aside; let cool.

4. Repeat Steps 1-3 to create another piece of fused plastic.

5. Place pieces of fused plastic with edges matching. Trim edges even, forming desired size matching rectangles.

6. Using a straight stitch and ½-in. seam allowance, sew around three sides of the fused plastic pieces joining them together. If desired, fold down opening edge 3/4-in. and stitch hem in place.

7. (Optional) Cut stripes, flowers or other desired shapes from duct tape or sheets to decorate exterior sides of bag.

8. For handles, mark a dot about 1-in. down and 2-in. in from each top corner on each side of the bag. Use a craft knife to cut a very small "X" shape on the four marked dots. Cut two identical pieces of ribbon at desired length. On one side of the bag, thread a few inches of each end of a ribbon piece through the two small "X"-shaped cuts. Knot each ribbon end to secure handle in place. Repeat with other ribbon piece on other side of bag. Trim ribbon ends as desired. If needed, secure handles with a drop of tacky glue at the base of each knot.

At the very first sign of summer, you see them: eager cooks who can't wait to fire up the grill and savor that enticing flame-kissed flavor. Nothing brings out the true essence of meat, fish, veggies—even fruit—like grilling.

Add depth and dimension to basic ingredients as you transform them into barbecued masterpieces that prove your grill isn't just for great burgers and hot dogs.

Flaky and flavorful Tuscan-Style Grilled Trout sets the tone for this succulent summer spread. Then, page through the rest of the chapter to find other delights such as Grilled Vegetable & Goat Cheese Napoleons, Grilled Shrimp Salads with Coconut Vinaigrette, Ginger Pound Cake S'Mores and more.

FLAME-KISSED FAVORITES
Tuscan-Styled Grilled Trout (p. 210)

GRILLING WITH A TWIST

tuscan-style grilled trout
(PICTURED ON PAGE 208)

My husband is an avid fisherman, so I am challenged to create recipes featuring his catch of the day. The Tuscan accents really shine through in this one, making it a favorite grilled entree.

ROXANNE CHAN | ALBANY, CALIFORNIA

4   pan-dressed trout (about 8 ounces each)

1   tablespoon olive oil

½   cup shredded zucchini

¼   cup chopped roasted sweet red peppers

2   tablespoons tapenade or ripe olive bruschetta topping

1   tablespoon minced fresh parsley

1   garlic clove, minced

1   teaspoon balsamic vinegar

RELISH

2   large tomatoes, chopped

½   cup chopped fennel bulb

1   green onion, thinly sliced

2   tablespoons pine nuts, toasted

2   tablespoons minced fresh basil

1   teaspoon lemon juice

½   teaspoon lemon-pepper seasoning

1. Rub trout with oil. In a small bowl, combine the zucchini, red peppers, tapenade, parsley, garlic and vinegar; spoon into fish cavities.

2. Place fish in a well-greased grill basket. Grill, covered, over medium heat for 8-10 minutes or until fish is browned on the bottom. Turn; grill 5-7 minutes longer or until fish flakes easily with a fork.

3. In a small bowl, combine the relish ingredients; serve relish with trout.

YIELD: 4 SERVINGS (3 CUPS RELISH).

THE PERFECT CATCH FOR GRILLING

Grilling fish is simple when you follow a few helpful hints.

• Use two very big spatulas to aid in flipping the fish.

• Watch fish closely; it cooks quickly.

• Thick steaks and slabs, preferably with skin, and many kinds of whole fish, gutted and cleaned but not boned, are best for grilling.

grilled vegetable & goat cheese napoleons

Vegetarian or not, your guests will savor this meatless entree at your next summer soiree.

JOAN MEYER | NEW YORK, NEW YORK

2 plum tomatoes, halved lengthwise

¼ cup olive oil, divided

⅛ teaspoon dried oregano

⅛ teaspoon dried basil

¾ teaspoon salt, divided

½ teaspoon pepper, divided

1 large zucchini, cut into ½-inch slices

1 large yellow summer squash, cut into ½-inch slices

4 large portobello mushrooms

4 slices eggplant (½ inch thick)

1 package (5.3 ounces) fresh goat cheese

1 teaspoon minced fresh parsley

1 teaspoon minced garlic, divided

4 ounces fresh mozzarella cheese, cut into 4 slices

1 package (10 ounces) fresh spinach

¼ cup balsamic vinaigrette

1. Brush tomatoes with 2 teaspoons oil; sprinkle with herbs and ¼ teaspoon salt and pepper. Transfer to 15-in. x 10-in. x 1-in. baking pan. Bake at 350° for 20-25 minutes.

2. Brush zucchini and yellow squash with 2 tablespoons oil; sprinkle with ¼ teaspoon salt. Place vegetables in a grill wok or basket. Grill, uncovered, over medium heat for 8-12 minutes, stirring occasionally.

3. Remove and discard the mushroom stems and gills. Brush the mushrooms and eggplant with 1 tablespoon oil; sprinkle with remaining salt.

4. Grill mushrooms, covered, over medium heat for 12-15 minutes. Grill eggplant, covered, over medium heat for 4-5 minutes on each side. Combine goat cheese, parsley, ½ teaspoon garlic and remaining pepper. Place mushrooms on a greased baking sheet; spread each with 2 teaspoons cheese mixture. Layer with zucchini, squash, 2 teaspoons cheese mixture, eggplant and remaining cheese mixture. Top with mozzarella cheese and tomato. Bake at 350° for 8-10 minutes or until cheese is melted.

5. Saute remaining garlic in remaining oil for 1 minute. Add spinach; cook for 4-5 minutes or until wilted. Divide among four plates; top each with a mushroom stack. Drizzle with vinaigrette.

YIELD: 4 SERVINGS.

Editor's Note: *If you do not have a grill wok or basket, use a disposable foil pan. Poke holes in the bottom of the pan to allow liquid to drain.*

ginger pound cake s'mores

Kids and adults won't be able to resist this fun twist on campfire s'mores. Pound cake replaces the traditional graham cracker, while crystallized ginger adds a unique touch.

PETER HALFERTY | CORPUS CHRISTI, TEXAS

8 large marshmallows

5 ounces bittersweet chocolate candy bars, broken into eight pieces

8 teaspoons crystallized ginger, optional

16 slices pound cake (¼ inch thick)

3 tablespoons butter, softened

1. Cut each marshmallow lengthwise into four slices. Place the chocolate, four marshmallow slices and ginger if desired on each of eight cake slices; top with remaining cake. Spread outsides of cake slices with butter.

2. Grill, covered, over medium heat for 1-2 minutes on each side or until toasted.

YIELD: 8 SERVINGS.

italian meatball kabobs

When the temperatures are high—and so is your craving for Italian fare—turn to these deliciously different kabobs. A green salad and rustic bread are all you need to complete this summer meal.

MARIE RIZZIO | INTERLOCHEN, MICHIGAN

2 eggs, lightly beaten

⅔ cup seasoned bread crumbs

½ cup grated Parmesan cheese

¼ cup minced fresh parsley

4 teaspoons Italian seasoning

½ teaspoon salt

½ teaspoon garlic powder

2½ pounds ground beef

1 medium onion, cut into 1-inch pieces

1 medium sweet red pepper, cut into 1-inch pieces

1 medium zucchini, cut into 1-inch pieces

½ small eggplant, cut into 1-inch pieces

½ cup balsamic vinegar

½ cup olive oil

1. In a large bowl, combine the first seven ingredients. Crumble the ground beef over mixture and mix well. Shape into 1½-in. balls.

2. On 12 metal or soaked wooden skewers, alternately thread meatballs and vegetables. In a small bowl, combine the vinegar and oil.

3. Grill kabobs, covered, over medium heat for 8-10 minutes or until meatballs are no longer pink and vegetables are tender, basting frequently with vinegar mixture and turning occasionally.

YIELD: 12 KABOBS.

MAKING MEATBALLS OF EQUAL SIZE

Meatballs that are equal size cook more evenly. First, lightly pat the meat mixture into a 1-in.-thick rectangle. Then, cut the rectangle into the same number of squares as meatballs in the recipe. Gently roll each square into a ball. Or if you have a 1-1/2 or 1-3/4-inch-diameter scoop, scoop the mixture into equal-sized portions. Gently roll each into a ball.

mexican flank steak tacos

Here's a new take on a traditional Mexican main dish! The fruity salsa cools off the spicy pesto.

STEVE MEREDITH
STREAMWOOD, ILLINOIS

1   medium onion, chopped

¼   cup lime juice

2   tablespoons lemon-pepper seasoning

2   tablespoons minced fresh cilantro

2   garlic cloves, minced

¼   teaspoon salt

¼   teaspoon pepper

1   beef flank steak (1 to 2 pounds)

CILANTRO PESTO

1   cup fresh cilantro leaves

1   habanero pepper

1   garlic clove

½   teaspoon salt

½   teaspoon pepper

3   tablespoons olive oil

SALSA

1   medium mango, peeled and halved

⅔   pound fresh pineapple, cut into 3 spears

2   medium ripe avocados, peeled pitted and halved

1   medium red onion, chopped

8   corn tortillas (6 inches)

1. In a resealable plastic bag, combine the first seven ingredients. Add steak; seal bag. Turn to coat. Refrigerate for at least 6 hours.

2. Place cilantro, habanero, garlic, salt and pepper in a small food processor. Cover; pulse until chopped. While processing, gradually add oil in a steady stream.

3. For salsa, grill mango, pineapple and avocados, covered, over medium heat for 2-3 minutes on each side or until tender; set aside.

4. Drain and discard marinade from steak. Moisten a paper towel with cooking oil; using long-handled tongs, lightly coat the grill rack. Grill steak, covered, over medium heat for 6-8 minutes on each side or until meat reaches desired doneness (for medium-rare, a meat thermometer should read 145°; medium, 160°; well-done, 170°). Let stand for 10 minutes.

5. Place onion in a small bowl. Chop the grilled fruit and avocado; add to bowl. Grill tortillas, uncovered, over medium heat for about 1 minute on each side or until warm.

6. Thinly slice beef across the grain; place on tortillas. Top with salsa and pesto.

YIELD: 4 SERVINGS.

EDITOR'S NOTE: *Wear disposable gloves when cutting hot peppers; the oils can burn skin. Avoid touching your face.*

grilled chorizo pizzas

I love grilling in the summer and this recipe incorporates some of my favorite flavors. It's a little more work to grill the corn and chorizo ahead of time, but the smoky flavor they add to the final dish makes it worth the effort.

NEEMA ENRIQUEZ | WASHINGTON, WASHINGTON DC

1 large ear sweet corn in husk

2 uncooked chorizo links (4 ounces each)

4 whole wheat pita breads (6 inches)

Cooking spray

1 medium sweet red pepper, chopped

2 cups (8 ounces) shredded Manchego cheese

1 tablespoon minced fresh cilantro

1. Carefully peel back corn husk to within 1 in. of bottom; remove silk. Rewrap corn in husk and secure with kitchen string. Grill corn and chorizo, covered, over medium-low heat for 25-30 minutes or until a meat thermometer reads 160° and corn is tender, turning occasionally.

2. Cut corn from cob; place in a small bowl. Chop chorizo; place in another bowl.

3. Coat both sides of pita breads with cooking spray. Grill pitas, covered, over medium-low heat for 2-3 minutes or until warm. Turn pitas; top with corn, chorizo, red pepper, cheese and cilantro. Cover and cook 3-5 minutes longer or until cheese is melted.

YIELD: 4 SERVINGS.

grilled shrimp salads with coconut vinaigrette

I first tried a salad very similar to this when visiting a friend in Florida. When I returned, I was determined to create the same refreshing combination at home. The secret is the coconut-milk marinade—makes the shrimp incredibly tender and flavorful!

SARAH VASQUES | MILFORD, NEW HAMPSHIRE

1 cup coconut milk

⅓ cup honey

2 tablespoons rice vinegar

1 tablespoon canola oil

¼ teaspoon salt

1 pound uncooked large shrimp, peeled and deveined

SALAD

4 cups spring mix salad greens

1 cup green grapes

½ cup flaked coconut

½ cup dried cranberries

¼ cup sliced almonds, toasted

1. In a small bowl, combine the first five ingredients. Pour ¾ cup into a large resealable plastic bag. Add the shrimp; seal bag and turn to coat. Refrigerate for up to 30 minutes. Cover and refrigerate remaining vinaigrette.

2. Drain and discard vinaigrette. Thread shrimp onto four metal or soaked wooden skewers. Moisten a paper towel with cooking oil; using long-handled tongs, lightly coat the grill rack.

3. Grill shrimp, covered, over medium heat or broil 4 in. from the heat for 6-8 minutes or until shrimp turn pink, turning once. Divide the salad ingredients among four plates; top with shrimp. Serve with reserved vinaigrette.

YIELD: 4 SERVINGS.

feta & tomato-topped greek burgers

A cooking class that taught me to make my own pita bread inspired me to create this "Greek" burger. The beef-lamb mixture is an interesting change of pace, and the fresh tomato-feta salad adds a delightful, summery taste.

DONNA MARIE RYAN | TOPSFIELD, MASSACHUSETTS

4   medium tomatoes, sliced

1   medium red onion, sliced

⅓   cup pitted Greek olives, coarsely chopped

3   ounces feta cheese, cut into ½-inch cubes

3   tablespoons olive oil

2   tablespoons minced fresh basil

2   tablespoons minced fresh parsley

2   tablespoons white wine vinegar

1   teaspoon salt

½   teaspoon pepper

BURGERS

¼   cup olive oil

¼   cup dry red wine or beef broth

2   tablespoons red wine vinegar

1   tablespoon fresh thyme leaves

1   tablespoon snipped fresh rosemary leaves

2   garlic cloves, peeled

½   cup panko (Japanese) bread crumbs

1½   teaspoons salt

1¾   pounds ground beef

¼   pound ground lamb

6   whole pita breads, warmed

1. In a large bowl, combine the first 10 ingredients; set aside. For burgers, place the oil, wine, vinegar, thyme, rosemary and garlic in a food processor; cover and process until blended.

2. In a bowl, combine the oil mixture, bread crumbs and salt.

3. Crumble beef and lamb over mixture and mix well. Shape into six patties.

4. Grill burgers, covered, over medium heat or broil 4 in. from the heat for 5-7 minutes on each side or until a meat thermometer reads 160° and juices run clear. Serve burgers on pita breads with tomato mixture.

YIELD: 6 SERVINGS.

grilled wasabi oysters

My recipe for grilled oysters is easy to make, but incredibly elegant.
The wasabi-flavored butter mixture makes it an extraordinary appetizer for your next party.

PERRY PERKINS | WILSONVILLE, OREGON

½   cup white wine

1   shallot, finely chopped

1   tablespoon white wine vinegar

1   tablespoon wasabi mustard

1½ teaspoons reduced-sodium soy sauce

½   cup butter, cubed

½   cup minced fresh cilantro

⅛   teaspoon salt

    Rock salt

18 fresh oysters in the shell, washed

1. In a small saucepan, combine the wine, shallot and vinegar. Bring to a boil; cook until liquid is reduced by half. Strain liquid, discarding shallot.

2. Return to pan; stir in mustard and soy sauce. Cook and stir over low heat. Add butter; whisk until melted. Stir in cilantro and salt; set aside.

3. Spread rock salt into an ungreased 15-in. x 10-in. x 1-in. baking pan; set aside. Place oysters, flat side up, on grill rack. Grill, covered, over high heat for 3-6 minutes or until shells open.

4. Transfer to prepared pan. To loosen oysters, cut muscles from top shell; place on bottom shell in juices. Discard top shell. Spoon 2 teaspoons butter mixture over each oyster; serve immediately.

YIELD: 1½ DOZEN.

grilled red potato salad with blue cheese and bacon

Grilling potatoes is an all-too-rare means of preparing America's
most popular vegetable, but nothing says summer like grilling and potato salad.
The blue cheese and bacon add unique flavor to this traditional side dish.

LINDSAY SPRUNK | NOBLESVILLE, INDIANA

3   pounds small red potatoes, quartered

1   small red onion, thinly sliced

2   tablespoons olive oil

1   teaspoon kosher salt

1   teaspoon pepper

1   cup mayonnaise

¼   cup minced chives

¼   cup white balsamic vinegar

2   teaspoons sugar

2   teaspoons Dijon mustard

1   cup (4 ounces) crumbled blue cheese

6   bacon strips, cooked and crumbled

1. In a large bowl, toss the potatoes, onion, oil, salt and pepper. Divide mixture between two double thicknesses of heavy-duty foil (about 18 in. square). Fold foil around mixture and seal tightly.

2. Grill, covered, over medium heat for 40-45 minutes or until potatoes are tender, turning once. Open foil carefully to allow steam to escape. Transfer potato mixture to a large bowl.

3. In a small bowl, combine the mayonnaise, chives, vinegar, sugar and mustard; pour over potatoes and toss to coat. Sprinkle with blue cheese and bacon.

YIELD: 9 SERVINGS.

brown sugar grilled peaches with white chocolate

When I decided to host a family barbecue, I was determined to create an original dessert I could take straight off the grill. This fruity finale is absolutely divine, especially when topped with whipped cream or a scoop of peach ice cream.

TONYA BURKHARD | DAVIS, ILLINOIS

¼ cup butter, melted

2 tablespoons brown sugar

½ teaspoon ground cinnamon

4 medium peaches, halved and pitted

⅓ cup chopped white baking chocolate

3 tablespoons chopped pecans

Whipped cream, optional

1. In a small bowl, combine the butter, brown sugar and cinnamon. Add peaches, one half at a time, and toss to coat. Reserve remaining butter mixture.

2. Moisten a paper towel with cooking oil; using long-handled tongs, lightly coat the grill rack. Place peaches cut side down on grill rack. Grill, covered, over medium heat for 5 minutes.

3. Turn and fill peaches with white chocolate. Drizzle with reserved butter mixture. Cover; grill peaches for 4-5 minutes longer or until the peaches are tender and begin to caramelize.

4. Sprinkle the peaches with pecans and serve with whipped cream if desired.

YIELD: 8 SERVINGS.

Sweet, juicy and simply delicious, the strawberry is undoubtedly the jewel of summer. The only thing better than spending a breezy afternoon picking basketfuls of the sun-ripened rubies is turning them into a host of tasty treats.

Fans of strawberry shortcake will "ooh" and "ahh" over Strawberry Pistachio Towers, a fun take on the classic dessert. Strawberry Pot Pie will tempt taste buds from the moment its heavenly aroma first rises from the oven right up until its mouthwatering berry filling and tender crust hit your tongue.

And because summertime and ice cream go hand in hand, this menu simply had to include creamy and cool Strawberry Ripple Ice Cream.

STRAWBERRY BLISS

STRAWBERRY FARM
SENSATIONS

strawberry pistachio towers

(PICTURED ON PAGE 218)

I once received a standing ovation for this impressive and unique dessert that features layers of homemade pistachio wafers, whipped cream and fresh berries. You might expect the same response.

JEANNETTE SABO | LEXINGTON PARK, MARYLAND

2 eggs

½ cup sugar

5 tablespoons butter, melted

¼ teaspoon vanilla extract

¼ cup all-purpose flour

¼ teaspoon salt

½ cup ground pistachios

FILLING

1½ cups heavy whipping cream

1 vanilla bean, halved lengthwise

¼ cup sugar

3¼ cups sliced fresh strawberries

Confectioners' sugar and chopped pistachios

1. In a large bowl, beat the eggs, sugar, butter and vanilla until smooth. Combine flour and salt; gradually add to egg mixture and mix well. Fold in ground pistachios.

2. Drop by rounded teaspoonfuls 4 in. apart onto greased baking sheets. Spread into 3-in. circles. Bake at 325° for 7-9 minutes or until golden brown. Remove wafers to wire racks to cool completely.

3. In a large bowl, beat cream until it begins to thicken. Split vanilla bean and scrape seeds into bowl. Add sugar; beat until soft peaks form.

4. On each of 12 serving plates, layer one wafer, a dollop of whipped cream and three strawberry slices. Repeat layers. Top with remaining wafers; dust with confectioners' sugar. Arrange the remaining strawberries over tops. Garnish with chopped pistachios; serve immediately.

YIELD: 12 SERVINGS.

strawberry pot pie

(PICTURED ON PAGE 219)

Despite an impressive appearance, these cute individual pies couldn't be simpler!

JACKIE SCHWARTZINGER | ZURICH, ILLINOIS

9 cups halved fresh strawberries

¾ cup sugar

½ cup all-purpose flour

1 package (14.1 ounces) refrigerated pie pastry

4½ teaspoons 2% milk

4½ teaspoons coarse sugar

1. Place strawberries in a large bowl. Combine sugar and flour; sprinkle over strawberries and gently toss to coat. Transfer to six greased 8-oz. ramekins.

2. On a lightly floured surface, unroll one pastry sheet. Using an 8-oz. ramekin as a pattern, cut out three pastry circles to ½ in. beyond edge of ramekin. Repeat with the remaining pastry sheet.

3. Place one pastry circle over each ramekin; press to seal edges to ramekin. Cut slits in each. Brush with milk; sprinkle with sugar. Place on a baking sheet.

4. Bake at 350° for 25-30 minutes or until crust is golden brown and filling is bubbly. Serve warm.

YIELD: 6 SERVINGS.

bocconcini & strawberry bruschetta

Talk about the perfect summer appetizer! Tender greens, mozzarella pearls infused with a sweet tangy marinade and fresh juicy strawberries top these crunchy toasts drizzled with homemade vinaigrette.

RAYMONDE BOURGEOIS | SWASTIKA, ONTARIO

¼ cup walnut oil

3 tablespoons balsamic vinegar

1 tablespoon minced fresh gingerroot

1 tablespoon water

1 tablespoon lemon juice

1 tablespoon maple syrup

1 teaspoon pepper

1 carton (8 ounces) bocconcini (fresh mozzarella balls), drained and sliced

48 slices French bread baguette (¼ inch thick)

12 fresh strawberries, sliced

3 cups spring mix salad greens

1. In a small bowl, combine the first seven ingredients. Pour ⅓ cup into a small resealable plastic bag. Add the cheese; seal bag and turn to coat. Refrigerate mixture for 30 minutes. Cover and refrigerate the remaining vinaigrette.

2. Meanwhile, place baguette slices on an ungreased baking sheet. Bake at 350° for 8-10 minutes or until crisp. Drain and discard marinade from cheese. Combine marinated cheese and strawberries.

3. Top the toasts with the salad greens and cheese mixture; drizzle with the reserved vinaigrette. Serve immediately.

YIELD: 4 DOZEN.

strawberry cilantro lemonade

(PICTURED AT RIGHT)

I'm not certain whether it's the pretty pink color or the lip-puckering tartness
that makes this beverage such a standout, but it's lovely, refreshing and laced with cilantro.

STEVIE DUVALL | MALVERN, ARKANSAS

1½ cups lemon juice

1¾ cups sugar

6 cups fresh or frozen strawberries, thawed

¾ cup fresh cilantro leaves

3 quarts cold water

Ice cubes

1. Place the lemon juice, sugar, strawberries and cilantro in a blender; cover and process until blended. Strain; discard pulp.

2. In two pitchers, combine equal amounts of strawberry mixture and water. Serve over ice.

YIELD: 15 SERVINGS (1 CUP EACH).

french berry torte

For a showstopping dessert that highlights the peak of berry season, turn to
my scrumptious meringue dressed with jam and sweetened whipped cream and strawberries.

GALELYNN PETERSON | LONG BEACH, CALIFORNIA

3 egg whites

1½ teaspoons vanilla extract, divided

½ teaspoon cream of tartar

1 cup sugar

½ cup finely chopped pecans

10 saltines, crushed

1 package (8 ounces) cream cheese, softened

1 cup heavy whipping cream, divided

½ cup confectioners' sugar

⅔ cup seedless raspberry jam, divided

1 pound fresh strawberries, sliced

1. Place egg whites, 1 teaspoon vanilla and cream of tartar in a large bowl; let stand at room temperature for 30 minutes. Beat egg white mixture until soft peaks form. Gradually beat in sugar, 1 tablespoon at a time, on high until stiff speaks form. Fold in pecans and saltines.

2. Spread into a greased 9-in. springform pan. Bake at 350° for 25-30 minutes or until lightly browned. Cool on wire rack.

3. In a large bowl, beat cream cheese and 2 tablespoons cream until smooth. In another bowl, beat remaining cream until it begins to thicken. Add confectioners' sugar and remaining vanilla; beat until stiff peaks form.

4. With a spatula, stir a fourth of the sweetened whipped cream into cream cheese mixture. Fold in remaining whipped cream until combined. Spread ½ cup jam over meringue shell. Top with cream cheese mixture. Cover and refrigerate for at least 3 hours.

5. Carefully run a knife around edge of pan to loosen. Remove sides of pan. Arrange strawberries over top. In a small microwave-safe bowl, microwave remaining jam in 10-second intervals until melted; brush over strawberries.

YIELD: 12 SERVINGS.

strawberry chicken salad croissants

Crunchy almonds add delicious texture to this chicken salad with fresh strawberries. Pack a basketful of the picnic-perfect sandwiches the next time you head to the park.

ABIGAIL ROE
CHULA VISTA, CALIFORNIA

4   cups shredded cooked chicken breasts

½   cup mayonnaise

2   tablespoons sweet pickle relish

2   tablespoons seedless strawberry jam

¼   teaspoon salt

12 fresh strawberries, quartered

½   cup salted roasted almonds

9   lettuce leaves

9   croissants, split

In a large bowl, combine the chicken, mayonnaise, pickle relish, strawberry jam and salt. Stir in the strawberries and the almonds. Place one lettuce leaf onto each croissant bottom; spoon ½ cup chicken salad onto lettuce. Replace tops.

YIELD: 9 SERVINGS.

strawberry ripple ice cream

(PICTURED ON PAGE 218)

Nothing beats the heat—or showcases ripe strawberries—better than my homemade frozen treat. Once you try it, you'll be amazed how easily it comes together!

AGNES WARD | STRATFORD, ONTARIO

4 cups heavy whipping cream

1 can (14 ounces) sweetened condensed milk

1 teaspoon vanilla extract

3 cups crushed strawberries

1. In a large bowl, combine the cream, milk and vanilla. Refrigerate until chilled.

2. Fill cylinder of ice cream freezer two-thirds full; freeze according to the manufacturer's directions. When ice cream is frozen, pour into a freezer container; drop strawberries by tablespoons over ice cream. Cut through ice cream with a knife to swirl. Freeze for 8 hours or overnight before serving.

YIELD: 1¾ QUARTS.

strawberry risotto

For a fun twist on a classic Italian dish, try this creamy, rich risotto brightened with the bold flavors of strawberry, basil and white wine.

BRUCE NEWCOMER | FREDERICKSBURG, VIRGINIA

5½ to 6 cups reduced-sodium chicken broth

1 large onion, chopped

2 tablespoons butter

1½ cups uncooked arborio rice

1 pint fresh strawberries, hulled and sliced, divided

2 shallots, minced

½ cup dry white wine or additional reduced-sodium chicken broth

1 cup grated Parmesan cheese

⅓ cup minced fresh basil

1 teaspoon grated lemon peel

½ teaspoon salt

¼ teaspoon pepper

⅛ teaspoon ground nutmeg

Additional sliced fresh strawberries and fresh basil, optional

1. In a large saucepan, heat broth and keep warm. In a large skillet, saute onion in butter until tender. Add the rice, 1 cup strawberries and shallots; cook and stir for 2 minutes. Reduce heat; stir in wine. Cook and stir until all of the liquid is absorbed.

2. Add heated broth, ½ cup at a time, stirring constantly. Allow the liquid to absorb between additions. Cook just until risotto is creamy and rice is almost tender. (Cooking time is about 20 minutes.)

3. Add the cheese, basil, lemon peel, salt, pepper, nutmeg and remaining strawberries; heat through. Garnish with additional strawberries and basil if desired. Serve immediately.

YIELD: 6 SERVINGS.

MAKING PERFECT RISOTTO

The first step toward perfect risotto is "toasting" the rice—cooking it in hot butter or oil before adding any liquid. The process heats the exterior of the rice grains quickly, preventing the rice from becoming soggy.

grilled salmon
with herbed strawberry hollandaise

Traditional hollandaise sauce gets a sunny twist in this delightful entree. After being marinated in a fresh strawberry vinaigrette, salmon fillets are grilled and dressed with a strawberry-herb sauce.

PATRICIA HARMON | BADEN, PENNSYLVANIA

6   fresh strawberries, hulled

½   cup rice vinegar

3   tablespoons canola oil

1   tablespoon minced fresh cilantro

½   teaspoon salt

⅛   teaspoon cayenne pepper

1½   teaspoons Dijon mustard, divided

4   salmon fillets (6 ounces each)

2   egg yolks

¼   cup heavy whipping cream

1   tablespoon lemon juice

¼   cup butter, melted

1½   teaspoons minced fresh tarragon or ½ teaspoon dried tarragon

Optional garnishes: chopped green onions and additional fresh strawberries

1. Place strawberries in a food processor. Cover and process until pureed; set aside 2 tablespoons for sauce. Pour remaining puree into a large resealable plastic bag. Add the vinegar, oil, cilantro, salt, cayenne and 1 teaspoon mustard. Add the salmon; seal bag and turn to coat. Refrigerate for 30 minutes.

2. Drain and discard marinade. Moisten a paper towel with cooking oil; using long-handled tongs, lightly coat the grill rack. Place salmon skin side down on grill rack. Grill salmon, covered, over medium heat or broil 4 in. from the heat for 12-14 minutes or until fish flakes easily with a fork. Keep warm.

3. In a double boiler or metal bowl over simmering water, constantly whisk the egg yolks, cream, lemon juice and remaining mustard until mixture reaches 160° or is thick enough to coat the back of a metal spoon. Reduce heat to low. Very slowly drizzle in warm melted butter, whisking constantly. Stir in tarragon and reserved strawberry puree.

4. Serve immediately with salmon. Garnish with green onions and additional strawberries if desired.

YIELD: 4 SERVINGS.

strawberry shortbread pizza

Pizza—it's delicious any time of day, and this dessert variety is no exception!
A crisp pecan crust is treated to a creamy layer of vanilla-flavored mascarpone,
then it's topped with berries, whipped cream and chocolate curls.

PRISCILLA GILBERT | INDIAN HARBOUR BEACH, FLORIDA

1 cup butter, softened

½ cup packed brown sugar

2 cups all-purpose flour

¾ cup chopped pecans, toasted

2 tablespoons cornstarch

1 teaspoon ground cinnamon

½ teaspoon salt

TOPPING

1 carton (8 ounces) mascarpone cheese

½ cup plus 2 tablespoons confectioners' sugar

1 teaspoon vanilla extract

½ cup strawberry preserves

¼ cup orange juice

1 pound fresh strawberries, sliced

Chocolate curls and sweetened whipped cream

1. In a large bowl, cream butter and brown sugar until light and fluffy. Combine the flour, pecans, cornstarch, cinnamon and salt. Gradually add to the creamed mixture just until it is combined.

2. On a greased baking sheet, roll dough into a 13-in. x 9-in. rectangle. Bake at 350° for 20-25 minutes or until edges are lightly browned. Remove to a wire rack to cool completely.

3. Meanwhile, in a small bowl, cream the mascarpone, confectioners' sugar and vanilla until smooth. Spread mascarpone mixture over crust.

4. In a food processor, puree preserves and orange juice until smooth. Add strawberries; toss to coat. Spread over crust. Cut into pieces. Garnish with chocolate curls and whipped cream. Serve immediately.

YIELD: 18 SERVINGS.

bountiful berry sips

Served as a sweet appetizer or mini dessert, these berry and
wine-splashed sips will lend a refreshing touch of class to any occasion.

DONNA NOEL | GRAY, MAINE

1 pint fresh strawberries, hulled

½ cup plus 2 tablespoons cold water, divided

1 tablespoon cornstarch

½ cup white wine

¼ cup sugar

2 teaspoons lemon juice

2 tablespoons minced fresh mint

1. In a small saucepan, bring strawberries and ½ cup water to a boil. Reduce heat; cover and simmer for 7-9 minutes or until softened. Remove from the heat; cool slightly. Transfer to a blender; cover and process until blended. Strain and discard seeds and pulp.

2. Combine the cornstarch and the remaining water. Return strawberry puree to saucepan. Add the wine, sugar, lemon juice and cornstarch mixture. Bring to a boil; cook and stir for 4-6 minutes or until thickened. Stir in mint.

3. Cool to room temperature; cover and refrigerate until chilled. Serve in shot glasses.

YIELD: 8 SERVINGS.

strawberry cheesecake pancakes

More a dessert than a breakfast item, these scrumptious pancakes really know how to make the most of summer strawberries! Both the sauce and cream cheese topping are loaded with them.

SHIRLEY WARREN
THIENSVILLE, WISCONSIN

- 6 ounces cream cheese, softened
- 1 tablespoon sugar
- ½ cup crushed strawberries

PANCAKES

- 2 cups all-purpose flour
- ¼ cup sugar
- 4 teaspoons baking powder
- ½ teaspoon salt
- 2 eggs
- 1½ cups 2% milk
- 1 cup (8 ounces) sour cream
- ⅓ cup butter, melted
- 1 cup chopped fresh strawberries

SAUCE

- 3 cups crushed strawberries
- ¼ cup seedless strawberry jam
- ¼ cup water

1. In a small bowl, beat cream cheese and sugar until smooth; stir in strawberries. Chill until serving.

2. In a large bowl, combine the flour, sugar, baking powder and salt. Combine the eggs, milk, sour cream and butter. Stir into dry ingredients just until moistened. Fold in strawberries.

3. Pour batter by ¼ cupfuls onto a greased hot griddle; carefully turn when bubbles form on top. Cook until the second side is golden brown.

4. For sauce, in a small saucepan, combine the strawberries, jam and water; heat through. Spread cream cheese mixture over pancakes; top with sauce. (Refrigerate remaining sauce for another use.)

YIELD: 20 PANCAKES (¾ CUP SPREAD AND 3 CUPS SAUCE).

P unch up the flavor of your favorite dishes with a bounty of fresh herbs. The easy-to-grow kitchen garden favorites not only taste great, they are incredibly versatile, too. Take Almond Tarragon Pesto for instance. It's a favorite over noodles, but also stands out when drizzled over thinly cut slices of grilled meat or served with cream cheese and crackers.

If you think homegrown basil is just for seasoning Italian fare, you're in for a treat when you sip a glass of Botanical Infusion. The bubbly, summery beverage stars basil, mint, lemon verbena, thyme and rosemary.

FRESH HERB FLAVOR
Almond Tarragon Pesto (p. 230)
Botanical Infusion (p. 230)

HARVEST OF HERBS

almond tarragon pesto

(PICTURED ON PAGE 228)

Most pesto is made from basil, which makes my recipe unique. Try it over whole wheat pasta or meat.

LIZA AMOR | LAS VEGAS, NEVADA

3 shallots, chopped

½ cup grapeseed or olive oil

1¾ cups sliced almonds

¼ cup tarragon leaves

¼ cup grated Parmesan cheese

1 tablespoon honey

1¾ teaspoons salt

½ teaspoon pepper

2 cups olive oil

1. In a large skillet, saute shallots in grapeseed oil until tender; set aside.

2. Place the almonds, tarragon, cheese, honey, salt and pepper in a food processor; cover and pulse until chopped. While processing, gradually add shallot mixture and olive oil in a steady stream. Transfer pesto to ice cube trays. Cover and freeze for up to 1 month.

3. To use frozen pesto: Thaw in the refrigerator for 3 hours.

YIELD: 3 CUPS.

botanical infusion

(PICTURED ON PAGE 229)

Summer means cookouts to our family. I wanted to use fresh herbs to create a refreshing beverage that had simple ingredients and could accompany any grilled meal. This was the tasty result.

JENNIFER KUTSCH | NEWPORT NEWS, VIRGINIA

4 cups water

2 cups sugar

½ cup fresh mint leaves

2 tablespoons minced fresh lemon verbena

2 tablespoons minced fresh basil

2 tablespoons minced fresh thyme

2 tablespoons minced fresh rosemary

2 bottles (1 liter each) club soda, chilled

¾ cup citrus vodka

Ice cubes

1. In a large saucepan, bring the first seven ingredients to a boil. Reduce heat; simmer, uncovered, for 10 minutes, stirring occasionally. Remove from the heat; strain. Transfer to a large bowl and cool to room temperature. Cover and refrigerate for at least 1 hour.

2. Pour syrup into a large pitcher; stir in club soda and vodka. Serve over ice.

YIELD: 16 SERVINGS (¾ CUP EACH).

HARVESTING HERBS

Kitchen herbs, such as basil, tarragon, oregano, etc., taste best if harvested before the plant begins to flower. So pinch and use the leaves often—even young plants need to be pinched back to encourage growth. If your herb plants have overflowered, shear back a third of the plant and start using the leaves more often.

mint papaya sorbet

While looking for new ways to use my favorite herb, fresh mint, I decided to create a frosty treat that was healthy, too. A dish of my pretty sorbet is the perfect ending to a summer meal!

JESS APFE | BERKELEY, CALIFORNIA

- 1 cup water
- ½ cup sugar
- ½ cup fresh mint leaves
- 2 cups chopped peeled papaya
- ¼ cup lime juice
- 3 tablespoons minced fresh mint

1. In a small saucepan, bring the water, sugar and mint leaves to a boil. Cook and stir until sugar is dissolved; set aside to cool. Strain; discard mint leaves.

2. Place the papaya in a food processor; add sugar syrup and lime juice. Cover and process for 2-3 minutes or until smooth. Stir in chopped mint.

3. Fill cylinder of ice cream freezer; freeze according to manufacturer's directions. Transfer to a freezer container; freeze for 4 hours or until firm.

YIELD: 5 SERVINGS.

triple-herbed biscuits

(PICTURED AT RIGHT)

*If the tender flakiness of these biscuits isn't reason enough to fall for them,
the robust herb flavor is! Serve them with any number of main dishes, or just enjoy one all by itself.*

ROBLYNN HUNNISETT | GUELPH, ONTARIO

1½ cups all-purpose flour

½ cup All-Bran

2 tablespoons sugar

2 tablespoons minced fresh parsley

1 tablespoon baking powder

1 tablespoon minced fresh thyme

1½ teaspoons minced fresh rosemary

¼ teaspoon salt

½ cup cold butter

1 egg

⅔ cup plus 2 teaspoons 2% milk, divided

1. In a large bowl, combine the first eight ingredients. Cut in butter until mixture resembles coarse crumbs. Whisk egg and ⅔ cup milk; stir into flour mixture just until moistened. Turn onto a floured surface and knead 10 times.

2. Pat or roll out to ¾-in. thickness; cut with a floured 2½-in. biscuit cutter. Place on a greased baking sheet. Brush tops with remaining milk. Bake at 425° for 12-15 minutes or until golden brown. Serve warm.

YIELD: 8 BISCUITS.

blue cheese and blueberry tossed salad

(PICTURED AT RIGHT)

*In this deliciously different salad, fresh herbs and arugula create a flavorful bed for ripe
blueberries and crunchy almonds. Drizzled with raspberry vinaigrette, it's simply divine!*

DIANE DAVIS | VENICE, FLORIDA

4 cups fresh arugula

2 cups fresh blueberries

1 cup packed fresh flat-leaf parsley sprigs

1 cup loosely packed basil leaves

¾ cup coarsely chopped chives

¾ cup crumbled blue cheese

½ cup coarsely chopped fresh tarragon

½ cup raspberry vinaigrette

1 cup salted roasted almonds

In a large bowl combine the first seven ingredients. Drizzle with dressing; toss to coat. Sprinkle with almonds.

YIELD: 8 SERVINGS.

ADD PEP WITH ARUGULA

Not familiar with arugula? Then you're in for a treat! This small, tender, leafy green has a peppery taste. It's fabulous in salads, sandwiches and pesto, and it even makes a great change-of-pace addition to pizza sauce. It also pairs well with prosciutto, goat cheese, figs, sun-dried tomatoes and Parmesan cheese.

mango salad
with mint yogurt dressing

*An abundant planter full of mint inspired me to create this summery salad.
The flavors pair together so well, and really let the freshness of the mint shine.*

NATALIE KLEIN | ALBUQUERQUE, NEW MEXICO

3   medium mangoes, peeled
    and cut into ¼-inch slices

3   medium Gala apples, cut into
    ¼-inch slices

2   tablespoons lime juice,
    divided

½   cup plain yogurt

2   tablespoons honey

1   teaspoon minced fresh
    gingerroot

¼   teaspoon salt

¼   cup fresh mint leaves, thinly
    sliced

1. In a large bowl, combine the mangoes and apples. Drizzle with 1 tablespoon lime juice; toss to coat.

2. In a small bowl, combine the yogurt, honey, ginger, salt and remaining lime juice. Stir yogurt mixture into mango mixture. Sprinkle with mint and toss to coat. Refrigerate for at least 15 minutes before serving.

YIELD: 8 SERVINGS.

dilly red potato bundles

Some of my best recipes happen by accident. This side came about when I attempted to cook an entire meal on the outdoor grill. Fresh dill adds wonderful flavor and a heavenly aroma.

DONNA GIBLIN | MIDDLETOWN, NEW JERSEY

8   medium red potatoes, cubed

⅓   cup chopped onion

¼   cup snipped fresh dill

½   teaspoon salt

½   teaspoon pepper

¼   cup butter, cubed

1. In a large bowl, combine the first five ingredients. For each of four bundles, place 2 cups potatoes mixture on a double thickness heavy-duty foil (about 18 in. x 12 in.). Dot with butter. Fold foil around potato mixture and seal tightly.

2. Grill, covered, over medium heat for 30-35 minutes or until the potatoes are tender. Open the foil carefully to allow the steam to escape.

YIELD: 8 SERVINGS.

athenian chicken grilled cheese sandwiches

Mozzarella and feta cheese make one delicious duo in this upscale grilled cheese that also features tender chicken and fresh herb flavor.

MICHAEL COHEN | LOS ANGELES, CALIFORNIA

1   pound boneless skinless chicken breasts, cubed

¼   teaspoon kosher salt

¼   teaspoon pepper

3   garlic cloves, minced

1   tablespoon plus ¼ cup olive oil, divided

6   ounces fresh mozzarella cheese, shredded

½   cup crumbled feta cheese

½   cup grated Parmesan cheese

½   cup fresh mint leaves, chopped

2   tablespoons minced fresh oregano

2   tablespoons capers, drained

8   slices olive or Italian bread (½ inch thick)

1. Sprinkle chicken with salt and pepper. In a large skillet, cook chicken and garlic in 1 tablespoon oil over medium heat until meat is no longer pink. Set aside and keep warm.

2. In a small bowl, combine the cheeses, mint, oregano and capers. Spread four bread slices with half of the cheese mixture. Layer with chicken and remaining cheese mixture. Brush outsides of sandwiches with remaining oil.

3. On a griddle, toast sandwiches for 2-3 minutes on each side or until cheese is melted.

YIELD: 4 SERVINGS.

KEEP HERBS FRESH

If you know you won't be able to use an entire bunch of fresh herbs right away, wrap them in a slightly damp paper towel and place in a resealable plastic bag. Press the air out of the bag and seal. They should keep in the refrigerate for up to 7 days.

tilapia with basil oil and summer salsa

Tilapia is one of my favorite fish, especially as it's prepared here. The light entree blends full flavor and beautiful color, and can be served with any number of sides, such as pasta, couscous or rice. I've even enjoyed it over a bed of greens.

JEANNINE SANCHEZ | ENCINITAS, CALIFORNIA

½ cup fresh or frozen corn, thawed

½ cup chopped nectarine

½ cup cubed avocado

½ cup chopped tomato

2 tablespoons minced fresh basil

2 tablespoons lime juice

1½ teaspoons grated lime peel

1 teaspoon finely chopped seeded jalapeno pepper

¼ teaspoon salt

¼ teaspoon pepper

BASIL OIL

1 cup loosely packed basil leaves

2 tablespoons lime juice

1½ teaspoons grated lime peel

1 garlic clove

½ teaspoon salt

⅓ cup olive oil

TILAPIA

4 tilapia fillets (6 ounces each)

¼ teaspoon salt

¼ teaspoon pepper

2 tablespoons olive oil

1. In a small bowl, combine the first 10 ingredients; chill until serving.

2. For basil oil, place the basil, lime juice, peel, garlic and salt in a small food processor; cover and pulse until chopped. While processing, gradually add oil in a steady stream.

3. Sprinkle tilapia with salt and pepper. In a large skillet, cook tilapia in oil over medium heat for 5-6 minutes on each side or until fish flakes easily with a fork. Serve tilapia with basil oil and salsa.

YIELD: 4 SERVINGS.

EDITOR'S NOTE: *Wear disposable gloves when cutting hot peppers; the oils can burn skin. Avoid touching your face.*

fresh chili salsa

*Looking for a fresh-tasting appetizer? My salsa makes good use of
locally grown tomatillos, serranos and cilantro. Enjoy it with corn chips or crackers.*

MOLLY SEIDEL | EDGEWOOD, NEW MEXICO

2 to 3 serrano peppers

3 to 4 tomatillos, husks removed

4 medium tomatoes

½ cup finely chopped onion

½ cup minced fresh cilantro

2 tablespoons lime juice

3 garlic cloves, minced

¼ teaspoon salt

Tortilla chips

1. Broil peppers 4 in. from the heat until skins blister, about 4 minutes. With tongs, rotate peppers a quarter turn. Broil and rotate until all sides are blistered and blackened. Immediately place peppers in a small bowl; cover and let stand for 15 minutes. Peel off and discard charred skin. Remove stems and seeds. Finely chop peppers.

2. Place tomatillos in a small saucepan; cover with water. Bring to a boil. Reduce heat; simmer, uncovered, for 5-7 minutes or until tomatillos begin to soften; drain. Cool to room temperature.

3. Chop tomatillos; place in a small bowl. Add the tomatoes, onion, cilantro, lime juice, garlic, salt and roasted peppers. Serve with chips.

YIELD: 3 CUPS.

EDITOR'S NOTE: *Wear disposable gloves when cutting hot peppers; the oils can burn skin. Avoid touching your face.*

herbed ciabatta croutons

*Homemade croutons add a special touch to soups and salads. Loaded with
fresh rosemary, thyme and sage flavor, these crunchy toppers won't disappoint.*

TASTE OF HOME TEST KITCHEN

4 garlic cloves, minced

⅓ cup olive oil

4 teaspoons minced fresh sage

1 tablespoon minced fresh thyme

2 teaspoons minced fresh rosemary

1 loaf ciabatta bread (14 ounces), cut into ¾-inch cubes

¼ cup grated Parmesan cheese

½ teaspoon salt

⅛ teaspoon pepper

1. In a small skillet, saute garlic in oil for 1 minute. Stir in the sage, thyme and rosemary. Place bread cubes in a large bowl; drizzle with oil mixture. Add the cheese, salt and pepper and toss to coat.

2. Transfer to two ungreased 15-in. x 10-in. x 1-in. baking pans. Bake at 325° for 12-16 minutes or until lightly browned, stirring once. Cool. Store in an airtight container.

YIELD: 10 CUPS.

cooking with fresh herbs

Growing a windowsill or outdoor herb garden not only looks lovely, it's a budget-friendly way to add a delicious spark to your favorite foods. Let this chart help you add fresh flavor to all your cooking.

ROSEMARY: Pungent aroma and slight pine flavor; most used in poultry, lamb, fish and stews as well as in hearty Mediterranean dishes.

PARSLEY: Subtle peppery flavor; often used on salads, vegetables and pasta.

MINT: Cool and refreshing flavor; commonly found in desserts, but also pairs nicely in beverages and a variety of savory dishes.

THYME: Minty and citrusy in flavor; most often found in stews, eggs, seafood and poultry dishes that offer a bit of Mediterranean flair.

SAGE: Woodsy in flavor; excellent in fresh sausage, stuffing and rich meats.

BASIL: Sweet and slightly spicy, it's wonderful with tomatoes, vegetables, poultry, pizza, pasta and salads.

CHIVES: Flavor resembles onion; sprinkle on egg dishes, potatoes, soups and fish.

MARJORAM: Aromatic and slightly sweet flavor that resembles oregano; use with roasted meats and eggs.

DILL: Slightly sharp flavor; use to perk up tuna salad, cucumbers, eggs, vegetables and vinegars.

CILANTRO: Sharp, pungent and aromatic flavor; especially good in Mexican, Southwestern, Asian and Indian dishes.

OREGANO: Earthy and aromatic; frequently used in Italian and other tomato-based dishes, also works well with beef, lamb, eggs and vegetables.

TARRAGON: Slight licorice flavor; used in poultry, fish, shellfish, vegetables, eggs and flavored vinegars.

Once upon a time, there was a tasty Halloween get-together that was anything but "Grimm." Spooky fun lurks down every path when you transform your backyard into a haunted fairy-tale forest.

Is that the wind howling through the trees, or is the Big Bad Wolf nearby? Tame his appetite—and yours—with some spellbinding eats! Sassy and flavorful Cranberry BBQ Pulled Pork topped with Sweet & Tart Slaw will scare away hunger of even beastly proportions!

Still not satisfied? My what a big appetite you have. How about a bowl of Sweet Potato Chili and Flaky Whole Wheat Bicuits topped with Butternut Squash Butter? Wash it all down with something wickedly different, such as hot Pear Cider, and your spooky storybook evening is sure to stay on everyone's mind for years to follow.

HOWLING GOOD EATS

INTO THE WOODS

butternut squash butter

(PICTURED AT RIGHT)

Looking for a tasty way to use up pumpkins? My homemade butter is delicious on biscuits or freshly baked bread. It also makes a tempting filling for miniature tart shells.

WANDA RICHARDSON | SOMERS, MONTANA

6 cups mashed cooked butternut squash or pumpkin

2 cups apple cider or juice

1¼ cups packed brown sugar

1 teaspoon ground cinnamon

½ teaspoon ground ginger

½ teaspoon ground nutmeg

⅛ teaspoon ground cloves

Place all ingredients in a Dutch oven. Bring to a boil. Reduce heat; simmer, uncovered, for 1 to 1½ hours or until mixture reaches a thick, spreadable consistency. Cool to room temperature. Cover and store in the refrigerator for up to 3 weeks.

YIELD: 6 CUPS.

flaky whole wheat biscuits

(PICTURED ON PAGE 239 & AT RIGHT)

Whole wheat flour gives these biscuits a nutty, home-style flavor. Ever since I started making this recipe, white flour biscuits just don't taste as good! Pair them with soup or slather them with whipped cream and sweetened berries for a dessert treat.

TRISHA KRUSE | EAGLE, IDAHO

1 cup all-purpose flour

1 cup whole wheat flour

3 teaspoons baking powder

1 tablespoon brown sugar

1 teaspoon baking soda

½ teaspoon salt

¼ cup cold butter

1 cup whole milk

1. In a large bowl, combine the first six ingredients. Cut in butter until mixture resembles coarse crumbs. Stir in milk just until moistened. Turn onto a lightly floured surface; knead 8-10 times.

2. Pat or roll out to ½-in. thickness; cut with a floured 2½-in. biscuit cutter. Place 2 in. apart on an ungreased baking sheet. Bake at 425° for 8-10 minutes or until golden brown.

YIELD: 10 BISCUITS.

BETTER BISCUITS

For biscuits to bake properly, arrange your oven rack so that the baking sheet is in the center of the oven. Be sure to use a hot oven (425°-450°) and a baking time of 10-12 minutes for standard-size biscuits. Insulated baking sheets will not allow the bottom of biscuits to brown like regular baking sheets do.

sweet potato chili

My friends and I created this warming chili one rainy day in Seattle. The sweet potatoes may be left out, but they are the secret ingredient that makes this recipe fabulous.

JONELL TEMPERO
OMAHA, NEBRASKA

2 medium sweet potatoes, peeled and cubed

2 pounds ground beef

2 celery ribs, chopped

1 large onion, chopped

1 medium green pepper, chopped

4 garlic cloves, minced

1 jalapeno pepper, seeded and minced

2 cans (14½ ounces each) reduced-sodium chicken broth

1 can (14½ ounces) diced tomatoes, undrained

2 tablespoons chili powder

2 tablespoons tomato paste

¾ teaspoon ground cumin

½ teaspoon salt

½ teaspoon pepper

¼ teaspoon cayenne pepper

1 can (16 ounces) kidney beans, rinsed and drained

2 tablespoons butter

1. Place potatoes in a greased 15-in. x 10-in. x 1-in. baking pan. Bake, uncovered, at 400° for 20-25 minutes or until tender, stirring once.

2. Meanwhile, in a Dutch oven, cook the beef, celery, onion, green pepper, garlic and jalapeno over medium heat until meat is no longer pink and vegetables are tender; drain.

3. Stir in the broth, tomatoes, chili powder, tomato paste and seasonings. Bring to a boil. Reduce heat; cover and simmer for 30 minutes. Add the potatoes, beans and butter; heat through.

YIELD: 6 SERVINGS.

EDITOR'S NOTE: *Wear disposable gloves when cutting hot peppers; the oils can burn skin. Avoid touching your face.*

peanut & popcorn balls

(PICTURED AT RIGHT)

*Young and old alike enjoy munching—and making—
these chewy popcorn balls. Little goblins especially delight in the touch of lemon flavor.*

LISA ALLBRIGHT | CROCKETT, TEXAS

4 quarts popped popcorn

2 cups dry roasted peanuts

1 package (10½ ounces) miniature marshmallows

¼ cup butter, cubed

1 to 2 teaspoons light corn syrup

1 package (3 ounces) lemon gelatin

1. Place popcorn and peanuts in a large bowl. In a large microwave-safe bowl, heat marshmallows, butter and corn syrup on high for 2 to 2½ minutes or until melted; stir in gelatin powder until dissolved. Pour over popcorn mixture and toss to coat.

2. With lightly buttered hands, quickly shape mixture into twelve 2½-in. balls. Let stand at room temperature until firm before wrapping in plastic wrap.

YIELD: 12 SERVINGS.

cranberry bbq pulled pork

(PICTURED ON PAGE 239)

*Cranberry sauce adds a yummy twist on traditional pulled pork—my family can't get enough of it!
The pork cooks to tender perfection in the slow cooker, which also makes this dish conveniently portable.*

CARRIE WIEGAND | MT. PLEASANT, IOWA

1 boneless pork shoulder roast (4 to 6 pounds)

⅓ cup cranberry juice

1 teaspoon salt

SAUCE

1 can (14 ounces) whole-berry cranberry sauce

1 cup ketchup

⅓ cup cranberry juice

3 tablespoons brown sugar

4½ teaspoons chili powder

2 teaspoons garlic powder

1 teaspoon onion powder

½ teaspoon salt

¼ teaspoon ground chipotle pepper

½ teaspoon liquid smoke, optional

14 hamburger buns, split

1. Cut roast in half. Place in a 4-qt. slow cooker. Add cranberry juice and salt. Cover and cook on low for 8-10 hours or until meat is tender.

2. Remove roast and set aside. In a small saucepan, combine the cranberry sauce, ketchup, cranberry juice, brown sugar, seasonings and liquid smoke if desired. Cook and stir over medium heat for 5 minutes or until slightly thickened.

3. Skim fat from cooking juices; set aside ½ cup juices. Discard remaining juices. When cool enough to handle, shred pork with two forks and return to slow cooker.

4. Stir in sauce mixture and reserved cooking juices. Cover and cook on low for 1 hour or until heated through. Serve on buns.

YIELD: 14 SERVINGS.

cherry oat bars

The addition of dried cherries and cherry preserves gives these homemade granola bars a sweetness everyone enjoys. Each bar provides a delicious pick-me-up and lasting energy.

KEVIN JOHNSON | GLENDORA, CALIFORNIA

2 cups all-purpose flour

2 cups old-fashioned oats

1 cup chopped pecans

½ cup toasted wheat germ

½ cup packed brown sugar

1 teaspoon salt

1 teaspoon baking soda

1 teaspoon ground cinnamon

½ teaspoon ground allspice

1 cup butter, melted

½ cup honey

2 eggs, beaten

1 teaspoon vanilla extract

1 jar (12 ounces) cherry preserves

⅓ cup dried cherries, chopped

½ cup flaked coconut

1. In a large bowl, combine first nine ingredients. In another bowl, combine butter, honey, eggs and vanilla. Stir into oat mixture until combined. Set aside 1⅓ cups for topping.

2. Press remaining oat mixture into a greased 13-in. x 9-in. baking pan. Combine preserves and dried cherries; spread over crust. Sprinkle with coconut and reserved oat mixture; press down lightly.

3. Bake at 350° for 25-30 minutes or until golden brown. Cool on a wire rack. Cut into bars.

YIELD: 2 DOZEN.

pear cider

(PICTURED ON PAGE 239)

A wonderful alternative to traditional apple cider, our perfectly spiced pear-flavored beverage will warm you from head to toe.

12 cups unsweetened apple juice

4 cups pear nectar

8 cinnamon sticks (3 inches)

1 tablespoon whole allspice

1 tablespoon whole cloves

1. In a 6-qt. slow cooker, combine juice and nectar. Place the cinnamon sticks, allspice and cloves on a double thickness of cheesecloth; bring up corners of cloth and tie with string to form a bag. Place in slow cooker.

2. Cover and cook on low for 3-4 hours or until heated through. Discard spice bag. Serve warm cider in mugs.

YIELD: 20 SERVINGS (¾ CUP EACH).

sweet & tart slaw

(PICTURED ON PAGE 239)

For family gatherings and potlucks I am usually expected to bring a salad, as that's my specialty. The unusual combination of shredded cabbage, red apples, carrots and celery make this recipe a conversation-starter and crowd-pleaser.

KATHY RAIRIGH | MILFORD, INDIANA

7 cups shredded cabbage

2 medium red apples, shredded

2 medium carrots, shredded

¾ cup dried cranberries

1 tablespoon celery seed

¼ cup cider vinegar

2 tablespoons sugar

2 tablespoons finely chopped onion

1 teaspoon salt

1 teaspoon ground mustard

½ cup canola oil

1. In a large bowl, combine the cabbage, apples, carrots, cranberries and celery seed.

2. Place the vinegar, sugar, onion, salt and mustard in a food processor; cover and process until pureed. While processing, gradually add oil in a steady stream. Drizzle over cabbage mixture and toss to coat.

3. Refrigerate for at least 2 hours. Toss before serving.

YIELD: 12 SERVINGS (¾ CUP EACH).

SHRED AND DICE VEGGIES—FAST!

To avoid shredding carrots when a recipe calls for them, I put pieces of cut raw carrot into my blender, then blend until they're finely chopped.

gourd & apple candleholders

Cast an eerie glow on your Halloween festivities with these simple gourd and apple candleholders. The largest step is cutting a hole in the center for a candle!

- ☐ assorted gourds, carnival squash, miniature pumpkins or apples
- ☐ pumpkin carving tools (a lid-cutter saw)
- ☐ apple corer (if using apples)
- ☐ sharp knife
- ☐ taper and votive candles

1. Insert the knife into the center of the gourd near the stem. Be careful, as gourds are very hard. Wedge the knife back and forth a little until you have a slit of about an inch. Remove the knife.

2. Insert lid-cutter saw and gently and patiently saw—using an up-and-down sawing motion (don't try to slice)—a circle in the center of the gourd. Don't push too hard or the saw may break. If this happens, try to finish the work with a grapefruit knife or apple corer. When ends of the circle meet, remove that section of the gourd.

3. If using apples, core the apple first, then use a knife or pumpkin carving tools to hollow out the apple.

4. Place a votive candle into the hole as shown.

reference index

Use this index as a guide to the many helpful hints, food facts, decorating ideas and step-by-step tips throughout the book.

general recipe index

This handy index lists every recipe by food category, major ingredient and/or cooking method.

APPETIZERS & SNACKS

COLD APPETIZERS
Apple and Peanut Butter Stackers, 167
Bocconcini & Strawberry Bruschetta, 221
Ham and Cheese Cream Puffs, 43
Marinated Antipasto Medley, 38
Mini Tomato Sandwiches, 194
Pistachio Gorgonzola Cheesecake, 93

DIPS
Crab & Artichoke Dip, 24
Fresh Chili Salsa, 236
Yogurt Cheese Dip, 40

HOT APPETIZERS
Asian Chicken Dumplings, 96
Autumn Squash Tartlets, 111
Chicken Sliders on Pecan Biscuits, 83
Crab & Artichoke Dip, 24
Cranberry Hot Wings, 42
Edamame Peanut Falafel with Peanut
   Yogurt Sauce, 87
Goat Cheese Egg Rolls, 42
Grilled Wasabi Oysters, 216
Holiday Sweet Potato Skins, 48
Honeyed Fig & Ricotta Appetizers, 14
Lemon Risotto Fritters with Lemon-
   Cilantro Dipping Sauce, 44
Moroccan Stuffed Mushrooms, 36
Parmesan-Stuffed Artichokes, 204
Rustic Tomato Cheese Tart, 9
Seafood Cakes with Herb Sauce, 38
Shrimp Spring Rolls, 98
Spicy Beef Satay, 36
Sweet & Sour Turkey Meatballs, 22

SNACK MIXES, CRACKERS & CHIPS
Almond Pesto Crackers, 86
Blueberry Pancake Snack Mix, 28
Peanut & Popcorn Balls, 242

SPREADS
Artichoke Hummus, 39

APPLES
Apple and Peanut Butter Stackers, 167
Apple and Walnut Stuffed Pork
   Tenderloin with Red Currant Sauce, 84
Apple Pie Bundles, 123
Apple Salad With Peanut Butter
   Dressing, 30
Blue Cheese Apple Slaw, 126
Blue Cheese-Apple Strudels, 187
Fruit & Nut Harvest Stuffing, 14
Rotkohl (Red Cabbage), 10
Sweet & Tart Slaw, 244
Toffee Apple French Toast with Caramel
   Syrup, 28

ARTICHOKES
Artichoke & Green Bean Penne, 48
Artichoke Hummus, 39
Crab & Artichoke Dip, 24
Parmesan-Stuffed Artichokes, 204

ASPARAGUS
Asparagus with Creamy Garlic Mustard
   Sauce, 152
Chicken and Asparagus Crepes, 184
Shaved Asparagus Salad, 206

BACON & PANCETTA
Broccoli with Garlic, Bacon &
   Parmesan, 12
Grilled Red Potato Salad with Blue
   Cheese and Bacon, 216
Holiday Sweet Potato Skins, 48
Kale & Bacon Salad with Honey-
   Horseradish Vinaigrette, 11
Orange-Glazed Bacon, 32
Sweet & Sour Turkey Meatballs, 22

BANANAS
Banana Cream Pies, 160
Chocolate-Hazelnut Banana Crepes, 197
Crumb-Topped Banana Bread, 170

BARS & BROWNIES
Cherry Oat Bars, 243

BEANS & LEGUMES
Artichoke Hummus, 39
Seared Tuna with Nicoise Potato
   Salad, 196
Spiced Split Pea Soup, 21
Sweet Potato Chili, 241
Winter Country Soup, 51

BEEF & GROUND BEEF
Beef Osso Bucco, 25
Feta & Tomato-Topped Greek
   Burgers, 215
Italian Meatball Kabobs, 212
Mexican Flank Steak Tacos, 213
Rustic Ribeyes, 178
Sweet Potato Chili, 241

BERRIES

BLACKBERRIES
Berry Breakfast Parfaits, 185

BLUEBERRIES
Berry Breakfast Parfaits, 185
Blue Cheese and Blueberry Tossed
   Salad, 232
Rainbow Spritzer, 169

RASPBERRIES
Chocolate-Raspberry Creme Brulee, 60
Pine Nut Dumplings in Raspberry
   Sauce, 89
Raspberry Ricotta Pies, 161

STRAWBERRIES
Berry Breakfast Parfaits, 185
Bocconcini & Strawberry Bruschetta, 221
Bountiful Berry Sips, 226
French Berry Torte, 222
Grilled Salmon with Herbed Strawberry
   Hollandaise, 225
Mozzarella Strawberry Salad with
   Chocolate Vinaigrette, 179
Rainbow Spritzer, 169
Strawberry Cheesecake Pancakes, 227
Strawberry Chicken Salad Croissants, 223
Strawberry Cilantro Lemonade, 222
Strawberry Pistachio Towers, 220
Strawberry Pot Pie, 220
Strawberry Ripple Ice Cream, 224
Strawberry Risotto, 224
Strawberry Shortbread Pizza, 226
Vanilla Bean Cake with White Chocolate
   Ganache, 188

BEVERAGES

COLD
Botanical Infusion, 230
Bountiful Berry Sips, 226
Cherry Cobbler Smoothies, 30
Cranberry-Jalapeno Martini, 41
Creamsicle Mimosa, 184
Easy French Iced Coffee, 196
Kiwi-Mint Sparkling Water, 202
Make-Ahead Eggnog, 19
Pomegranate Champagne Cocktail, 180
Rainbow Spritzer, 169
Strawberry Cilantro Lemonade, 222

HOT
Chocolate-Caramel Rum Coffee, 40
Pear Cider, 244

BISCUITS & SCONES
Cherry Almond Streusel Scones, 186
Cinnamon Roll Biscuits, 133

BREADS (see Biscuits & Scones; Crepes & Pancakes; French Toast & Waffles; Muffins; Quick Breads; Yeast Breads & Rolls)

BREAKFAST & BRUNCH
Berry Breakfast Parfaits, 185
Bocconcini & Strawberry
   Bruschetta, 221
Cheese Grits & Sausage Breakfast
   Casserole, 31
Cherry Almond Streusel Scones, 186
Cherry Cobbler Smoothies, 30
Cherry Oat Bars, 243
Chicken and Asparagus Crepes, 184
Christmas Morning Oatmeal, 32
Cinnamon Roll Biscuits, 133
New Year's Kick-Off Omelet, 33
Pistachio Granola, 86
Spinach Hash Brown Frittata, 190
Strawberry Cheesecake Pancakes, 227
Sweet Potato Hash, 190
Sweet Potato-Cranberry
   Doughnuts, 29
Toffee Apple French Toast with
   Caramel Syrup, 28

BROCCOLI
Broccoli with Garlic, Bacon &
   Parmesan, 12

CABBAGE & SAUERKRAUT
Asian Chicken Dumplings, 96
Asian Sugar Snap Peas and
   Cabbage, 100
Blue Cheese Apple Slaw, 126
Pork Stir-Fry with Noodle Nests, 101
Rotkohl (Red Cabbage), 10
Shrimp Spring Rolls, 98
Sweet & Tart Slaw, 244

CAKES (also see Cheesecakes; Cupcakes)
Chocolate-Caramel Pumpkin Torte, 115
Decadent Chocolate Crepe Cake, 58
Dirt Ball Pops, 167
Double Shot Espresso Ganache
   Cake, 66
Famous Chocolate Cupcakes, 65
French Berry Torte, 222
Grapefruit Layer Cake, 13
Molten Chocolate Cakes with Mint Fudge
   Sauce, 68
Pistachio-Date Cake with Chantilly
   Creme, 88
Tangerine Cream Roulade, 103
Vanilla Bean Cake with White Chocolate
   Ganache, 188

CANDIES
Chocolate Cherry Truffles, 59
Chocolate-Covered Apricot-Pecan
   Pretzels, 74
Cranberry Caramels, 74
Dirt Ball Pops, 167
Heavenly Chocolate-Fudge Cake
   Balls, 73
Neapolitan Fudge, 75

CARAMEL
Cranberry Caramels, 74

CARROTS
Beef Osso Bucco, 25
Carrot Cake Tarts with Cream Cheese
   Topping, 162
Roasted Carrots with Dill Weed, 116
Sweet & Tart Slaw, 244

CASSEROLES
BREAKFAST
Cheese Grits & Sausage Breakfast
   Casserole, 31
Toffee Apple French Toast with Caramel
   Syrup, 28
SIDE DISHES
Minted Parsnip Souffles, 49
Moist Corn Spoon Bread, 23

CHEESE (see also Cream Cheese)
APPETIZERS
Bocconcini & Strawberry Bruschetta, 221
Goat Cheese Egg Rolls, 42
Gruyere & Caramelized Onion Tarts, 194
Ham and Cheese Cream Puffs, 43
Holiday Sweet Potato Skins, 48
Honeyed Fig & Ricotta Appetizers, 14
Pistachio Gorgonzola Cheesecake, 93
Rustic Tomato Cheese Tart, 9
DESSERTS
Blue Cheese-Apple Strudels, 187
Raspberry Ricotta Pies, 161
MAIN DISHES
Artichoke & Green Bean Penne, 48
Favorite Deep-Dish Pizza, 166
Grilled Vegetable and Goat Cheese
   Napoleons, 211
Hearty Ham Mac and Cheese, 168
New Year's Kick-Off Omelet, 33
Pine-Nut Parmesan Chicken with
   Rosemary Beurre Blanc, 198
Spinach Hash Brown Frittata, 190
SALADS
Amazing Spinach Salad, 113
Blue Cheese and Blueberry Tossed
   Salad, 232
Mozzarella Strawberry Salad with
   Chocolate Vinaigrette, 179

SANDWICHES
Athenian Chicken Grilled Cheese
   Sandwiches, 234
Chicken Sliders on Pecan Biscuits, 83
Feta & Tomato-Topped Greek
   Burgers, 215
SIDE DISHES
Blue Cheese Apple Slaw, 126
Broccoli with Garlic, Bacon &
   Parmesan, 12
Fennel-Stuffed Twice-Baked Potatoes, 50
Garlic Fontina Bread, 152
Grilled Red Potato Salad with Blue
   Cheese and Bacon, 216
Onion-Garlic Herb Rosettes, 130
Parmesan-Stuffed Artichokes, 204
Scalloped Potatoes and Parsnips, 150
Shaved Asparagus Salad, 206
Two-Cheese Corn Muffins, 132

CHEESECAKES
Amaretto Cheesecake, 142
Blissful Peanut Butter-Chocolate
   Cheesecake, 140
Holiday Sweet Potato Cheesecake, 139
Pear-Topped Caramel Cheesecake, 143
Salted Butterscotch Cheesecake, 138
Turtle Pumpkin Cheesecake, 142

CHERRIES
Black Forest Icebox Cookies, 37
Cherry Cobbler Smoothies, 30
Chocolate-Covered Cherry Parfaits, 61

CHICKEN
Athenian Chicken Grilled Cheese
   Sandwiches, 234
Barbecued Turkey, 122
Chicken and Asparagus Crepes, 184
Chicken Sliders on Pecan Biscuits, 83
Cranberry Hot Wings, 42
Pine-Nut Parmesan Chicken with
   Rosemary Beurre Blanc, 198
Strawberry Chicken Salad Croissants, 223
Tea-Smoked Peking Chicken, 104
Turducken, 114

CHOCOLATE
BEVERAGES
Chocolate-Caramel Rum Coffee, 40
CAKES, CHEESECAKES & CUPCAKES
Blissful Peanut Butter-Chocolate
   Cheesecake, 140
Dirt Ball Pops, 167
Double Shot Espresso Ganache Cake, 66
Famous Chocolate Cupcakes, 65
Heavenly Chocolate-Fudge Cake Balls, 73
Molten Chocolate Cakes with Mint Fudge
   Sauce, 68

DOUGHNUTS
Sweet Potato-Cranberry Doughnuts, 29

DRIED FRUIT
APRICOTS
Chocolate-Covered Apricot-Pecan
   Pretzels, 74
Coconut Croissant Bread Pudding, 151
Fruit & Nut Harvest Stuffing, 14

CHERRIES
Cherry Almond Streusel Scones, 186
Cherry Oat Bars, 243

CRANBERRIES
Chicken Sliders on Pecan Biscuits, 83

CURRANTS
Apple and Walnut Stuffed Pork
   Tenderloin with Red Currant Sauce, 84
Moroccan Stuffed Mushrooms, 36

FIGS
Honeyed Fig & Ricotta Appetizers, 14

RAISINS
Carrot Cake Tarts with Cream Cheese
   Topping, 162
Cranberry Rum-Raisin Relish, 126
Fruit & Nut Harvest Stuffing, 14
Spinach with Pine Nuts and Raisins, 176

DUCK
Turducken, 114

EGGS
Cheese Grits & Sausage Breakfast
   Casserole, 31
Chocolate-Raspberry Creme Brulee, 60
French Berry Torte, 222
Ginger Egg Drop Soup, 96
Minted Parsnip Souffles, 49
Mushroom Fried Rice, 100
New Year's Kick-Off Omelet, 33
Pecan French Silk Pies, 162
Peppermint Meringue Cookies, 77
Spinach Hash Brown Frittata, 190
Tangerine Cream Roulade, 103
Toffee Apple French Toast with Caramel
   Syrup, 28

FISH & SEAFOOD
Catfish with Brown Butter-Pecan Sauce, 92
Grilled Lobster Tails, 176
Grilled Salmon with Herbed Strawberry
   Hollandaise, 225
Macadamia-Crusted Mahi Mahi with
   Coconut "Beurre Blanc", 90
Mushroom Scallop Primavera, 202
Seared Tuna with Nicoise Potato Salad, 196
Tilapia with Basil Oil and Summer
   Salsa, 235
Tuscan-Style Grilled Trout, 210

FRENCH TOAST & WAFFLES
Toffee Apple French Toast with Caramel
   Syrup, 28
Waffled Soft Pretzels, 170

FRUIT (also see specific kinds)
Kiwi-Mint Sparkling Water, 202
Mango Salad with Mint Yogurt
   Dressing, 233
Mint Papaya Sorbet, 231
Rainbow Spritzer, 169

GOOSE
Roast Goose with Sweet Glaze, 10
Turducken, 114

GRAPEFRUIT, ORANGE & TANGERINE
Cranberry Hot Wings, 42
Grapefruit Layer Cake, 13
Macadamia-Crusted Mahi Mahi with
   Coconut "Beurre Blanc", 90
Radish, Cucumber and Grapefruit
   Salad, 153
Rainbow Spritzer, 169
Roast Goose with Sweet Glaze, 10
Tangerine Cream Roulade, 103

GREEN BEANS & SOYBEANS
Artichoke & Green Bean Penne, 48
Edamame Peanut Falafel with Peanut
   Yogurt Sauce, 87

GRILLED RECIPES
APPETIZERS
Grilled Wasabi Oysters, 216

DESSERTS
Brown Sugar Grilled Peaches with White
   Chocolate, 217
Ginger Pound Cake S'mores, 212

MAIN DISHES
Barbecued Turkey, 122
Feta & Tomato-Topped Greek
   Burgers, 215
Grilled Chorizo Pizzas, 214
Grilled Lobster Tails, 176
Grilled Salmon with Herbed Strawberry
   Hollandaise, 225
Grilled Vegetable and Goat Cheese
   Napoleons, 211
Italian Meatball Kabobs, 212
Mexican Flank Steak Tacos, 213
Tuscan-Style Grilled Trout, 210

SIDE DISHES
Dilly Red Potato Bundles, 234
Farmer's Market Corn Salad, 203

Grilled Red Potato Salad with Blue
   Cheese and Bacon, 216
Grilled Shrimp Salads with Coconut
   Vinaigrette, 214

HAM & PROSCIUTTO
Ham and Cheese Cream Puffs, 43
Hearty Ham Mac and Cheese, 168
Mozzarella Strawberry Salad with
   Chocolate Vinaigrette, 179
New Year's Kick-Off Omelet, 33
Pineapple-Glazed Ham, 150

HERBS
Almond Pesto Crackers, 86
Almond Tarragon Pesto, 230
Broccoli with Garlic, Bacon &
   Parmesan, 12
Butternut Squash with Whole Grain
   Pilaf, 22
Celeriac & Garlic Mashed Potatoes, 112
Dilly Red Potato Bundles, 234
Glazed Rosemary Pork Roast, 18
Kiwi-Mint Sparkling Water, 202
Macadamia-Crusted Mahi Mahi with
   Coconut "Beurre Blanc", 90
Mango Salad with Mint Yogurt
   Dressing, 233
Mint Papaya Sorbet, 231
Onion-Garlic Herb Rosettes, 130
Pine-Nut Parmesan Chicken with
   Rosemary Beurre Blanc, 198
Roasted Carrots with Dill Weed, 116
Strawberry Cilantro Lemonade, 222
Tilapia with Basil Oil and Summer
   Salsa, 235
Triple-Herbed Biscuits, 232

HONEY
Holiday Sweet Potato Skins, 48
Honey Walnut Butter, 91
Honeyed Fig & Ricotta Appetizers, 14
Kale & Bacon Salad with Honey-
   Horseradish Vinaigrette , 11
Radish, Cucumber and Grapefruit Salad,
   153

ICE CREAM & SHERBET
Mint Papaya Sorbet, 231
Strawberry Ripple Ice Cream, 224
Two Layer Baked Alaska, 62
What-a-Nut Brittle Ice Cream, 85

JAMS, JELLIES & PRESERVES
Apple and Walnut Stuffed Pork
   Tenderloin with Red Currant Sauce, 84
Cherry Oat Bars, 243
French Berry Torte, 222
Roast Goose with Sweet Glaze, 10

alphabetical index

Refer to this index for a complete alphabetical listing of all recipes in this book.

Here's Your Chance to Be Published!

Send us your special-occasion recipes, and you could have them featured in a future edition of this classic cookbook.

Year after year, the recipe for success at every holiday party or special-occasion celebration is an attractive assortment of flavorful food. So we're always on the lookout for mouthwatering appetizers, entrees, side dishes, breads, desserts and more...all geared toward the gatherings you attend or host throughout the year.

Here's how you can enter your family-favorite holiday fare for possible publication in a future ***Holiday & Celebrations Cookbook***:

- Print or type each recipe on one sheet of 8-1/2-in. x 11-in. paper. Please include your name, address and daytime phone number on each page. Be specific with directions, measurements and sizes of cans, packages and pans.
- Please include a few words about yourself, when you serve your dish, reactions it has received from family and friends and the origin of the recipe.
- Send to "Celebrations Cookbook," 5400 S. 60th Street, Greendale WI 53129 or email to recipes@reimanpub.com. Write "Celebrations Cookbook" on the subject line of all email entries and include your full name, postal address and phone number on each entry.

Contributors whose recipes are printed will receive a complimentary copy of the book—so the more recipes you send, the better your chances of being published!